BOURBON

The Evolution of
Kentucky Whiskey

BOURBON

The Evolution of
Kentucky Whiskey

Sam K. Cecil

TURNER
PUBLISHING COMPANY

Turner Publishing Company

445 Park Avenue, 9th Floor
New York, NY 10022
Phone: (646)291-8961   Fax: (646)291-8962

200 4th Avenue North, Suite 950
Nashville, TN 37219
Phone: (615)255-2665   Fax: (615)255-5081

www.turnerpublishing.com

Bourbon: The Evolution of Kentucky Whiskey

Library of Congress Control Number: 2010941791

ISBN: 978-1-59652-769-0

Printed in the United States of America

10 11 12 13 14 15 16 17—0 9 8 7 6 5 4 3 2 1

Contents

Acknowledgments

Special thanks to Captain Paul Bland USN and Rose Mary Bland, who did the final editing and computerizing of the manuscript; my son Tony, who provided the reproduction of pictures; and my daughter Bernadine Strange, who provided a volume of typing and other reproductions. Also thanks to my wife, Jean, who has assisted me and prodded me to complete the book, along with other members of my family. Donald Parrish also provided valuable assistance in selecting a publisher and providing a number of pictures that appear throughout the book.

Rose Mary Bailey	Jack Beam
George Barry	Jo Anne Beam
Mitchel F. Bass	Walter (Toddy) Beam
Charles L. Beam	Sam S. Boldrick
David Beam	Chuck Brauch

David Burg

Teresa Cecil

Pike Conway

H. L. (Whit) Coyte

Bill Creason

Marion Davis Creech

Margie Cross

William Cross

Charlie and Rosalie Cummins

Frank Dailey

Phil Dant

Walter Doerting

Joe Pat Downs

Sara Cummins Edwards

Jim Fothergill

Mary Ann Gentry

Lorene D. Goepper

Phillip Greenwell

Hugh Grundy

Shirley B. Guthrie

Paul Hagan

Sara Harris

Mary Simpson Hite

Kenny Ice

Shirlee Isaacs

Dr. James Klotter

Paul Kraus

Steve Lowery

Nancy G. McKay

Joe Eddie Masterson

Charles Medley

Yancey Cummins Moore

Bill Nagle

Flaget Nally

Johnny Newcomb

Booker Noe

Freddie Noe

Ed O'Daniel

Bill Padgett

Donald Parrish

Alice Patterson

Mary W. Perkins

Henry and Betty Pogue

Jack and Jean Pogue

Kenny Rapier

Dr. Sherril Redmon

Mrs. Guy Ritchie

Orville Schupp

Jack Smart

Francis X. Smith

Robin Smith

Robert E. Snyder

Gerry Werner

Cecilia Marie R. Wheeler

Hugh Wheeler

Donna Wilhite

Thompson Willett

C. P. Williams

Jean Yeager

Introduction

Much has been written about the origin of bourbon and its definition, as well as all other spirituous products that have been created over the years, including all types of distilled beverages ranging from Scotch, Irish, vodka, rum, tequila, sake, liqueurs, brandies, and cordials, as well as other fermented and undistilled products, which all compete with one another.

Under the Internal Revenue Code of the United States, bourbon is described as that which contains a corn content no less than 51 percent nor more than 80 percent. The remainder of the formula can be made of rye, wheat, and malted barley or malted rye. It is to be distilled at less than 160 degrees of proof and entered into new white-oak charred barrels at no more than 125 degrees proof. Whiskey is not to be bottled at less than 80 degrees proof. In order to be called *straight whiskey*, it must be stored for a minimum of two years in charred new oak containers. Bottled-in-Bond whiskey, which has become quite rare, must be stored for no less than four years and bottled at 100 proof.

When standards were first established, whiskey was to be stored in bonded warehouses under government supervision for a maximum of eight years, after which time it was required to be removed from bond and the tax paid whether it was to be bottled or not. However, this was changed by the Forand Bill, which permitted this storage to be extended to twenty years.

Most bourbon whiskeys are withdrawn between four and eight years since this is considered the ideal aging period. However, some whiskey is marketed at older periods, sometimes because of an imbalance in inventories and for some clientele who prefer an older whiskey. Depending on storage conditions, older whiskeys ordinarily carry a more heavily wooded taste that some prefer. It must be remembered that cost is a factor, since it is considerably more expensive to carry the product for a longer period of time and since there is an additional loss of the product, due to soakage and evaporation. An old rule of thumb was that one should expect a normal loss of approximately 20 percent the first four years, with the percentage diminishing somewhat afterward.

Kentucky has remained the largest bourbon-producing state in the union. The region where most bourbon is produced was first established by Virginia, which had named the territory Fincastle County, Virginia. Later the name was changed to Kentucky County. In 1780, the county was divided into Jefferson, Lincoln, and Fayette counties. Bourbon County spun off from Fayette County and included a larger portion of north central Kentucky. This all took place prior to 1792, when Kentucky became a state. Later, Bourbon County was subdivided into thirty-three separate counties, which became Kentucky's main whiskey-producing counties.

On May 4, 1964, by a joint resolution in the Congress of the United States, bourbon whiskey was proclaimed "a distinctive product of the United States." This was done to prevent any encroachment on the type, as well as to put it on an even footing with Scotch of Scotland, Irish of Ireland, and even Cognac of the Cognac area of France.

Harry Harrison Kroll, a University of Tennessee professor, wrote the most comprehensive book on the Kentucky Distilleries I have ever read, *Blue Grass, Belles and Bourbon*. He was both a prolific writer and a great instructor, having taught Jesse Stuart at the old Lincoln Institute, and he was the author of many other books himself. He spent a lot of time in the Kentucky area in the mid-1960s. In his research he interviewed a wide variety of people in the whiskey industry as well as some historians. Unfortunately, he died about six months before his book was published in 1967.

The one person I know who has done more to catalog a complete, so far unpublished, record of all the Kentucky distilleries prior to Prohibition is H. L. (Whit) Coyte of Paris, Kentucky, who died on August 17, 1987. He seemed to be such an unlikely person to develop this wealth of information, except for the fact that the subject intrigued him. He retired from AT&T and devoted his time principally to the collection of this data, in addition to collecting vintage telephones, which he had connected to his own PBX in the basement of his home—all in working order.

Mr. Coyte and I became friends in the early 1960s when he was doing some of his research. It could be that I impressed him with my own telephone system, which I had installed in 1955. I had about fifteen vintage phones hooked up in a series located throughout the facility and used mainly for an intercom system. Each department was assigned a ring, and I could keep in touch with each one without having to go in search of the foreman for information. The system worked well, since the telephone company serving us at that time had no modern equipment to furnish us, and it did not become obsolete until the mid-1980s.

After Mr. Coyte's death in 1987, I was able to get a copy of his records, and I am relying heavily on his early work while expanding it to bring it up-to-date based on my own knowledge of the whiskey business. My association with the whiskey business started actively in 1937 and continued until 1980. Growing up in Nelson County and being in such close contact with the distilleries during Prohibition, I have picked up a lot of information. There are very few distilleries in Kentucky that I have not visited over the years. I have also visited the Tennessee distilleries of Jack Daniel and George Dickel, McCormick in Weston, Missouri, Hiram Walker in Peoria, Illinois, and Michter's in Schaefferstown, Pennsylvania, as well as Canadian, Irish, Scotch, New Zealand, and Australian distilleries. Of course, there are many that I have missed. I have seen many changes from this association and have seen the rise and fall of many firms: the small plants that just couldn't make it, the changes in ownership for various reasons, and the complete loss of all the independents in a final swallow by the conglomerates and foreign interests.

I talked to Vicki Hermann, the chief librarian for the Bureau of Alcohol, Tobacco, and Firearms in Washington, and she informed me that the library contained great volumes of historical information on distilleries and that it would be a great source of data for compiling a complete and accurate history. However, she also informed me that access to this data would need approval from the director. I then spoke with the director, Mr. Stephen Higgins, by phone, and he asked me to put my request in writing. This I did. After reviewing it, the ATF disapproved my request with the excuse that this was proprietary information. I followed up with another letter stating that I only wanted the dates of origin and the transfers from one proprietor to another plus their mashing capacity, which I felt should have been available under the Freedom of Information Act, but I was still turned down.

My search continued through the Kentucky Distillers Association and the Distilled Spirits Council of the U.S., but this quest yielded no fruit. I then made several trips to the Nelson County Courthouse and began a search of the deed books, but this effort turned out to be an interminable job. One could spend a lifetime in one whiskey-producing county and still not be able to get a completely accurate record.

As a result, my information has been derived from records that I have been able to obtain and interviews with knowledgeable people in the industry. Owing to the magnitude of this project, some mistakes are inevitable and some distilleries will be overlooked. In some cases very little information is available, particularly about those distilleries that did not survive Prohibition and are lost in time. Many small operations seen as insignificant at the time were not kept in available records, and they too are lost. In any event, the better-known distilleries are fairly well documented.

For the sake of clarity, permit me to explain that prior to Prohibition, the state of Kentucky was divided into districts for the purpose of federal government supervision and control of the operations and collection of the federal excise tax. Within each district, each distillery was assigned a number for identification. In addition, most distilleries had a separate Internal Revenue Bonded Warehouse number and also a tax-paid bottling house number if such was appropriate. For example, in some instances the same Registered Distilleries Number (RD No.) was assigned to a distillery in another district and was differentiated by the district number. This continued after repeal of Prohibition, but some districts were redesignated with a different number.

In 1956, the Internal Revenue Service was revamped and a system of area offices was established. These were located in Louisville, Frankfort, Owensboro, and Bardstown, with an area coordinator in charge. At this time, the distilleries were redesignated as Distilled Spirits Plants, followed by the state and number.

A central office for Kentucky was established in Louisville for problems that could not be reconciled locally, and from there they were forwarded to Cincinnati, which was the regional office. The regional office would then direct inquiries to Washington, DC., if necessary. Requests for label approvals remained the province of the national office in Washington for review regarding mandatory information, adherence to regulations on format, and infringements on prior approvals. For the purposes of this book, all distilleries are referred to as Registered Distilleries (RD).

Chapter 1

The Early Years

The bourbon whiskey industry had its humble beginnings with the early pioneers, principally immigrants from Ireland. As they migrated into the wilderness they carried with them their own distilling apparatus and set it up wherever they established their homestead. This was an important part of their meager possessions, but was designed for a very small output and not intended for any large-scale production. The apparatus consisted of a copper pot used to distill the fermented wort and a worm for collecting the vapor when it was immersed in a cooling tank or condenser.

Historical records show that the art of distilling whiskey was developed in Ireland. It was in 1608 that a license was issued to Old Bushmills in County Antrim near the Giants Causeway in Northern Ireland. The true origin of the art is lost to history, however, because it is thought that distilling began in the Near East or Mediterranean area and was brought to Ireland by Phoenician traders or by missionary monks around a.d. 500. It moved to England around the twelfth century and from there to Scotland.

Irish and Scotch whiskeys were made mostly from barley and malted barley, although other grains may have been employed. Scotch whiskey varied from the Irish, being somewhat "smoky," a characteristic derived from their method of drying malt over peat moss fires. These distilleries used a pot still for their distilling process, and, of course, many still do.

In 1830, Aeneas Coffee of Dublin developed the first continuous still, which not only speeded up the process, but also afforded a more consistent product. It differed from the original pot or batch still in that the fermented beer is introduced into a top chamber while steam is injected at the base. As the beer courses across a number of perforated plates into pots placed alternately on the plates it moves to the bottom. Steam is driven through the perforations and it heats the beer to the boiling point of alcohol, which is driven off the top as a vapor into a condenser. The first distillation, or low wine, is condensed back to a liquid and flows to a second still, or doubler, and is further vaporized; it passes through a second condenser and is collected as the finished product. The first distillation is a lower proof and contains more impurities; concentrating the alcohol at a higher proof on the second still and removing the undesirable products makes it more palatable.

The pot stills in the beginning were charged and heated by open fires, and even after the three-chambered still was designed it was still heated by fires. Steam was not available for these early operations because the operators had no boilers or steam-generating equipment, so they made do with what was available. Another handicap that they had to overcome was the lack of electricity in the rural areas, and even after steam engines were introduced all systems were operated with steam pumps and steam-driven equipment.

The danger of fire was an everpresent hazard in the early days, but comes as little surprise. With no electricity, it was not uncommon to light the distilling areas with open kerosene lanterns. Even after electricity became available, explosion-proof wiring was unheard of. It was not until the late 1930s that the more rural areas were furnished power by rural electrification. This was usually a single-phase current, and motors of some sizes could not be obtained with explosion-proof features. Dust explosions in the milling equipment were also quite common. I have heard of the practice of hanging a lantern on the tail boxes of distillation equipment in order to check the proof of the whiskey coming off the stills. Maintenance workers often used acetylene torches for welding or brazing in hazardous areas.

The slop, also known as spent beer, feed mash, and by other names, was recovered from either method of distilling and generally fed to cattle, which was a side benefit for the business. A portion of the slop was returned in the mashing and fermentation process, initially for the liquid content and the heat, but it proved quite advantageous as a means of increasing the acidity of the mash, thus giving rise to the sour mash process.

The whiskey-making art developed in a very crude way. Without any temperature control, the fermentation was quite erratic, and it was only by trial and error that distillers were able to create a suitable product. Since the yeast in the mash fermented better under acidic conditions, they soon found that the addition of a portion of their previous run produced the desired effect of increasing the acidity, thereby making a more palatable liquor. Another contributing factor in the use of slop was a shortage of water. By utilizing the heat of the freshly run slop to reset their next batches, they were able to overcome both hurdles. There are many references to sweet mash whiskey in the late eighteenth century and early nineteenth century, but it was not long before this whiskey was discontinued in favor of the better sour mash product.

In 1659, Silvius de le Boe, a French chemist, distinguished fermentation from other gas-emitting reactions in his laboratory, but it was not until 1682 that another chemist named Becker found that only sweet liquids fermented. In 1680, Leuenbeck discovered some different forms of yeast under a microscope, but he gave no particular significance to them except to classify them as a reagent. It was more than a century later in 1790 when Lavoisier established the theory of fermentation, which is still being used today.

J. L. Gay Lussac, in 1824, invented the hydrometer for determining proof of liquor, which is another term for specific gravity based on the Archimedes principle of displacement, and it became the common instrument to accurately determine the alcohol content of whiskey. These instruments are in general use today but have been improved over the original to give precise readings calibrated to a fraction of a point in proof and adjusted by a table for variations in temperature. It is doubtful if many of the original instruments were in use in the early days in Kentucky, where distillers used the old gun powder methods or tried shaking the product and watching how the beads appeared on the top of the liquid.

Whiskey producers in the newly founded United States knew nothing of the scientific approach. Having learned their trade from experience, and by passing it on to succeeding generations, they gradually improved the product. It is still common to find that several generations of the same family are involved in whiskey making, because that is what they learned to do.

The early distilleries were usually established in conjunction with a milling operation and were designed for the farmers' own use for so-called medicinal purposes or to barter for other supplies or necessities of life. Each mill was set up on a stream where part of the water could be diverted to a mill race and used to operate either an undershot or overshot water wheel. The wheel was connected by a wooden shaft to a gear mechanism called a ring gear and pinion, which turned the mill stones for grinding the grain. A miller would grind grain for his neighbors and, as payment, would be given a portion of the flour. No money changed hands. As the farmer accumulated grain in excess of his needs, he found it profitable to convert it into whiskey; thus a distillery was established on the same site.

All distilleries started out very small—able to process anywhere from four or five bushels of grain up to ten—and did not require the elaborate facilities of today. They were also seasonal, since grain was harvested in the fall and with the availability of cold water for cooling the distillate they could operate more efficiently. As distillers became more proficient and their reputations spread, they soon found that there was a demand for the product throughout the country. In the next fifty years, the business expanded and larger distilleries were built. At this time distillers were devoting full time to their operations. Kentucky in particular was becoming commercially important, as trade down the Ohio River and Mississippi River to New Orleans quickly developed. With the advent of the L & N Railroad, which began operations in 1849, the trade soon moved back over the mountains to Virginia and Maryland.

The water wheel for grinding continued for a while, but with the advent of steam-operated equipment and the increase of operations, burr mills were replaced by roller mills, and pot stills gave way to three-chambered charged stills and later to the columnar stills.

Distilleries in Pennsylvania and Maryland began making whiskey using rye as the dominant grain. With the migration of these farmer-distillers to Kentucky they began growing more corn. When they found that it was a suitable grain for whiskey production, the use of rye was mostly abandoned. Some distilleries over the years continued to produce a small amount of rye whiskey, but corn dominated. It is now a requirement by federal regulation that, in order to be a bourbon, whiskey must contain at least 51 percent corn. The regulation further requires that in order to be a straight bourbon whiskey it must be distilled at less than 160 proof and stored in new, white-oak, charred barrels for a minimum of two years.

According to Dr. Thomas D. Clark, in his *History of Kentucky* published in 1937, there were 2,000 distilleries in Kentucky by 1810. An article in the December 1974 *Wooden Barrel,* a cooperage trade magazine, stated that there were 3,000 distilleries in Pennsylvania at about the same time. I don't know the source of this latter information, but it was a quotation from the *Derrick,* an Oil City paper dated October 1974. According to Dr. Clark, before 1865, 166 distilleries in Kentucky were producing 3,348,000 gallons of whiskey valued at the time at nearly $1 million. By 1910, production was valued at $11 million and from 1914 to 1919, it had increased from $44 million to nearly $49 million annually. This was a tremendous boon to the labor market, was quite advantageous for the disposal of farm products, and made Kentucky commercially important.

In 1791, after the end of the Revolutionary War, the young nation found itself strapped for funds to finance the new federal establishment and to pay the war debts, so the government decided to impose a tax of 7 cents a gallon on whiskey and 54 cents per wine gallon on the capacity of all whiskey stills. Alexander Hamilton, secretary of the treasury, was the instigator of this law, which immediately aroused the ire of distillers, particularly in Pennsylvania. The farmers united against this taxation, known in American history as the Whiskey Rebellion, so Hamilton sent a contingent of federal troops under U.S. Marshal Major William Lenox to quell the uprising and collect the tax. Of course, he was successful. Some distillers, realizing the need for the money, settled down and submitted to the tax. Others who were a little more militant continued to resist, and still others simply pulled up stakes and migrated to Kentucky, farther from the seat of government. The biggest problem was that the law required that the tax be paid in specie, which the early settlers did not have since their trade was generally conducted on the barter system. The tax, always unpopular and difficult to collect, was repealed when Thomas Jefferson became president, then reinstated again during the Civil War.

Jere Beam compiled a list of distilleries that were in existence in 1899 in the Fifth District of Kentucky. The registered distillery numbers correspond to the numbers that I have described in my listings, but in some cases the names do not coincide. Many transfers of ownership occurred from time to time that were impossible to keep track of, and in some cases, the names simply refer to a trade name under which the distillery was doing business at the time. Some were tenant lessees who might have been a wholesaler or some other company outside the state that wanted to make whiskey under their own name.

Reference is made to some of these distilleries in business after Prohibition—such as Heaven Hill, which operated under the names of Stonegate Distillery Company of Chicago and Alfred Hart of San Francisco. T. W. Samuels had a tenant lessee of Clear Springs Distilling Company of Chicago, Illinois, and Star Hill Distilling Company operated for a period as Laurel Springs Distill-ing Company, whose headquarters were in St. Louis. Many oth-ers were operated in the same way in order to be able to use their name as "distilled and bottled by" mainly for the sake of using the name for bottled-in-bond products. Since there is practically no whiskey bottled in bond anymore, this has lost its significance, but some distilleries who still have their whiskey produced elsewhere or lack the facilities still want to maintain their own name on the distillation.

Registered Distilleries in the Old Fifth District of Kentucky 1899
Compiled by T. Jeremiah Beam
(The 5th District included Bullitt, Henry, Jefferson, Larue, Laurel, Marion, and Nelson counties.)

Registered Distillery Number	Distiller	Address
1	Sidney F. Westheimer	28th & Broadway, Louisville, Ky., Jefferson County
2	C. W. Tribble	40th & High, Louisville, Ky.
4	The Nelson Distillery Co., Inc. J. & J. M. Safell	Hamilton & Gregory, Louisville, Ky.
5	Sunny Brook Distillery Co., Inc.	28th & Broadway, Louisville, Ky.
6	Wm. O. Bonnie - Park & Tilford	Ashland & Tyler, Louisville, Ky.
7	J. H. Beam	Early Time, Ky., Nelson County
8	Julius Kessler	30th & Garland, Louisville, Ky.
9	E. J. Wiley	7th Street Road, Louisville, Ky.
10	Willow Springs Distillery Co.	Coon Hollow, Ky., Nelson County
11	Mary J. Blair	Chicago, Ky., Marion County
14	The Brown-Forman Distillery Co., Inc.	St. Mary, Ky., Marion County
17	Stitzel Distilling Co., Inc. Crigler & Crigler O'Bryan Brothers A. Ph. Stitzel	Johnson & Story, Louisville, Ky.
19	Richard E. Wathen	7th Street Road, Louisville, Ky.
34	Mellwood Distillery Co., Inc.	Mellwood & Frankfort, Louisville, Ky.
47	Orene-Parker Co.	Gethsemane, Ky., Nelson County

F. M. Head & Co.

87	Julius Kessler	Athertonville, Ky., Larue County
97	Anderson Distillery Co., Inc.	Hamilton & Gregory
	George C. Buchanan	Louisville, Ky.
	Allen-Bradley Co.	
106	Jacob Stitzel	26th & Broadway
	Louisville, Ky.	
107	Eminence Distillery Co., Inc.	Eminence, Ky., Henry County
111	Daniel & James S. McKenna	Fairfield, Ky., Nelson County
145	Leslie B. Samuels	Deatsville, Ky., Nelson County
146	New Hope Distillery Co., Inc.	New Hope, Ky., Nelson County
	E. L. Miles & Co., Inc.	
168	H. Sutherland	Bardstown, Ky., Nelson County
	Bonnie & Co.	
169	The Dant Distillery Co., Inc.	Dant, Ky., Marion County
170	William R. Schmidt	Dant, Ky., Marion County
174	Smith Distillery Co., Inc.	Chicago, Ky., Marion County
	Farm Springs Distillery Co.	
229	A. Mayfield & Co., Inc.	Athertonville, Ky., Larue County
	Boldrick, Callaghan Co.	
230	The Clear Spring Distilling Co.	Bardstown, Ky., Nelson County
	James B. Beam	
239	Graeme McCowan	Greenbrier, Ky., Nelson County
240	Taylor & Williams, Inc.	Gethsemane, Ky., Nelson County
241	W. B. Samuels & Co., Inc.	Samuels, Ky., Nelson County
266	Marion E. Taylor & Wm. G. Miller	Chapeze, Ky., Bullitt County
270	Wathen, Mueller & Co.	Lebanon, Ky., Marion County
271	Belle of Nelson Distillery Co., Inc.	New Hope, Ky., Nelson County
272	Mattingly & Moore Distillery Co., Inc.	Bardstown, Ky., Nelson County

294	The Nelson Co., Ky. Distillery Co., Inc.	Coon Hollow, Ky., Nelson County
297	Associated Distilleries of Ky., Inc.	28th & Broadway, Louisville, Ky.
	E. I. Jackman	
	Sunny Brook Distillery Co., Inc.	
299	Charles Kobert & Co.	Lebanon, Ky., Marion County
329	W. H. Head Distillery Co., Inc.	Raywick, Ky., Marion County
354	D. Meschendorf	Work House Road, Louisville, Ky.
	Old Kentucky Distillery, Inc.	
355	Thomas S. Moore	Bardstown, Ky., Nelson County
	Hamilton C. Applegate	
	M. & F. J. Herrmann	
	George & Otmar G. Stark	
	Thixton & Millett Co., Inc.	
357	R. Cummins & Co., Inc.	Loretto, Ky., Marion County
360	E. M. Babbitt	36th & Missouri, Louisville, Ky.
363	W. J. O'Hearn	26th & Baker, Louisville, Ky.
368	R. G. Shipman	Southall & Thorne, Louisville, Ky.
369	J. P. Rocke	Southall & Thorne, Louisville, Ky.
	Allen-Bradley Co., Inc.	
370	Boldrick, Callaghan Co.	Calvary, Ky., Marion County
371	N. M. Uri & Co.	Hunters Depot, Ky., Nelson County
372	Julius Kessler	31st & Rudd, Louisville, Ky.
379	The Nelson Co. Ky. Distillery Co.	Coon Hollow, Ky., Nelson County
401	Moses Crabfelder	Clermont, Ky., Bullitt County
405	M. C. Beam & Co.	Gethsemane, Ky., Nelson County
	Taylor & Williams, Inc.	
409	Joseph Schwab, Jr.	Logan & Breckenridge, Louisville, Ky.
410	F. G. Walker & Co., Inc.	Bardstown, Ky., Nelson County
	R. H. Edelen	
412	Belmont Distillery Co., Inc.	17th & Lexington, Louisville, Ky.
414	Samuel A. Hoffheimer	18th & Howard, Louisville, Ky.

415	S. P. Lancaster, Inc.	Bardstown, Ky., Nelson County
	Louis Poock	
420	M. A. Wathen	Hobbs, Ky., Bullitt County
422	Thixton, Millett & Co.	Bardstown, Ky., Nelson County
440	George R. Burke	Loretto, Ky., Marion County
	T. F. & F. M. Smith	
	John C. Weller Co., Inc.	
442	B. McClaskey & Son	Bloomfield, Ky., Nelson County
470	Samuel A. Hoffheimer	18th & Howard, Louisville, Ky.
471	R. C. Dick	Baldrock, Ky., Laurel County
472	S. A. Douglas	Baldrock, Ky., Laurel County
473	Roy & Luttrell	Catherine, Ky. (Unidentified)

Chapter 2

Prohibition

The abuse of whiskey led to the rise of several temperance movements across the nation. They were particularly active in the period around 1832, and legislation was enacted to regulate the industry by taxation. In some areas, business was completely outlawed.

Largely forgotten during the War Between the States, it flared up again in 1869. The Good Templars was organized in 1851 in Utica, New York, and quickly spread across Canada and Great Britain. (This and other temperance movements, the W.C.T.U. and Anti-Saloon League, gained strength after the war, and by 1890 they were the most active.) Carrie Nation, a former native of Garrard County, Kentucky, who had moved to Eureka Springs, Arkansas and later to Kansas, gained notoriety through her anti-saloon raids with her hatchet-wielding antics, especially in Kansas and Missouri, her self-described Den of Iniquity in the Midwest.

Indulgence in liquor became the scourge of the army, particularly in the lonely outfits out on the plains during the Indian Wars in the 1880s. The soldiers usually spent several months on their forays to keep the Indians in line, and then, when they returned to their frontier forts, proceeded to blow their pay in the local saloons.

As a result of the growing strength of the temperance leagues and the abuses so rampant brought on by the Whiskey Trust, a bill was introduced in the House of Representatives on October 18, 1919, by an ardent dry from Minnesota by the name of Andrew J. Volstead. The law was passed over Woodrow Wilson's veto, and the nation went bone dry at 12:01 a.m. Saturday, January 20, 1920. At the same time, a tax of $6.40 a gallon was placed on beverage alcohol, which was to be dispensed through drugstores by prescription only. Volstead received credit for introducing the bill, but Wayne Wheeler from Brookfield, Ohio, had been devoting his life to prohibition since 1893 and was the principal author.

The trouble was just beginning. John F. Kramer of the Internal Revenue Bureau of Alcohol in Washington ordered some 2,500 watchmen to be employed to guard the whiskey in bonded storage. They estimated that, by selling the remaining liquor by prescription at drugstores, by 1925 all stocks would be depleted.

Some of the distillers, recognizing that Prohibition was imminent, began early to remove stocks for bottling and shipped it out.

They removed whiskey regardless of owner when a large amount of it was on warehouse receipt and unknown to the owner. They paid the taxes, bottled the whiskey, and sold it.

Bill Kennedy became director of the Internal Revenue Bureau at a later date, and I became well acquainted with him. After his retirement he moved back to his home "Top O'The Hill" in Tell City, Indiana, and became a liaison with the Distilled Spirits Institute. He called on me a number of times and related that the bureau received inquiries for years afterward inquiring about the status of the whiskey they held receipts for. Since the tax had been paid on the whiskey, the federal government had no interest in the matter. Their object was to collect taxes, and they never had any control over ownership. Most of these receipt holders held one to five barrels, which was not a sufficient quantity to institute an expensive lawsuit; and, not knowing or having access to other holders in order to file a class action suit, they were left with the loss of their whiskey and investment.

As the Prohibition years began to unfold, a considerable amount of whiskey was still in the bonded warehouses, and the feds padlocked the warehouses and placed guards to patrol the premises. Evidently this was not effective, particularly in the rural areas. The guards were either bribed or incapacitated, and the locks were broken and the whiskey removed. Eventually this activity became so rampant that all the whiskey in the more isolated areas was ordered to be transferred to consolidated warehouses in the larger cities of Frankfort, Lexington, and Louisville. These locations organized under the American Medicinal Spirits Company established bottling operations until stocks were depleted.

Prohibition took its toll on the distilleries. All the rural plants were closed down, and most were dismantled and their equipment salvaged. Some buildings were converted to other uses or left to deteriorate if they had no further value for re-use.

Prohibition of the sale, manufacturing, or importation of intoxicating liquors was expected to solve all the evils of the United States, according to the popular thinking of the day, at least according to the dry forces. They must have been in the majority, but the veterans of World War I felt that Prohibition was steamrollered in their absence. Had they been at home, so the thinking went, they would not have permitted it to happen.

In spite of all dissent, on January 16, 1919, the Volstead Act was ratified by Nebraska, which was the 36th state to join, giving it a 75 percent majority. The industry was given one year to close out their operations and find new occupations. The only exceptions were special permits to bottle the remaining whiskey for medicinal purposes. Only four times during the fourteen years of Prohibition were distillers allowed to operate and replenish stocks that had been exhausted.

The effort to curb the lawlessness and social problems caused by the abuse of alcohol backfired, ushering in the most violent and anti-law period the country had ever seen. Depriving people of their drinks infringed upon their rights, and drunkenness among young people soared. The new law fostered a disrespect for government as Americans determined to imbibe found ways to flout it. Rival gangs in the business of producing illegal liquor or smuggling it in through the Canadian provinces turned parts of the nation into a battleground and the weapon of choice was the Thompson sub-machine gun. Legs Diamond and Dutch Schultz of New York and "Scarface" Al Capone of Chicago were a few of the more notorious gangsters cashing in on the contraband. During Capone's reign in Chicago there were at least 400 gangland murders. The most publicized of these was the St. Valentine's Day Massacre of 1929, when Capone's gang gunned down six of the O'Banion gang in their liquor warehouse. Capone was never convicted of any of these crimes but was finally indicted and convicted of income tax evasion, for which he spent time in the federal penitentiaries in Atlanta and Alcatraz.

Alcatraz was established as a penitentiary for incorrigibles and men who were unable to be rehabilitated. On a visit to Alcatraz a few years ago, after it was abandoned as a penal institution, I asked a guide the reason for moving Capone to that location. The answer was that with his still vast financial resources, he could obtain anything he wanted and could bribe his way through any other institution. If he wanted to pay someone $50 for a cigar, it meant nothing to him.

While the big cities received most of the attention, the small towns and rural areas also participated. Speakeasies and bribery of law officials and enforcement agents were quite common, and an attitude of "devil may care" abounded.

During the administration of Jimmy Walker as mayor of New York, conditions really got out of hand. The flamboyant Walker encouraged the proliferation of the gangs, which were engaged not only in the illicit whiskey trade but in just about every other vice imaginable. Bribery of public officials was commonplace. When they were discovered with an unusually large amount of money in relation to their salary, a simple explanation was furnished that it was an inheritance left by a grandmother or other relative and had been stored in a tin box. This became known as the "Tin Box Parade."

At the age of five, in 1881 George Remus immigrated to America with his parents, who were German. When he was fourteen he started to work in a drugstore owned by his uncle. The uncle decided to sell it to him five years later, and Remus was able to pass the examination for a pharmacist's license by lying about his age. He acquired another drugstore about five years later and then married. He decided to become a lawyer and completed a three-year law course in eighteen months of night school and was then admitted to the Illinois bar in 1900. His law practice as a criminal lawyer for the next twenty years was quite profitable, but he tired of it, and when the Volstead Act was enacted, he began to study the provisions of the act.

In one section the Volstead Act stated that nothing would prohibit the purchase and sale of warehouse receipts covering distilled spirits on deposit in government bonded warehouses. The only problem was to find a way to get the whiskey out, since the act further provided that whiskey could be removed only by a permit from the Commissioner of Internal Revenue and bottled and used for medicinal purposes. This was a natural for Remus's former experience in the drug business and would fit perfectly into his plan to re-enter the drug business. By buying the warehouse receipts, he could then sell them to himself as a legitimate wholesale druggist and have the whiskey delivered to his account. In addition, he was able to acquire a number of distilleries with sufficient inventory to furnish him easy access to what he needed. In the meantime he moved to Cincinnati in order to be closer to the supply of whiskey, and he set up his business on his Death Valley farm. He was able to procure permits by bribing officials, and he amassed a considerable fortune.

Violations of the prohibition law were not confined to the gangs and hoodlums in the large cities, or to the small-town moonshiners and bootleggers throughout the rest of the country.

The Montagne brothers (Morgan, Rene, and William respectively) had legal residence in Paris, France, but lived in New York City. All were great sportsmen and socially prominent. They were well known among the French vintners and achieved great success in the operation of a fleet of freight vessels. They had also inherited a liquor business from their father, known as the E. La Montagne's Sons, Inc. which controlled the operations of the Green River Distillery, RD No. 9, in Owensboro, Daviess County, Kentucky, and the Fible & Crabbe Distillery, RD No. 107, in Eminence, Henry County, Kentucky.

Since they belonged to all the private clubs in New York and had access to all the fashionable hotels and speakeasies, it was natural for them to be able to supply these outlets from their own inventory during the first few years of Prohibition. They were apprehended, however, for serving alcoholic beverages at one of their clubs but received only a light sentence. So many prominent people came to their defense that it became politically and socially incorrect to do otherwise. They remained on the social register until the late 1920s and were then dropped, but President Coolidge restored their citizenship rights with a full pardon.

Several books published after Prohibition was repealed give a very graphic description of the lawlessness of the period and of the rackets that proliferated:

The Long Thirst: Prohibition in America 1920-1933
John Abler

Ardent Spirits: The Rise and Fall of Prohibition
John Kabler

The Rum Running Years
Ted R. Hennigar

The End of the Roaring Twenties: Prohibition and Repeal
Bill Severn

Prohibition brought a great rise in moonshine operations in the state of Kentucky. This is thought to have been a mountain industry because of the federal taxes that had been imposed on legal operations.

The people of the Appalachian region felt that the tax was unconstitutional and that the government had interfered with their livelihood, so they had continued to produce whiskey and had avoided the tax ever since it was first legislated in 1791. When Prohibition was enacted, it then followed for the same reason that many farmers would set up their own stills out in the country and continue to make their own. The enforcement division of Internal Revenue maintained a fairly large force in breaking up their illicit operations, not only destroying their equipment and prosecuting the offenders, but also assessing tax on the finished product that they confiscated.

This business was not confined strictly to the rural areas, but spilled over into the urban areas. Operations were found within the area of legal distilleries where their stills were camouflaged by the smell from the legal operations. A story appeared in *True* magazine in June 1961, condensed from the *Purveyor* written by John Starr wherein he describes some of the more elaborate operations taking place in large cities. They had operations that were so well organized that the legal distilleries could learn from their methods. The transportation of supplies and the production and distribution were as efficient as that of any legal business. In fact, the increase in federal taxes encouraged illegal businesses to proliferate. Because it was possible to profit as much as 400 percent illegally, the taxes faced by the legal industry left them unable to compete.

The traffic in illegal liquor did not end with repeal of Prohibition, but continued for several years afterward. The ring of moonshiners in the Golden Pond area of Land Between the Lakes was not broken up until the early 1960s. John Baize and Quinn Pearl, both enforcement agents, spent a considerable time in the area before the illegal traffic was finally cracked.

"Big Six" Henderson, another enforcement agent, didn't join the force until 1941. He spent a great deal of his time in western Kentucky around Edmonson County and is reputed to have destroyed many a still. I used to deer hunt with him in the 1960s on his farm on Second Creek not far from Brownsville where he knew everybody. Some of them he had caught at one time or another at their stills.

Fiscal Year	Stills Seized	Illicit Spirits Seized (Gallons)	Mash Seized (Gallons)
1965	7,432	156,544	3,637,881
1970	5,228	86,415	1,956,170
1975	889	16,046	283,043
1980	106	N/A	48,470
1985	8	218	6,065
1990	0	4	0

Federal Liquor Excise Taxes 1791 to the Present	
Jan. 25, 1791, through May 7, 1792	9¢ a gallon
May 8, 1792, through June 30, 1802	7¢ a gallon
July 1, 1802, through September 18, 1814	all liquor excise tax abolished
Sept. 19, 1814, through November 30, 1817	20¢ per proof gallon
Dec. 1, 1817, through July 31, 1862	no liquor excise taxes
Aug. 1, 1862, through March 6, 1864	20¢ per proof gallon
March 17, 1864, through June 30, 1864	60¢ per proof gallon
July 1, 1864, through Dec. 31, 1864	$1.50 per proof gallon
Jan. 1, 1865, through July 19, 1868	$2 per proof gallon
July 20, 1868, through July 21, 1872	50¢ per proof gallon

Aug. 1, 1872, through March 2, 1875	70¢ per proof gallon
March 3, 1875, through Aug. 26, 1894	90¢ per proof gallon
Aug. 27, 1894, through Jan. 15, 1920	$1.10 per proof gallon
Jan. 16, 1920, through Dec. 5, 1933	National Prohibition
Dec. 6, 1933, through June 30, 1938	$2 per proof gallon
July 1, 1938, through June 30, 1948	$2.25 per proof gallon
July 1, 1940, through Sept. 30, 1941	$3 per proof gallon
Oct. 1, 1941, through Oct. 31, 1942	$4 per proof gallon
Nov. 1, 1942, through March 31, 1944	$6 per proof gallon
Apr. 1, 1944, through Oct. 31, 1951	$9 per proof gallon
Nov. 1, 1951, through Sept. 30, 1985	$10.50 per proof gallon
Oct. 1, 1985, through Dec. 31, 1990	$12.50 per proof gallon
Jan. 1, 1991, to the present	$13.50 per proof gallon

In 1937, I was on a surveying crew for Ray W. Chanaberry, who was one of the contractors surveying for rural electric lines. We always kept a right-of-way man with us who was a local farmer. Several times when we were operating in southern Nelson County he suggested that we move our line a few degrees so as to avoid disturbing some of the boys at work.

I can't say exactly when the moonshining operations discontinued or at least slowed to a trickle, but I think one thing that influenced it was the amount of labor involved. This was really hard work, and the fear of being caught was always present. One moonshiner I knew told me that fear was the worst thing. He said he got caught because fear caused him to start drinking too much and he got careless.

Some brands of bourbon whiskey during this period were produced in Canada, including Old Grand-Dad and Old Crow, under the name of Consolidated Distilleries, Ltd., Montreal. These were National Distillers brands and National was the offshoot of the Kentucky Distillers and Warehouse Co., part of the original trust. Also the Waterfill and Frazier Distillery of Anderson County was moved to Juarez, Mexico, and operated for a time by Joe Beam and his son Harry from Bardstown.

Congress passed a ruling in 1964 proclaiming bourbon whiskey a distinctive product of the United States, in order to put it on the same footing as scotch in Scotland, Irish Whiskey in Ireland, and Cognac in Cognac, France. According to this ruling, the production of bourbon whiskey in Canada would be illegal today, but during Prohibition legality meant nothing. It was no secret that very large quantities of Scotch and Canadian whiskies were smuggled into the United States and operated by the very people who became so prominent in the industry after repeal.

Joe Kennedy, father of future president John F. Kennedy, was a large investor in Somerset Importers and was a big supporter of Franklin D. Roosevelt. He was in a prime position to have ships loaded with Scotch whiskey laying off shore in New York, ready to be unloaded when Roosevelt became president and Prohibition was repealed. This proved particularly advantageous for Kennedy because it took American distillers several years to accumulate any aged whiskey. By that time, a large segment of the drinking public had become accustomed to the taste of Scotch and they were hard to convert. Naturally they preferred Scotch, which had been aged for several years, to the younger bourbons that were put on the market before they had matured.

Roosevelt appointed Robert Worth Bingham, publisher of the *Louisville Courier,* as Ambassador to Great Britain, and he held that job until he became ill and died in December 1937. At this time, Roosevelt appointed Joe Kennedy to succeed Bingham.

There are a lot of stories circulating around the Nelson County area about whiskey being removed from warehouses and then the warehouses being set on fire to conceal the theft. In one such case the legal whiskey was replaced with moonshine, and when the moonshine aged for a while they returned and stole the moonshine. In another case, the whiskey barrels were refilled with water, and when all the whiskey was gone the warehouse was set afire. When the superstructure burned and reached the barrels, the water extinguished the blaze. These stories seem pretty farfetched and I question their validity. It is not likely that once the whiskey was removed the culprits would go to all that trouble.

Lewis Guthrie, who had bought the Early Times Distillery at the beginning of Prohibition, still lived on the premises in 1926. Nancy Guthrie McKay relates a story of a robbery that occurred at their residence in April of that year. It seems her father had a large number of tax-paid, bottled case goods in a vault in his basement. Somebody, evidently with firsthand knowledge of the vault, decided to relieve him of his inventory.

A social gathering was being held on the night involved, with several local guests attending, including Will and Nannie Stiles.

The perpetrators arrived early in the evening, but since there was a party going on, they didn't want to risk exposure. They waited until after midnight, when all the guests had departed, then forced their way in at gunpoint and took all the whiskey. It was loaded onto a truck they had stolen from Reginald Grigsby's garage on East Arch Street, now Flaget in Bardstown, and they made their escape. No one was injured in the encounter, and after the thieves had left, Lewis Guthrie sought out Henry Shain, who lived nearby, to take him to Bardstown to report the theft. His own automobile had been disabled and the telephone torn from the wall.

Heavy Tong and Chuck Haviland, local lawmen, were able to apprehend the culprits, and they were lodged in the Nelson County Jail. One young man by the name of Paul Vernon, with a very appealing personality, was among the group. He was a fine looking lad, clean cut, and supposedly a college man. Will Stiles visited him in the jail, and Vernon must have conned him. When Vernon complained that the food in the jail was no good, Stiles had his meals delivered to him from the Talbott Tavern nearby. I think Lewis gave Stiles a good cussing for buying meals for the man who stole his whiskey.

Thompson Willett and Hugh Wheeler filled me in on some of the later details. In addition to Vernon, W. A. Roby, Marion (Joe) Hall, and Sam Fleeters were involved. A trial was held in Nelson Circuit Court. Ernest Fulton prosecuted the case and Ronald Oldham from Louisville pled for the defense. The trial went on for several days and in Ernest's closing statement he set up the jury for a guilty verdict. "As I stand here and look at those defendants with their fancy city lawyer, I am just thinking what a great party will be held on Eastern Parkway in Louisville tonight when they win their acquittal from these rubes down in Nelson County." I understand the rube jury didn't deliberate long before they returned the verdict of guilty.

Nancy told me one other thing: the whole episode took place at their home without any of the five children of her dad's knowing, except Newman, the oldest. They were asleep upstairs and their mother and father wouldn't even tell them about it. When they went to school the next morning everybody else had heard about it as the news spread through town.

The repeal of Prohibition has not eliminated all the vices and corruption that took place, but one would think that Americans would have learned a lesson. It is a well-known fact that to prohibit something makes it more enticing. Teaching good habits is more important than an absolute prohibition against bad ones.

Chapter 3

The Whiskey Trust

The Whiskey Trust was the outgrowth of a group of investors determined to control the production of industrial alcohol in the Midwest, particularly in Peoria, Illinois, where transportation, grain, and fuel were plentiful. They intended to limit the amount of production in order to fix prices at a high level that would net considerable profit. In 1887, this group formed the Distillers and Cattle Feeders Trust to accomplish their ends, but for lack of a consensus the effort was not completely successful.

Two important laws were enacted at the time the trust was operating. The Interstate Commerce Act of 1887 was aimed mainly at railroads and utilities that by their nature had no competition because of the investment and possible diluted return if spread too thin. In this case the price of service was to be regulated by the Interstate Commerce Commission to prevent a gouging of the public.

The other law, the Sherman Antitrust Law of 1890, was designed to accomplish just the opposite. Since competition usually did a pretty fair job of regulating prices, in order to enforce active competition the act outlawed restraints of trade, monopolies, and attempts to monopolize. Monopolies were declared illegal, and persons conspiring in such efforts were guilty of a misdemeanor.

The Supreme Court held that the Distiller and Cattle Feeders Trust was in violation of the Sherman Act. In 1890 they changed the name to the Distilling and Cattle Feeding Company to eliminate the stigma, but the result was the same.

As I understand it, the Whiskey Trust and its successor companies skirted the law by trading shares of stock in the member companies in exchange for shares in the trust. I assume that this put them within the law. However, their very act of selling below cost to force out financially strapped companies or forcing them into insolvency seems to be prima-facie evidence of violation.

The trust had been interested only in the larger operations of industrial alcohol and cattle feeding at these plants, and they did not enter into the whiskey business in Kentucky until about 1890. They bought out a few distilleries and attempted to modify them to produce both whiskey and alcohol, but their cutthroat methods of selling below cost to freeze out competition were unsuccessful and they were forced into receivership. Sometime later they reorganized as Distillers Security Company and established the subsidiaries of Kentucky Distillers and Warehouse Company and Julius Kessler Company. This time they were more successful.

Distillers made a valiant effort to compete with these companies, but they lacked a united front, and with no organization to support them and with their slim profits fanned by overproduction, they faced a losing battle. As a result, they started falling one by one, for various reasons. They grew tired of fighting the competition, and finances, fires, or old age took their toll. Beginning about 1896 and through 1905, Kentucky Distillers and Warehouse Company had purchased more than forty distilleries.

Since they had no use for so many distilleries and they were able to concentrate production in larger plants, the small ones were simply shut down and abandoned. The larger ones, such as Newcomb Buchanan plant in Louisville and the No. 36 plant at Athertonville, received the bulk of their production, but they continued to maintain some operations in Anderson, Fayette, Harrison, Nelson, and Madison counties. The brands that had developed a good reputation over the years were transferred around to other plants and completely lost their identification to the original producer, along with any distinctive characteristics of the whiskey.

As an example of the fight for survival that the distillers and wholesalers waged against the trust, I am reprinting an ad from a Kansas City, Missouri, paper dated February 9, 1913, by Marcel, calling themselves "the Trust Fighter." So many distilleries had joined the trust by this time that the remaining ones were holding their prices to stay in business while those controlled by the trust were raising their prices to whatever the traffic would bear.

Jere Beam of Jim Beam furnished a list of prices from their ledger dated 1906 showing prices that they were charging to various bars, saloons, and wholesalers.

1906 Sale Prices to Customers from J.B. Beam, Ledger

The Sealbach	4 cs Qts.	@ $8.50
Willard Hotel	4 cs Qts.	@ $8.50
George Toben	2 cs 5's	@ $7.50
F. A. Inder Stroth	5 cs 5's	@ $7.50
Dolph Mathey	2 cs 5's	@ $7.50
Al Kolb	2 cs 4's	@ $8.50
Boston Saloon	5 cs 4's	@ $8.50
Whalan & Johnson	3 cs 5's	@ $7.50
A. L. Veeneman	5 cs Qts.	@ $8.50
	2 cs Pts.	@ $8.75
	3 cs 1/2 Pts.	@ $9.25

1913 Cost of Distillery Supplies

Coal	$1.55 per ton
Malt	.73 per bushel
Corn	.75 per bushel
Rye	.69 per bushel
Barrels	3.25 each
Lumber	18.00 per 1,000 feet

By 1916, when it appeared that Prohibition was approaching the horizon, the trust had reduced their entire operations to less than half of their original acquisitions and had discarded a large number of brands, retaining only the most popular ones. When

Prohibition actually arrived on January 20, 1920, the companies originally involved in the trust did not completely go out of existence. The American Medicinal Spirits Company was formed shortly after to manage the concentration warehouses and to bottle whiskey for prescription sales. This company was headed by R. E. Wathen, who was employed by the trust at the J. B. Wathen Brothers Company in Louisville. Others joining the group were Sunnybrook, Old Taylor, W. A. Gaines, and the Kentucky Distillers and Warehouse Company organization. American Medicinal Spirits Company later joined with Pennsylvania-Maryland Corporation and formed National Distillers. Some of their brands of bourbon whiskey were being produced in Canada during Prohibition, and it wouldn't require a genius to determine where it was eventually consumed.

Julius Kessler, who had retired to Austria and had been a part of the trust organization, returned to the United States. His firm became a subsidiary of Seagrams in 1933.

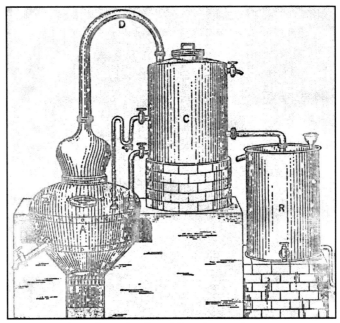

Pot still, used in French brandy manufacture.

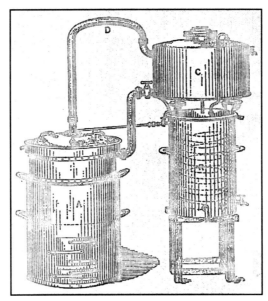

French brandy still, fitted with chaufee-vin.

A tailbox, an apparatus for receiving whiskey from a beer still.

Moonshine still, uncovered in Edmonson County.

The political power that brought on Prohibition was wielded chiefly by the alliance of Protestant churches formed by the Anti-Saloon League. Wayne B. Wheeler, second from left in the front row, is pictured with followers.

The drinks are on the house in Sloppy Joe's bar in downtown Chicago when news is flashed that Utah has just become the needed 36th state to ratify repeal of Prohibition on December 5, 1933. Of course, Sloppy Joe's had been in business all along.

A barrel of Ancient Age Kentucky Bourbon is gently rolled into storage where it will sleep away the days until it is ready for bottling.

Richard Cummins, second from left in the back, is pictured here with his employees of the Coon Hollow Distillery in Nelson County, 1890.

James B. Beam Distillery, Clermont, Kentucky, Bullitt County.

The baseball team of the Old Darling Distillery, 1911.

The 1,500,000th barrel of Barton Brands, April 22, 1961.

The 2,000,000th barrel of Barton Brands, January 11, 1967.

JAMES CROW, A NEW KIND OF PIONEER, ARRIVES IN KENTUCKY

A physician and chemist by training, James Crow reached Kentucky in 1825 and within a decade had revolutionized the making of Kentucky whiskey.

Smash Hit!

Every Ounce A Man's Whisky!

NOW! AMERICA'S LEADING
PREMIUM STRAIGHT WHISKY*

When you *swing* to Early Times, you'll find that you're always a hit as a host. For this wonderful whisky from the bluegrass is so distinctive that it's long been the favorite straight Bourbon in *all* Kentucky, where they have the best to choose from. Early Times is *hearty* but never heavy, *all* whisky, *fine* whisky, every ounce a *man's* whisky.

EARLY TIMES

*EARLY TIMES OUTSELLS ALL STRAIGHT WHISKIES AT OR ABOVE ITS PRICE

EARLY TIMES DISTILLERY CO. • LOUISVILLE 1, KENTUCKY • 86 PROOF

PRESENT IT PROUDLY

I. W. HARPER · The Gold Medal Whiskey

Chapter 4
After Repeal

Franklin D. Roosevelt campaigned for president in 1932 as the "Man of the Hour," and realizing that the economy needed a considerable jump-start, he promised to repeal Prohibition. The unprecedented experiment had been a dismal failure, adding the social problems created by the manufacture of and trafficking in illicit alcohol to those of alcohol abuse. The beer business run by organized crime as well as the moonshine and smuggling operations of distilled spirits helped inspire the "Roaring Twenties," when anything went. Speakeasies ran wide open, and a period of graft and corruption existed without parallel in the history of the nation.

The Twenty-first Amendment to the Constitution, enacted on

December 5, 1933, repealed the Eighteenth Amendment, otherwise known as the Volstead Act. The country had entered the period of the Great Depression, and Roosevelt was intent on finding ways through government action to use public dollars to stimulate the economy. There was still a segment of the population that opposed the repeal. Roosevelt opened the distilleries and saloons and closed the banks. The lingering thought of excessive consumption by individuals and the unscrupulous tactics of some distillers made the opponents skeptical of the repeal's chances of success. Nothing could have been more of a failure, however, than the fourteen-year experience of national prohibition. Some of the people who had been most active in the smuggling operations were the very ones who re-entered the legal trade and became leaders in the field.

One of the requirements for obtaining a license as a distiller, a wholesaler, or a retailer was that no officer or partner in the business could have a record of conviction for violation of any laws concerning the industry, and a thorough screening was conducted by inspectors of the Internal Revenue Service. Certainly some slipped through the cracks, and some should have been convicted but weren't. The ruling didn't apply to those who had not been caught and convicted. I think that the I.R.S. assumed that everyone had a tendency to circumvent the laws, and they placed such heavy restrictions on the newly organized distilleries that it was difficult to operate.

A government gauger held the keys to all access to the whiskey until the taxes were paid. Government seals were placed on all valves and flanges, and even the grain bins were locked. Production could not take place, nor was there any access whatever to the whiskey, unless a gauger was present. For operations to continue without serious inconvenience, this required a large number of federal employees to be available. In fact, the entire activity was based on complete distrust of everyone involved.

An elaborate system of applications for original registration or changes was established. Plats and plans required for every facet outlining the buildings and bonded premises had to be submitted for approval. Expensive bonds were required to insure the government for any breach of the laws or loss of whiskey.

The warehouses and bonded bottling premises in particular were targeted, with a focus on types of construction, including iron bars on windows and access doors secured with government sealed locks. The only thing not covered was the tax-paid storage rooms. Once the tax had been paid the government had no interest. If whiskey was lost at this stage, it was the proprietor's problem.

This system was later changed. In a complete reversal of the original, strict policy, storekeeper gaugers were removed from the premises, locks were removed, and so forth. The distiller is now treated just like any other taxpayer. Periodic reports are made showing withdrawals, the tax calculated, and the taxes submitted. The reporting method is patterned after the income tax except it is submitted bimonthly instead of quarterly or annually. It is still comparable to income tax payments, which are collected either on withholding at the time of payment or by estimation quarterly. Federal agents make semi-annual inspections of records and inventories of case goods they compare with whiskey dumped for bottling and cases shipped. If a shortage occurs at this time, an assessment is made and the tax is paid on the difference.

Early on, the various states also entered the picture and set up some very restrictive rules requiring permits and bonds along with a reporting system on transactions completed within the state. *True* magazine published an article in May 1962 called "The Red Tape Ambush of Your Right to Drink," which outlined some of the most ridiculous rules imaginable. Many of these rules have since been dropped, and the industry has come of age and is recognized as a legitimate business enterprise. Why would it ever have been considered otherwise except for the fact it is a permissive industry? After all, distilling is one of the most legitimate industries in the nation, because a majority of the people of this great country actually voted for repeal of prohibition.

In any event, the revived industry got off to a rocky start. The main restraint, of course, was lack of funds to re-enter the business. After fourteen years of inactivity, many of the older distillers were dying. The distilleries were either deteriorated or torn down and needed either rebuilding or massive renovation. Outside finances were sought, and in a number of cases the original owners lost their controlling interest.

One big obstacle the distillers were forced to cope with was the competition of already aged Scotch and Canadian whiskeys brought into the country not only during Prohibition but legally after repeal. The young, unmatured whiskey that U.S. distillers were forced to market was no competition for the already matured imports, and it took several years to build an inventory of aged bourbon. It was necessary to sell part of a distillery's production in order to support the inventory of older whiskey. The aim was to introduce a bottled-in-bond product at four years of age, which could not be accomplished until 1938 at the earliest. There is such a long holding period in the development of whiskey that recovering one's investment requires an optimistic entrepreneur able to predict what he can sell in future bottlings and able to hold on and reap a reasonable return. This was particularly true immediately after repeal, but it occurred again after World War II when distilleries were required to suspend whiskey production in favor of high proof alcohol for defense purposes. During this time as well, stocks of whiskey were very nearly depleted, and after the war ended, many brands were marketed at very young ages until distilleries could rebuild their inventories.

Immediately after repeal in 1933, the revival of the industry considerably alleviated the effects of the Great Depression for areas like Nelson and Anderson counties. Just prior to Prohibition there were 183 operating distilleries in the State of Kentucky—23 in Nelson, 23 in Jefferson, 17 in Bourbon, 12 in Anderson, and 10 in Franklin counties, with the others distributed throughout 26 counties. Of these, fewer than half survived the effects of prohibition, and some that did were on pretty shaky ground. The amount of money required to finance an operation is staggering. Size is also a determining factor, and small companies were just not able to compete.

Since the distilleries were all closed for whiskey production during the war, the Big Four began buying up the smaller ones mostly for their inventory of current production. However, their operations in the production of high proof spirits for defense were a pretty lucrative deal. They operated under the War Production Board and were given cost plus 10 percent. There was no uniformity in the cost of alcohol production because each distillery was different. Labor costs and transportation of fuel and grain all entered the picture, and I am sure that no reasonable price was ever questioned.

In addition, the Reconstruction Finance Corporation was established by the federal government at the end of World War II partly for the purpose of rehabilitating the distilleries when they discontinued production of high proof spirits. Many of the distilleries in the state profited by this largesse, which was intended to repay them for their part in the war effort. They rebuilt distillery buildings and installed dryer houses and many other portions of their facilities partially at government expense. It would seem that the cost plus 10 percent remuneration would have been sufficient when compared with the pay scale and hardships that some 16 million men and women who served in the armed forces during the same time were receiving. It was a little bit safer, too.

The distilleries have been very welcome in the economies of all whiskey-producing areas. I can say this without qualification about Nelson County. For years the city fathers discouraged other industries, and it was not until the mid-1950s when production started to decline and the smaller distilleries were closed, that other industries were brought in. Currently, with only three distilleries operating in this county, the new auto parts, greeting cards, and paper products industries have been a welcome boon.

The consumption of whiskey in the entire country has been reduced in favor of other alcoholic beverages. Distilleries have been consolidated to a point where very few are still operating, and ownership has changed hands from domestic to foreign interests. The only fully independent, family operated plant in Kentucky is Heaven Hill in Bardstown. They suffered a disastrous fire recently and lost their distilling operation and seven warehouses with a storage capacity of 108,500 barrels, but they now own warehouses at three other locations, all in Nelson County.

Brown Forman has large operations in Kentucky, including the Forester and Early Times plants in Louisville and the newly renovated Labrot & Graham Distillery on Glenn's Creek in Woodford County. Brown Forman also has operations outside the U.S.—for example, their Canadian Mist brand is manufactured in Ontario, Canada.

Jim Beam was bought out by American Brands in 1966. They now own all of the National Distillers plants of Old Crow, Old Grand-Dad, and Old Taylor, plus warehouses at two other locations in Nelson County, besides their main operating plants at Clermont in Bullitt County and Boston, Kentucky, in Nelson County. The parent company is now known as Fortune Brands.

Barton Brands has had a rash of changes over the years and at one time was owned by Argyle, a British subsidiary of Amalgamated, but is now owned by Canandaigua Wine of Canandaigua, New York. They own another plant, Barton Brands of Marietta, Georgia, and since the big merger of Glenmore with United Distillers, a subsidiary of Guinness of London, they have acquired the former Glenmore plants in Owensboro, Daviess County, and the small Viking Distillery in Albany, Georgia.

Boulevard Distillery, which was formerly J.T.S. Brown and before that T.B. Ripy, is the home of "Wild Turkey" and is owned by Pernod Ricard of Paris, France.

Maker's Mark in Marion County sold out to Hiram Walker of Walkerville, Ontario, in 1981. In addition to the Canadian Club plant they also ran a tremendous plant in Peoria, Illinois, which has since closed. This operation is now part of Allied Lyons of London.

All the operations once controlled by Schenley, including George Dickel in Tullahoma, Tennessee, are now part of United, whose parent company is Guinness. United also owns what's left of Glenmore and the Stitzel Weller or Old Fitzgerald plants. Stitzel Weller had been acquired by Norton Simon in the 1970s when they were operating the Kentucky River Distillery at Camp Nelson in Jessamine County.

The Ancient Age Distillery, RD no. 113 in Frankfort, was sold by Schenley to Robert Baranaska and Ferdie Falk of New York, and they sold it to Japanese investors headed by Takara Shuzo. It has since been sold to Sazerac of New Orleans.

The only other distillery operation in Kentucky is the Four Roses Distillery, RD no. 8, formerly Old Prentice. This is the only one being operated in Kentucky by Seagrams at this time. Seagrams has always been based in Canada, where they operate several plants making their most popular brands of Crown Royal and Canadian Lord Calvert. They have been engaged in spirit blends for many years and entered the straight Bourbon market for a period of time, but that has since been abandoned domestically. Seagrams owns a large warehousing complex under the name of Four Roses, formerly Lotus, in Bullitt County, but no distilling facilities are included. Recently they have become engaged in bottling a single barrel bourbon under the name of Four Roses for domestic distribution.

There are several other warehousing locations in the state that are still active, and a few small bottling facilities are engaged in specialty bottling, but that is the extent of Kentucky's whiskey business.

It has been a custom from the beginning among production people of the distilleries to cooperate with each other in furnishing information on construction, engineering, bottling, and so forth, and when any were in need of supplies, they could always borrow from one another. Lending anything that could help another out in a pinch was just standard procedure. My own experience was that I quite often provided analyses of whiskey and furnished advice whenever I was called on. In turn, many of my friends in competing distilleries did the same for me.

In 1940, H. McKenna had a theft of about 240 cases of whiskey from their tax-paid storage room. It wasn't long before the sheriff of Nelson County obtained a quantity of whiskey that they thought was the whiskey involved and, at the same time, apprehended the culprits. However, they had no proof that this was the same whiskey.

Andrew Nichols, county attorney at the time, asked me if I would analyze the whiskey and give my opinion of its origin. Of course, I was interested in doing so, and I asked that additional samples of the same lot be furnished for a comparative analysis. In a couple of days, Dr. Henry McKenna showed up with four quarts of the same day's production, and I ran the tests. I determined, without a doubt, that it was the same whiskey. However, I was a bit apprehensive about being called an expert witness. It ended that when the culprits were confronted with the evidence, and without my name being disclosed, the authorities were able to get a confession. For this I was very happy and relieved.

Chapter 5

The Master Distillers

In my description of the various distilleries that follows, I have listed the owners or proprietors as far as I have been able to ascertain them. In the early days, in most cases, these same people were the distillers who actually ran the operations. The plants were small, and the distillers could devote their time to propagating the yeast cultures needed to produce the fermentation. They oversaw the receipt and the cleaning of grain, grinding, mashing, fermentation, and distillation up to the final entry into the barrels in the cistern room. The barrels were then carried by conveyance or barrel runs for deposit in the warehouses for aging. Through experience and experimentation with different methods, these men acquired a special talent for improving the product.

In time, as the distilleries grew larger owing to demand, owners hired others who could be trained to perform these jobs, freeing them to handle the finances, sales, and administration. In many cases they passed these duties on to their sons or other relatives.

As these distillers gained experience, they were very much in demand, and, quite often, when one plant was shut down, they moved to another. It was not unusual to find a distiller who had supervised the production of whiskey at any number of distilleries. This is not to say that the whiskey would all be the same, because certain conditions and peculiarities prevailed that would alter the final product. However, the distiller could use his expertise in eliminating the undesirable features to arrive at a good product.

A number of distilleries passed into the hands of people who could supply the financial backing but lacked the know-how. In this case, it was not difficult to hire experienced people with a good reputation and develop a working relationship.

In some families not all the sons followed in the whiskey trade, and some may have skipped a generation. Daughters married into other whiskey families, and they carried on the tradition with in-laws and grandchildren.

Since the beginning of whiskey production in the state of Kentucky more than two hundred years ago, we have experienced such a drastic change in the business that very few of the original families are still represented—the Medleys, Browns, Samuels, and Beams being the exception. Automation and the computer age have also eliminated much of their role, but they are engaged in management and executive positions, if not in actual production.

The list of the older whiskey families is very impressive. Many of them have lasted through three, and as many as seven, generations. Here is a partial list:

Atherton	Cummins	Lancaster	Ripy
Beam	Dant	McGill	Samuels
Bixler	Dowling	McGowan	Stitzel
Blair	Edelen	McKenna	Sutherland
Boldrick	Hawkins	Mattingly	Taylor
Boone	Hayden	Medley	Thompson
Brown	Hollenback	Moore	Wathen
Callaghan	Johnson	Pepper	
Crow	Labrot	Pogue	

Jack Beam migrated from Maryland to Manton in Washington County around 1788 and set up a distillery about 1795. His son David followed and continued to operate the plant for a period. However, after David's son, David M., took over, they outgrew the facility and moved to Nelson County. Jack Beam and his son Edward spent their entire working lives at Early Times in Nelson County.

David M. had four sons, one of whom, Jim Beam, was operator of Beam & Hart or Clear Springs and F. G. Walker in Nelson County. After Prohibition he established the James B. Beam Distilleries at Clermont in Bullitt County. Parker, another son of David M., was active as a distiller and spent time at several other distilleries. Jere, son of Jim Beam, was associated with his father at Beam in Bullitt County. Booker Noe, son of Margaret, a daughter of Jim Beam, was distiller at the Beam No. 2 plant at Boston in Nelson

County for many years. Booker's son Freddie is presently at Beam No. 2 plant.

Parker Beam's son Carl was distiller at James B. Beam RD No. 230 at Clermont in Bullitt County as were Carl's two sons, Baker and David.

Earl, son of Parker, worked at T. W. Samuels RD No. 145, was also associated with brother Carl at Beam RD No. 230, and then was distiller at Heaven Hill RD No. 31 in Nelson County from 1946 until retirement. He was succeeded by son Parker and grandson Craig.

Joseph M. Beam had two sons, Minor and Joseph L. Son Minor owned the M. C. Beam Distillery at Gethsemane RD No. 405 and sold out to Bernard Dant, after which the distillery became Yellowstone.

Joseph L. Beam had seven sons and was distiller at any number of distilleries in and around Nelson County. During prohibition he and his son Harry operated for Waterfill & Frazier in Juarez, Mexico. He was associated with Stitzel in Louisville during the whiskey holidays in 1929 along with several of his sons. Joseph L. was one of the organizers of Heaven Hill Distillery in 1935, and he and other partners sold to the Shapiras during World War II. Harry was distiller at Heaven Hill until 1946, and he moved then to Sam Clay in Franklin County. Roy was at Stitzel in Louisville, and after prohibition he became distiller for Bill Veeneman at Frankfort Distillery in Louisville. He was later distiller at 21 Brands in Frankfort. Otis was at Buffalo Springs, Merchants Distillery in Vincennes, Indiana, and in later years was distiller at 21 Brands, Frankfort.

Desmond was associated with Park & Tilford in Midway and Old Lewis Hunter at Lair in Harrison County. Everett started out at Cummins-Collins RD No. 20 in Larue County and served for many years at Michter's in Schaefferstown, Pennsylvania. Wilmer was at Stitzel in Louisville but later joined the Dant operation of Yellowstone when they moved the plant to Louisville.

Roy had two sons who worked with him at Frankfort Distillery. Charles, the older, moved to Park & Tilford in Midway and from there he worked for Seagrams in Baltimore and Old Lewis Hunter at Lair in Harrison County and finally the Old Prentice Plant, or Four Roses, at Lawrenceburg in Anderson County. Jack, the second son, succeeded J. M. (Poss) Greenwell at Yellowstone, who retired from Yellowstone at the same time Wilmer Beam retired.

Jo Ann Beam, a daughter of Harry, youngest son of Joseph L., was employed by James B. Beam at Clermont in the bottling department for thirty-eight years. Jo has compiled a complete history of the Beam family and has detailed information on the distilleries they operated. This record is available at the Getz Museum of Whiskey History in Bardstown where she volunteers her time.

David Beam, son of Carl, was employed at James B. Beam RD No. 230 until he retired in 1996. He grew up on the premises and was a distiller there for nearly thirty-seven years. He now owns and operates the Old Kentucky Home Motel in Bardstown. Since the whiskey business was so ingrained in him (we call it a "blood disease") he decided to pursue it further. The Michter Distillery in Schaefferstown, Pennsylvania, had gone into receivership, and the equipment was sold. Back in 1976, during the nation's bicentennial celebration, Tom Sherman of Vendome Copper in Louisville had constructed a new pot still and allied equipment for them as a miniature-type operation. It was designed for a ten bushel capacity, or one barrel a day. This equipment included the mash tub, fermenters, condensers, and everything necessary for a complete distillery. David was able to purchase this distillery and move it to his premises next door to the motel and is preparing to put it in operation. The only thing lacking at present is a boiler plant and registration, and he is ready to go.

Guy Beam, a son of M. C. Beam, owner of RD No. 405 up to about 1910, was active in a number of distilleries prior to prohibition. After repeal, he worked with Joe Beam at Heaven Hill and also helped build the Fairfield Distillery RD No. 42 and was distiller there for a period of time. Afterward he and his son Burch teamed up with Paul Cummins Dant in 1946 to rebuild the Richwood Distillery at Milton in Trimble County, but this venture failed due to either lack of interest or finances of the financial backers.

Two other sons of Guy Beam were active in the whiskey business. Walter (Toddy) ran a retail package store in Bardstown for several years, and Jack was employed by Barton until he retired. During prohibition, Guy Beam was a distiller for A.M.S. in Canada.

Brothers Richard and Patrick Cummins came from County Carlow in Ireland in the mid-1800s after serving as apprentice yeast makers and distillers. Richard Cummins and Henry McKenna set up a distillery in Illinois, which they operated for about two years.

Richard moved to Marion County near Raywick and operated a distillery there for a period but then moved to Nelson County and established the Coon Hollow Distillery. He was a third partner in Mattingly & Moore and later bought out the Ballard & Lancaster plant at Loretto and moved all his operations there. Richard's son, J. P. Cummins, was associated with him as well.

Arthur, son of Patrick, was at the Coon Hollow plant and later moved to the Sam P. Lancaster Distillery and served at Crystal Springs in Louisville. Later he became owner of Willow Springs in Nelson County. Arthur J., son of Arthur, spent some time learning the trade at Willow Springs until 1920, when he established the Cummins Distillery at Athertonville and from there to the Louisville Distillery. His brother, Charles W., worked with him at the latter two plants as did his son Charles.

Samuel Bixler was the first known member of his family to enter the whiskey business. His first venture in this country was in Virginia, where he produced a sour mash whiskey. Later he migrated to Woodford County, Kentucky. In time, his four sons, Thomas, Milton, Otho, and Jerry, were taught the trade and made whiskey in Nelson, Anderson, Franklin, Scott, and Woodford counties.

Otho was employed at various stages at the Old Hermitage, J. H. McBrayer, and Old Jordan. His two sons, Coleman and Herman, followed, with Coleman being associated with H. McKenna in Nelson County, H. E. Pogue in Mason County, Old Poindexter in Meade, and last, J. W. Dant in Marion County. Coleman's son-in-law, Sam Sympson, served at H. McKenna and Tom Moore and retired from Barton. Herman Bixler was distiller originally at the Eagle Distillery in Owensboro owned by Tom Moore, and after Prohibition he was distiller at Tom Moore in Bardstown until his retirement.

Jerry Bixler served at a number of distilleries in the Frankfort area, and his two sons, Claude V. and Thomas, both served at Labrot & Graham, Old Judge, and Old O.F.C. in the same area. Claude operated some distilling plants in Canada during Prohibition, and shortly after repeal he was associated with the O'Rears at Buffalo Springs Stamping Ground. John Bixler, son of Coleman, served with his father at the Pogue Plant in Maysville and the Poindexter Plant in Ekron in Meade County.

The Dant family has been represented in a very large number of distilleries since the original J. W. Dant started his operation at Dant in Marion County in 1836. Various members of the Dant family have been involved in either management, finance, or production in such distilleries as Yellowstone, Dant & Head, Cummins, Ballard & Osbourne, Dant & Dant of Kentucky, John P. Dant, Shawhan, Park & Tilford, and Richwood. If detailed records were available, I'm sure that the Dants could be found in many more.

Henry E. Pogue and John N. Thomas operated their distillery in Maysville from 1869 to 1891, when the reins were turned over to H. E. Pogue II. The company was incorporated in 1876 and remained the same until prohibition. H. E. Pogue III succeeded his father and grandfather until 1925, when he moved to the New England Distillery of Covington, producers of rum, which was generally used for flavoring for the tobacco and food industries. H. E. Pogue III later joined the J. T. S. Brown Company.

The first member of the Medley family entering the whiskey

business was William, father of George E. Medley. This distillery was reported to be located in Washington County on Cartwright Creek near St. Rose. William died in 1853, and the date of his distilling venture cannot be determined.

George E. Medley was born in 1850, and in 1898 he accepted a position with Mattingly & Moore of Bardstown. However, in 1901 he joined with Dick Meschendorf in purchasing the Daviess County distillery, where he stayed until he died in 1910. His son, Thomas A., succeeded him and kept the corporation alive even during prohibition.

The original Daviess County Distillery Company was sold in 1928, and in 1933 the Medleys acquired the property of the Old Rock Springs Distilling Company, which was nearby. This plant and the name were sold in 1940. However, the Medleys had bought the property vacated by the Old Green River Distillery owned by J. W. McCullock, and they established the Medley Distilling Company. Although Ben F. and George E. II, brothers of Thomas A., had been involved in the Old Daviess County Distillery, the six brothers who were sons of Thomas A. were owners of the new plant.

Thomas Jr. and Ben later broke away and started the Old Stanley Distillery. George E. III died in 1944 and Edwin, in 1953. Wathen and John stayed with the Medley Distillery until it was sold to Renfield in 1959. Charles W., son of Wathen, was associated with the Renfield operation and also after Schaecter bought it; but after Glenmore bought out the land and subsequently sold to United Distillers, Charles repurchased the facility with his son Sam W. and is presently occupying the premises. Two sons of John Medley,

Tom and Bill, have stayed in the business. Tom is associated with Barton, which owns a plant in Atlanta; and Bill ran a bottling operation for Fleischman at Palatine, Illinois, but has since resigned and developed a used equipment business.

The Samuels family had very few offspring, but apparently each generation produced at least one male to continue with the tradition. William I died the same year as his father, T. W., but Leslie B. continued in the business until Prohibition. After prohibition he and his son T. William built a new plant at Deatsville about a mile south of the original distillery and started production in 1934. Leslie B. died in 1936, and T. William stayed on until August 1943, when the distillery was sold to the Foster Trading Corporation. After a tour of duty in the Navy in World War II, Bill returned to become a representative of Pneumatic Scale, manufacturers of bottling and packaging equipment.

In 1953, Bill re-entered the business when he bought the Burks Spring, or Old Happy Hollow Distillery, at Loretto in Marion County and renamed it in succession Old Samuels, Star Hill, and Maker's Mark. Bill Jr. joined him in 1967. When the company was sold to Hiram Walker in 1981, he stayed on to run the company. Bill Sr. retired at this time. Since the acquisition of Maker's Mark along with the complete Hiram Walker Corporation by Allied Lyons, Bill Jr.'s son Rob has joined the Hiram Walker Company and is assigned to Houston.

Chapter 6

Cooperage and Warehousing

Two other businesses sprang up with the advent of the whiskey distilleries. They were cooperage plants and warehouse construction.

Cooperage had been in existence for many years principally as a container for shipping all kinds of commodities from Europe and the West Indies. The barrels were constructed in Europe. The industry did not emerge in America until around 1846, when James Hopkinson Hamlen conceived the idea of competing with the foreign producers.

Barrels, hogsheads, and puncheons were the original containers. Barrels carried sugar, hogsheads held molasses, and puncheons the rum. Tight or wet barrels held liquids, and slack or dry barrels were used for other contents.

No barrel-making machinery was available in the early days, and all the containers were made by hand using specially designed coopers tools. Production was quite slow and thus very expensive. Hoops were fashioned of wood until sometime in the late 1800s when steel was substituted. A hierarchy was devised wherein coopers made barrels, and a "white cooper" made pails, buckets, piggins, firkins, tubs, churns, tankards, and other staved vessels.

Since barrels were a natural for containing whiskey, it followed that the distilleries would adopt this container and warehouses would be designed accordingly. It is not known exactly when charred white oak began to be used by coopers, but it was eventually adopted as a standard by the federal government as a specification for straight and bonded whiskeys.

Staves and heading were cut by independent millers and sold to the cooperage companies. Since the whiskey business is somewhat unpredictable, with ups and downs in the projections for future requirements, this caused the stave millers and cooperage companies considerable hardship in their own operations. The millers needed to cut timber sometime in advance, and then the cooperage companies needed to air dry the staves up to a year in advance and then further kiln dry before assembling them into the finished barrels. As a result, the distilleries started buying up the cooperage plants in order to control their supply of barrels. Along with the demise of so many whiskey distilleries, the smaller independent cooperage companies disappeared as well.

According to Bill Milholland, an old timer in the cooperage field with more than forty years experience and now with Kentucky Cooperage in Lebanon, Kentucky, the only remaining privately owned plants are Independent Stave of Lebanon, Missouri, which runs the Kentucky Cooperage of Lebanon, Kentucky, and the Missouri Cooperage of Lebanon, Missouri. He reports that there are three more small operators: East Bernstadt Cooperage in East Bernstadt, Kentucky, owned by C. S. & Ronnie Robinson; Kentucky Furniture & Woodworking in Lebanon, Kentucky; and McGinnis Wood Products in Cuba, Missouri. Brown Forman operates Bluegrass Cooperage in Louisville, which is the only distillery-owned plant, and they supply some barrels to other distilleries as well.

Some of the cooperage companies that started up after repeal of Prohibition but which no longer exist are:

Bardstown Cooperage—strictly handmade and short-lived
J. H. Hamlen & Son—Little Rock
Kelly—Kansas City
Klausner—Cleveland
Owensboro Cooperage
Pioneer—Chicago
Terre Haute Cooperage—Indiana
Kimball Tyler—Baltimore

Schenley controlled the Louisville Cooperage and Chess-Wymond operations. National bought out Motor Wheel of Memphis and Chickasaw in both Kentucky and Tennessee. Fleischman owned Oker of Cincinnati. Bluegrass in Louisville was run by Brown Forman and is now the only distillery-owned plant. White Oak was owned by Seagrams. Hiram Walker had a company in Peoria. Glenmore started the Bourbon Cooperage in Campbellsville and then moved it to Lebanon, Kentucky. In 1981 they sold to Independent Stave of Lebanon, Missouri, which is still operating. D. W. Karp had a barrel facility at his Loretto distillery No. 41 during and shortly after World War II, but it was abandoned.

Shortly after Prohibition was repealed, a Mr. Van Winkle moved to Bardstown and contracted for a number of warehouses at different distilleries. He built the "A" warehouse at T. W. Samuels at Deatsville, but apparently it was not braced properly with lateral bracing in addition to the vertical buck bracing and alternating rick bracing and it creeled. With considerable difficulty, it was unloaded and the warehouse was razed.

Tom and Ray Parrish, local builders, got into the warehouse construction business and built nine twenty-thousand-barrel houses for T. W. Samuels. Tom got out of the business, but Ray continued, building three houses for Heaven Hill and all the houses of Shawhan and Greenbrier (Double Springs). Mickey McGuire of Lebanon Junction built nearly all the warehouses for James B. Beam, all the Lotus Warehouse complex in Bullitt County for D. W. Karp (later sold to Seagram), as well as seven houses for Heaven Hill and two for Maker's Mark.

Howard Farnsworth, a native of Bardstown, first entered the warehouse construction business when he was a foreman for Mickey McGuire in 1959, when warehouse "F" was built for Maker's

Mark. In 1961, when "G" house was contracted, Farnsworth bid on his own and was awarded the job. Subsequently, he bid on jobs for Heaven Hill and eventually built eleven more warehouses for them.

Cliff Buzick of Bardstown began warehouse construction in 1941 and probably built more than anyone else in the area. His son Donald carried on after his death, and the firm expanded to other distillery buildings, such as bottling houses, case storage rooms, distillery buildings, boiler rooms, dryer houses, and regauge rooms. According to Donald, they built the following:

26 at Barton—Bardstown

2 at Beam—Boston

3 at Fairfield Distillery—Bardstown

1 at Glencoe—Bardstown

16 at Jack Daniels—Lynchburg, Tennessee

4 at Kentucky River—Camp Nelson

2 at Maker's Mark—Loretto

2 at Old Joe—Lawrenceburg

The Buzicks also built warehouses and other facilities at 21 Brands, Frankfort, a new distillery building and bottling house at Old Boone in Meadowlawn, and two warehouses for Old Poindexter, Ekron, Kentucky. Their most recent job in the distillery field was the Labrot & Graham plant in Woodford County for Brown Forman.

Cliff Buzick came up with a very innovative idea for the time. Lacking mechanical equipment for entry and removal of barrels, he placed stub posts in the center aisle the full length of the building and raised the center aisle two feet, allowing the third tier to be removed from the center. In this way it was only necessary to remove the two lower tiers from the outside aisles with the use of skids, which were commonly in use at the time. This reduced the labor and hazard of the higher tiers.

Later on, Harry Rogers of Mac Construction Company, Lebanon Junction, designed an electric and hydraulic ricking machine called "Jere" hoist, named for Jere Beam. This took all the labor away from the entry and removal and eliminated the hazard. He extended the machine further to allow the same type equipment to be used in ricks going much higher, thus eliminating the need for center aisles entirely. Distillers have since built houses with no ricks at all, allowing barrels to be stored head up on pallets and thus utilizing a forklift truck, which further reduces labor and the hazard of handling barrels by hand.

Chapter 7
The Kentucky Distillers Association

Agroup of thirty-two distillers representing the 2nd, 5th, 7th, and 8th districts of Kentucky convened in Louisville on June 10, 1880, to organize the Kentucky Distillers Association. In addition, many of the distillers held interests in other districts of Kentucky, particularly the 6th district of Harrison County.

The first order of business was to elect officers and directors of the Association, who were as follows:

Officers

Thomas J. Megibben, President, Fayette County, 7th District, representing Ashland District 6, Wm. Tarr, RD No. 1;

George C. Buchanan, Vice President, Jefferson County, 5th District, representing Newcomb-Buchanan, RDs No. 368, 4, and 97;

W. S. Hume, 2nd Vice President, Madison County, 8th District, representing W. S. Hume, RD No. 54;

John Callaghan, Secretary and Treasurer, Marion County, 5th District, representing Boldrick & Callaghan RD No. 370 and Crystal Springs Distillery, RD No. 78.

Directors

George G. White—Bourbon County, 7th District, representing G. G. White Distillery, RD No. 14;

Richard Monarch—Daviess County, 2nd District, representing R. Monarch-Glenmore, RD No. 24;

John M. Atherton—Larue County, 5th District, representing J. M. Atherton Distillery, RD No. 87;

Thomas H. Sherley—Nelson County, 5th District, representing E. L. Miles Distillery, RD No. 146, and New Hope Distillery, RD No. 101;

G. W. Swearington—Jefferson County, 5th District, representing Mellwood Distillery, RD No. 34;

Julius Barkhouse—Jefferson County, 5th District, representing Kentucky Distillery and Beargrass Distillery, RD No. 1.

The following named Distillers were present and took part in the organization of the association:

T. J. Megibben	7th district
Megibben Bramble & Co.	7th district
The Newcomb-Bramble Co.	5th district
Anderson Distilling Co.	5th district
George C. Buchanan	5th district
W. S. Harris	2nd district
George W. Swearingen	2nd district
John G. Roach	5th district
John G. Roach & Co.	2nd district
E. H. Taylor, Jr., & Co.	7th district
T. J. Monarch	2nd district
Thomas Sheffer & Co.	2nd district
J. B. Bush	5th district
H. B. Moore	5th district
R. Monarch & Co.	2nd district
J. I. Moore	5th district
G. G. Foster	5th district
Bel Air Distillery	5th district
W. S. Hume & Co.	8th district
E. C. George & Co.	5th district
Kentucky Distillery Co.	5th district
D. F. Brooks & Co.	5th district
M. V. Monarch	2nd district
L. Van Hook & Co.	7th district
Wm. Tarr & Co.	7th district
Redmon Distilling Co.	7th district
E. L. Miles & Co.	5th district
New Hope Distilling Co.	5th district
J. M. Atherton & Co.	5th district
A. Mayfield & Co.	5th district
John Cochran & Co.	7th district
J. G. Mattingly & Sons	5th district

The next order of business was to establish a uniform rate on whiskey in storage held on warehouse receipt in bonded warehouses, which was mandated by the Carlisle Bill. Rate was set at five cents per barrel per month, plus a gaugers fee and an additional five cents per barrel for labor when the whiskey was regauged.

(The Carlisle Bill also established the rules for Bottled in Bond as well as a uniform table of allowances for loss while in storage. This latter part was abolished in 1951 when the regulations were changed to permit bulk dumping and gauging prior to bottling.)

According to the *Wine and Spirits Bulletin,* the objective of the association shall be "the protection and advancement of the interests of its members, the devising and soliciting of appropriate legislation and the modification or repeal of needless and obstructive laws and regulations, the guarding of the common interest against unjust legislations, state or national."

Very little information can be obtained about the activities of the K. D. A. in the years following because records are apparently lost. However, Michael Veach of the Filson Club in Louisville suggested that I search issues of the *Wine and Spirits Bulletin* on file in the Louisville Public Library.

The bulletins, published at 113 West Main Street in Louisville, consist of a number of volumes dating from 1891 to 1915. They contain a great deal of advertising for distillers' brands, cooperage, and bottling and distillery supplies, as well as personal notes on members of the wine and spirits industry.

One article from the *Wine and Spirits Bulletin* dated March 18,

1891, mentions a meeting of distillers on March 3, 1891, at the Galt House for the purpose of organizing an association. Another article published on May 3, 1891, gives the details of this meeting:

Distillers Meeting

The Kentucky Distillers Association Reorganized— Mr. T. H. Sherley Elected President.

On the 3d of March there was a meeting of distillers held at the Galt House in this city, called together for the purpose of considering the advisability of organizing an association. The meeting was harmonious, and the unanimous sentiment was in favor of getting up such an organization and of incorporating it under Chapter 56 of the General Statutes of Kentucky. Accordingly a committee was appointed to draft a plan and present it to a general meeting to be called by themselves. This committee consisted of T. H. Sherley, Chairman, R. Monarch, Jas. Cunningham, R. W. Wathen, T. B. Ripy, T. S. Burnam, R. P. Stoll, F. S. Ashbrook, and T. M. Gilmore, Secretary.

Having completed their work, this committee called a general meeting for the 22d ult. at the Galt House for its approval or amendment. At this last meeting, which was presided over by Mr. R. Monarch, the attendance was good, and, although the discussion at times was animated, the best of feeling prevailed, and the report of the committee, with some few amendments, was adopted.

The name of the association is the Kentucky Distillers Association. It will be incorporated and have the power to sue and be sued. Its objects are general rather than specific, and it is doubtful if any distiller in Kentucky can find anything in it to object to. The officers elected were T. H. Sherley, President; R. Monarch, Vice-President; directors, M. V. Monarch, Second District; J. M. Atherton, C. Stege, Jas. Cunningham, and Nick Miller, Fifth District; F. S. Ashbrook, Sixth District; R. P. Stoll, Seventh District, and Thomas S. Burnam, Eighth District.

The directors, of which the President and Vice-Presidents are members ex-officio, were directed to prepare a set of by-laws and call another meeting for their approval. This meeting will probably take place in this city during the races this month. No Treasurer or Secretary has as yet been appointed by the directors, but it is understood that Mr. T. M. Gilmore, of *Bonforts Circular,* will be tendered the former position.

An issue of the *Bulletin* dated May 3, 1891, suggested that a paid representative be hired by the association to look after the interests of the Distillers before the Internal Revenue Department and also before Congress, when so instructed. The article continues, "As for any prejudices that such a course upon the part of distillers might excite, it is doubtful if any more prejudice than already exists against our trade can be brought out."

Another article, dated April 1, 1902, mentions Colonel John B. Thompson, proprietor of Old Jordan. "As President of the Kentucky Distillers Association, he has been the central figure in most of the sweeping betterments that have been inaugurated in the Bourbon trade in recent years."

The next documentation comes from a copy of the Amended Articles of Incorporation dated June 26, 1969, when Ben Morris of Brown-Forman was president and Frank Dailey was secretary. This amendment refers to the K.D.A. as being organized on November 11, 1940. The principal office was previously located in Louisville with Millard Cox, a local attorney, acting as Secretary. At this meeting the office was moved to Frankfort, where Cox's successor, Frank Dailey, was domiciled. The attorney, acting as secretary, was later changed to president and the office of Chairman of the Board was rotated annually between the board members. When Ed O'Daniel succeeded Frank Dailey as president, the principal office was moved to Springfield, Kentucky.

The Kentucky Distillers Association has been active with the Kentucky Legislature as well as the U.S. Congress and is considered the watchdog for the interests of the distillers. Several bills in the Kentucky legislature have been passed with their aid, which amends previous legislation detrimental to the distillers.

In 1966, during the administration of Governor Ned Breathitt, Bernie Keene of the 50th legislative district co-sponsored H.B. 140 with Eugene Stuart of Louisville to amend K.R.S. 243.680, which repealed the ten cents per gallon production tax. Former Governor Lawrence Wetherby, who had become a state senator at this time, pushed the bill through the Senate. The bill provided for a phase-out of the tax, reducing it two cents a year for five years. As a compromise, the advalorem tax on spirits in bonded warehouses was to be paid annually, also being implemented over a period of five years and then paid currently after that. Previously, spirits had been assessed as of January 1 each year and a deferred method of payment made at the time and tax paid along with accrued interest at the time of withdrawal. This new method of paying advalorem taxes was a windfall to the county and city school systems since it resulted in earlier payment of taxes.

In another bill, No. 972, amending K.R.S. 132.020 during Governor John Y. Brown's administration and introduced by Kenny Rapier, Representative of the 50th district, the advalorem tax on whiskey in storage was reduced from 31.5 cents per $100 valuation to 22.5 cents beginning in 1982. It was further reduced to 11.25 cents in 1983 and from 1984 and after, was set at 0.001 cents per $100. Ed O'Daniel, current President of K.D.A., was a senator at the time and sponsored it through the Kentucky Senate.

Larry Clark, Representative from Okolona, introduced Bill No. 430 during Governor Paul Patton's first administration in 1996, which amends K.R.S. 243.010 to allow distillers to obtain a license to purchase from Wholesale Liquor Dealers a quantity of liquor to sell to visitors at the rate of one liter per day per customer. This allowed the distillers to promote their product the same as the wine industry had been doing for years. A further amendment passed in the 1998 session to raise this to three liters per day, and in the 2000 session the distillers were allowed to perform sampling on the premises.

In recent years, emphasis has been placed on developing and improving bourbon sales in the export market, especially since there has been a decline in domestic sales owing to competition with the many other alcoholic beverages on the market. In 1987, export sales amounted to 5,083,000 gallons, but by 1999 sales had more than tripled to 15,691,000 gallons. Japan continues to lead in bourbon consumption, followed by Germany and Australia.

Beginning about 1995, a great amount of promotion was launched in the United Kingdom, the Czech Republic, and Spain. In 1988 there was a mere 219,000 gallons shipped to the U.K., but by 1999 that had increased to nearly two million gallons. In 1990, only 254 gallons were shipped to Czechoslovakia, but by 1999 the new Czech Republic had received 65,000 gallons. Likewise, in Spain, there was an increase from 59,000 gallons to 421,000 gallons in the same period.

The K.D.A., along with the efforts of the distillers themselves, continues to promote and increase the awareness of what bourbon is through various promotions, sales seminars, and high profile publications throughout the Far East and Europe. It is obvious that the promotional campaign is producing results.

Chapter 8
Distilleries of Kentucky

Anderson County
8th District

Belle of Anderson County Dist. , RD No. 400

Built on the cliffs overlooking the Kentucky River seven miles northeast of Lawrenceburg in 1881 by Brewer & Ross. It was sold to T. B. Ripy, who sold it to Murphy & Dowling in 1883. In 1888, Ed Murphy bought out Dowling's interest. Murphy was born in Daviess County in 1850, the son of Frank and Catherine Black Murphy, natives of Ireland. He entered the whiskey business at the age of 21 but then moved to Louisville in 1877 to pursue the same business and later moved to Anderson County in 1880. He was head distiller at T. B. Ripy, W. H. McBrayer, and Bond & Lillard plants for a period before he bought the T. B. Ripy operation. In 1907, E. M. Flexner of Louisville contracted for his entire production for the next ten years, but in 1912 Murphy was bankrupt and the distillery was ordered sold at the courthouse door. Unknown parties bought the plant for $7,600.

Ripy Bros. Distillery, RD No. 27

J. W. Stevens built this plant at Tyrone overlooking the Kentucky River. In 1888, J. P. Ripy purchased it and immediately replaced it with a modern plant operating as Old Hickory Springs Distillery (J. P. Ripy, Prop.). His brands were "J.P. Ripy," "Sam Stephens," and "J.W. Stephens." In 1905, the company was reorganized by the sons of the late T. B. Ripy with E. F. as president, J. C. as vice president, and Forest as secretary-treasurer and also general manager. The plant capacity was 162 bushels per day or about 16 barrels. They produced brands "Ripy Bros.," "Old Hardie," and some private brands until 1918 and were shut down by Prohibition. The distillery was dismantled and the building partially razed. The distillery was rebuilt and reorganized about 1935 as Ripy Bros. RD No. 27.

The plant was bought out by Bob Gould and run as J.T.S. Brown for a period and then sold to Austin Nichols on July 1, 1972; they were distributors of Wild Turkey, which was owned by Tom Mc-

Carthy, Sr. and Jr. Ernie Ripy was the manager of the operation for many years and later relinquished the reins to John Senter, since succeeded by Gregg Snyder. Tom Perry is the engineer and Jim Russell distiller. Austin Nichols sold to Pernod Ricard of Paris, France, and is operating as Boulevard Distillery.

I asked Tom McCarthy, Sr., one time where his Wild Turkey distillery was and he admitted they did not own one but would not disclose where the whiskey was made. It was rumored that Jim Beam at Clermont and Barton in Bardstown were making some of it and that there were some 45,000 barrels stored at Bernheim on July 1, 1972, which had been produced there. After Gould sold the plant he moved his whiskey to the Old Joe Distillery No. 35 in Anderson County and to the RD No. 23 at Burgin in Mercer. He had a longtime relationship with Schenley, which owned these plants at the time.

Boulevard Distillery, producers of Wild Turkey whiskey, had a mashing capacity in 1999 of 3,500-plus bushels daily and approximately 250,000-barrel warehousing at this plant. However, they also owned the five warehouses at McBrayer, where the Old Joe Distillery once operated containing a total of 100,000 barrels, and the six warehouses containing 120,000 barrels at Camp Nelson in Jessamine County, formerly Kentucky River and Canada Dry. On December 21, 2001, Ripy Brothers operating as Boulevard Distillery changed their name to Wild Turkey.

T. B. Ripy & Co., RD No. 112 and 418

Here I must quote the Supplement to the *Anderson News* dated June 1906: "Within the corporate limits of the town of Tyrone, in a graceful curve of the beautiful Kentucky River, stand two distilleries, the property of Kentucky Distillers and Warehouse Co. known as The Anderson County Distillery Co. with the registry No. 418 and the T. B. Ripy Distillery Co. with the Registry No. 112. The product of these distilleries is known throughout the length and breadth of the land, and Tyrone owes its existence to the distillery enterprise which had its origin on the banks of the Kentucky River many years ago." In 1868, Distillery No. 112 of Walker, Martin & Co. mashing 100 bushels per day, was erected at Tyrone, proprietors being Monroe Walker, Sam P. Martin, and James Ripy, all of Anderson County. In 1869 the property was sold to Judge W. H. McBrayer and T. B. Ripy, son of the above James Ripy. T. B. Ripy bought out Judge McBrayer in 1870.

The mashing capacity was gradually increased due to demand, and by 1899 it had reached 1,500 bushels daily. In 1900, Ripy sold the operation to Kentucky Distillers and Warehouse Corp., the trust.

The Anderson County Distillery Co. RD No. 418 was built in 1881 by Waterfill, Dowling & Co., with Mr. T. B. Ripy a member of the firm. Mashing capacity was 300 bushels per day at this time. Mr. Ripy bought out the other partners in 1885 and gradually increased it to 1,500 bushels, or about 150 barrels per day, but in 1899 he sold this plant to the trust. After it was bought by Kentucky Distillers and Warehouse Corporation, the mashing capacity was increased to 4,000 bushels daily, a size unheard of anywhere in Kentucky at this time and even for some time after Prohibition was repealed. They employed some 125 men in the distillery and warehouses, as well as about 20 women in the bottling house, thus contributing considerably to the economy of Tyrone as well as all of Anderson County. Both plants were shut down with the onset of Prohibition and dismantled.

The Waterfill & Frazier Distillery, RD No. 41

This plant was built in 1810 on Baileys Run at Tyrone, just above the T. B. Ripy plants, by John Bond and his son David. They operated until about 1850 and then sold to Jeff Mountjoy. J. M. Waterfill and George H. Frazier bought it during the Civil War, producing brands under their names. In 1903 John Dowling purchased the plant and continued with the same brand. The still house was destroyed by fire in 1904 with a resultant loss of some $30,000 but was quickly rebuilt. The plant continued to operate until 1918, when it was shut down by Prohibition. Sometime in the 1920s, Mr. Joe Beam and his son Harry moved the plant to Juarez, Mexico, and continued to operate as Waterfill & Frazier during prohibition. After repeal, a new plant was built at Anchorage, Kentucky, on the site of the Grosscurth plant No. 26, by John Dowling, but it was later bought by Joe Makler, who moved the name to Bardstown, where he had bought the Independent or Shawhan Plant No. 28.

W. H. McBrayer, Cedar Brook Distillery, RD No. 44

About 1844, Judge W. H. McBrayer established this plant on Cedar Brook Run about 1.5 miles east of Lawrenceburg. Judge McBrayer died December 6, 1887, and the estate went to his grandchildren, whose father was Colonel D. L. Moore, who owned the No. 148 distillery near Burgin in Mercer County. Colonel Moore operated it for his children in 1888 and 1889 and at the end of that time sold it to the trust. In 1876, McBrayer had won a medal at the Philadelphia Centennial, and he awarded his distiller, Newton Brown, a gold watch.

When the trust bought the plant in 1899 they enlarged it from 800 bushels to 1,800 bushels per day and operated it until 1916. They also added new warehouses, a bottling house, and a pumping station with a 2.5-mile line to the Kentucky River for cooling water.

James Levy & Brothers of Cincinnati were sole distributors of the W. H. McBrayer brand, but McBrayer stipulated that his name not be used after three years following his death.

Bond & Lillard Distillers, RD No. 247

John Bond built a distillery in 1820 near the W. H. McBrayer plant of Cedar Brook. He moved it in 1836 a short distance away and operated until his death in 1842, when it was taken over by his son David. W. F. Bond succeeded his brother in 1849, and in 1869 he formed a partnership with his brother-in-law, C. C. Lillard, thus creating the name. Lillard died in 1896, and the company was sold to the trust in 1899. They improved the plant by replacing the water wheel and burr mill with steam-operated equipment and modern roller mills. According to the Supplement to the *Anderson News* of June 1906, the distillery was operated by Stoll & Company of Lexington, a part of the trust, and in 1904 they were awarded the grand prize of the Louisiana Purchase Exposition held in St. Louis. The distillery operated until Prohibition, and the brand name was used for a period after repeal by National Distillers.

W. B. Saffell Distillery, RD No. 123

W. B. Saffell started this plant on Hammond Creek just north of Lawrenceburg in 1889. He had been a yeast maker for W. H. McBrayer for some twenty years. He continued the operation until his death on August 31, 1910. His heirs continued to run the plant until Prohibition, but it was never revived afterward.

Old Prentice Distillery, RD No. 8

The distillery was established in 1855 near McBrayer on present Kentucky 513 and was bought by J. T. S. Brown in 1904 and operated until Prohibition. Shortly after repeal Gratz Hawkins, Agnes Brown, and her son Wilgus Naugher renovated the plant and started operations as Old Joe RD No. 8. Seagrams bought the distillery in 1942 and produced high proof spirits during World War II for defense purposes. Seagrams later renovated it, increasing the capacity to 2,400 bushels per day.

Charles Beam had been with his uncle, Desmond, at Park & Tilford in Midway, and they both transferred to the Old Lewis Hunter when Schenley bought Park & Tilford. He was put in charge of Old Prentice in 1962. Ova Haney succeeded Charles in 1982. Associated with him were Joe Weber, head of maintenance; Gerry Werner and Mike Bullock of New Haven were assistants. On February 19, 2002, Kirin Brewing Ltd. of Japan bought the Four Roses plant and also the Lotus Warehousing and bottling operation of Four Roses of Bullitt County from Seagrams.

Seagrams changed the name to Four Roses and is making bourbon whiskey for export—this is now the only Seagrams distillery operating in Kentucky. They continue to operate the warehousing in Bullitt County, formerly called Lotus and now Four Roses, where they store most of the whiskey they produce. This includes the Lawrenceburg, Indiana, plant as well.

Although the plant in Anderson County has a warehousing capacity of some 30,000 barrels, the warehouses in Bullitt County have a capacity of 426,000 barrels. Whiskey is transported in tank truck and entered in barrels at their cistern room. The Bullitt County complex also bottles a single barrel bourbon whiskey under the name of Four Roses for export and domestic distribution.

Old Joe Distillery, RD No. 35

Built by Joe Peyton in 1818 on Gilberts Creek near McBrayer, Peyton enlarged the plant and then sold it to Hawkins, who operated it until 1849-50. M. S. Bond, the son of John Bond and half-brother of W. F. Bond, bought the plant and operated it for a number of years, then sold it to T. B. Ripy in 1885. Ripy operated it for only about one year before selling it to Captain Wiley Searcy, a veteran of Company E, 21st Regiment, Kentucky Infantry.

Fire destroyed both bonded warehouses and a free house on March 22, 1909, with a loss of 3,000 to 4,000 barrels and a large number of case goods. Ripy Bros. purchased the property and rebuilt it in 1911 and continued operating until Prohibition. The plant was rebuilt after prohibition and was owned by Sam Friedman of Cincinnati, with his son-in-law Stanley Levy managing and Gene Stratton assistant. Toby Head, who had been at Dant & Head RD No. 47 when A. Hammer bought the distillery, went to Old Joe in the early 1950s for a short time but left and returned to Bardstown.

Schenley owned the plant for a period of time, and Jim Gatewood from the No. 113 plant in Frankfort was manager. Later when Gould sold the No. 27 plant, he moved part of his whiskey to Old Joe warehouses and part to the No. 23 in Mercer County. The warehouses were leased to Seagrams for a period, but later were sold to Boulevard Distillery.

In 1912, the distillery was incorporated with W. P. Frazier, N. E. Gee, J. H. Hawkins, and G. B. Hawkins, with capital of $5,000. In the early 1930s, G. B. Hawkins and others bought the Old Prentice plant newly designated as RD No. 8 and operated it as Old Joe. Pelham Hawkins, the son of J. H. and a nephew of Gratz (G. R.), was distiller.

J. S. Searcy & Co.

This plant was built at Boiling Springs on Hammonds Creek and operated from 1880 to about 1910. Brands were Boiling Springs and Old J.S. Searcy.

S.O. Hackley,
Hoffman & Hackley,
The Hoffman Distilling Co., RD No. 406 (Commonwealth No. 112)

S. O. Hackley established a distillery by that name in 1880 near the mouth of Hammonds Creek. Ike Hoffman became a partner in 1889, and the name changed. Several years later Hoffman gained full control but went into receivership in 1912. The plant was idled until 1916, when it was sold to a Cincinnati wholesaler who increased the capacity from 15 bushels to 50 bushels. Closed during Prohibition, the plant fell into complete disrepair. It was rebuilt about 1933 as RD No. 112 and operated as the Hoffman Distilling Co. In 1968, the distillery was operating as Ezra Brooks. I visited the distillery in the mid-1970s, and the still house was falling down. Ben Ripy was operating the bottling plant and was bottling the brand Fighting Cock as well as some private brands for Julian P. Van Winkle III, and some bottling is still being done for Van Winkle.

G. B. Hawkins, RD No. 124

G. B. Hawkins (apparently Sr.), operated this distillery near Ripyville. It is not mentioned in the June 1906 Supplement of the *Anderson News*.

Bonds Mill Distilling Co., RD No. 35

Established in 1934 near McBrayer and apparently taking the name from Bonds Flour Mill, this plant was engaged in bottling a six-month-old whiskey produced by Old Joe Distilling Co. In 1935, the firm built a 300-bushel house across the Salt River from Old Joe, and by 1940 they were bottling their own Bottled in Bond as Bonds Mill. In 1945, the name changed to Bond and Johnson Distilling Co. For a period, Bob Gould made J. T. S. Brown whiskey at this plant after Creel Brown sold out his plant No. 29 at Early Times in Nelson County.

Distillery and warehouses were in complete disrepair by the early 1970s.

Boone County
6th District

Boone County Distillery, RD No. 8

Sometime after the Snyder Distillery at Milton in Trimble County burned in July 1879, W. T. Snyder, the son of the owner, bought the property on the Ohio River at Petersburg and established the Boone County Distillery. The trust bought the distillery in 1907 and it operated until 1918. The W. T. Snyder brand was sold mostly in Cincinnati, and it was later bottled at the No. 36 plant at Athertonville in LaRue County.

Bourbon County
7th District

J. A. Miller,
G. G. White, RD No. 14

This plant was located on the Maysville Pike, now U.S. 68, about half a mile from Paris. It was built by a Mr. Foley in 1855 but went through a succession of owners, including J. A. Miller, Wm. Tarr, G. G. White, and C. Alexander, between 1856 and 1882. Mashing capacity was 400 bushels.

Ford & Bowen Distillery,
H. C. Clay,
Peacock Distillery, RD No. 10

This plant was built near Kiserton in 1857 by H. C. Bowen, who was succeeded by his son in 1869. An interest was sold to H. C. Clay and James K. Ford with their main brand of Peacock. The plant had a mashing capacity of 600 bushels and two warehouses of 12,000 barrels, one brick and the other of wood construction. The plant was sold in 1890 to parties in Cincinnati, who sold out to the trust in 1902. In 1905, KD&W installed two new boilers and new roller mills. H. E. Pogue Distillery of Maysville bought the plant in 1911, and it was salvaged in 1916 by Max Munich, a Paris junk dealer.

J. S. Shawhan, RD No. 11

Daniel Shawhan moved into Bourbon County from Pennsylvania in 1788, established himself near a spring behind Mt. Carmel Church, and built his distillery there. Daniel died some years later, and his sons, Joseph and John, who had entered the business with him, continued the operation. The firm's production was very small—in 1881 they produced only 232 barrels. In 1883, they did not operate at all because of dry weather and the resulting poor grain harvest. Shawhan and Brandon built the Excelsior Distillery in Harrison County in 1837 and sold it to T. J. Megibben in 1850.

The Shawhans moved to Weston, Missouri, in 1918, and after repeal of Prohibition they started the McCormick Distillery there. All remnants of the plant in Bourbon County have disappeared.

Tom Pendergast, boss of Kansas City, acquired the distillery in Weston, Missouri, and later moved the name to Bardstown when he bought the Independent Distillery No. 28. He ran this plant for a number of years and sold it to the states of Washington and Oregon. Cloud Cray, owner of Commercial Solvents, bought the Weston plant, which is still in existence.

Howard & Bowen Distillery,
H. C. Bowen,
Bourbon Dist. Co., RD No. 102

H. C. Bowen came to Kentucky from Maryland and plied his trade as a builder of houses and churches. In 1867, he built a distillery at Kiser Station that he sold. He built another at Ruddles Mill in 1869 and became part owner of this plant. His partner, J. Howard, sold out to him in 1879, at which time the capacity was 444 bushels with an 8,000-barrel warehouse capacity. In 1882, he produced 3,400 barrels. In 1890 the plant was sold to Wm. Adams and Joe Messer of Cynthiana, Robert House of Covington, Levi Weiskoph of Cincinnati, and B. F. Bowen of Ruddles Mill. They completely remodeled the plant and changed the name to Bourbon Distilling Co.

On February 4, 1891, the still house was destroyed by fire at a loss of $20,000. It was rebuilt and continued operations up to Prohibition.

Jacob Spears, W. H. Thomas, RD No. 84

Jacob Spears operated a distillery on Kiser Road between Jacksonville Road and what is now U.S. 27 in 1836. He sold it to Gov. Thomas Metcalfe, who, after the Civil War, sold it to a Major W. H. Thomas. The mashing capacity was 54 bushels, and in 1882 Thomas made 900 barrels, which meant that he operated no fewer than 200 days, a long season for the time. He owned one brick warehouse of 2,500 barrels, which is still in use as a tobacco warehouse. He operated a quart house from his home with a drive-through window, from which the old "Blind Tiger" was patterned during Prohibition. Many distilleries operated a quart house, or retail operation, to which the customer brought his own container to be filled from a barrel that had been tax paid. The Blind Tiger was used for selling illegal whiskey during prohibition. The building had no windows but a revolving shelf where the customer deposited money and came back later to pick up his bottle. One never saw the proprietor, who was thus protected from the revenuers.

The Paris Distillery, RD No. 77

Located on the Kentucky Central Railroad one mile from Paris and built by Geo. N. Bedford and W. T. Buckner, this distillery was operated from 1860 to 1880 as Buckner and Bedford and then sold to Sam Clay, Jr. Production had originally been a sweet mash whiskey, but Sam Clay produced a sour mash. In 1882, the capacity was 412 bushels with 15,000-barrel storage, making Paris Distillery handmade sour mash. Beginning in 1884, T. J. Megibben operated the plant until he died in 1890. In 1892, the plant was leased to N. J. Walsh of Cincinnati, whose manager was H. D. Haynes; it continued as Paris Distilling Co. In 1901, the company was bought by the trust and reorganized as Julius Kessler. Kessler bought the Peacock Distillery in Bourbon County and the Old Lewis Hunter plant in Harrison County in 1902 and used the brands Sam Clay and Paris Club.

In 1905 a storm blew down their boiler smokestacks and took the roof from a large warehouse, halting production until repairs were made. Another catastrophe occurred on May 2, 1913, when a granary fire destroyed the entire still house, with a loss of about $100,000. However, their warehouses were saved as well as 800 head of cattle in the slop pens nearby being fed distillery slop. In August of the same year, Sam Clay moved the operation to the Old Lewis Hunter plant No. 9 in Lair in Harrison County. Thus ended the company's distillery operations in Bourbon County.

The property was transferred to a Mrs. Robert Grogin and her two brothers, Carl and Thomas Wilmoth, in 1920, who sold it two years later to E. F. Spears.

Woodford, Spears & Clay

Stoner Creek, six miles southeast of Paris, Kentucky, was the location of this distillery. It had been a water-powered mill prior to 1867 and was built by E. F. Spears. J. T. Woodford, E. E. Spears, and Sam Clay converted it to a distillery and operated from 1867 to 1876. The warehouses were located on the northeast side of the creek on the opposite side from the distillery. It was reported by the *Paris True Kentuckian* that 370 barrels of whiskey were made in the 1878 season. No further record of whiskey production is available. The property was purchased by Ed Simms of the Xalapa Farms, and a residence was established there. Fire destroyed the residence in the 1940s, and it was rebuilt on the same site.

Wm. Davis & Co., The Millersburg Distillery, RD No. 30

Wm. Davis, who had been a successful whiskey peddler for a St. Louis wholesaler, built a 500-bushel plant at Millersburg in 1881, costing some $40,000. His plan was to produce 6,000 barrels of handmade sour mash annually under the brands Old Cabin, Kentucky Belle, and Daniel Boone. As of October 1, 1882, government records show an inventory of only 76 barrels, and the venture apparently failed.

George Pugh, RD No. 13

Located at the mouth of Townsend Creek where it empties into the South Fork of Licking River, this plant was built by Jacob Wilson in 1800. By the year 1880, it was believed to be the oldest operating distillery in Bourbon County. John Ewalt rebuilt the plant after it was washed away by a flood. It was sold to George Pugh in 1856. Supposedly operated by water power, the plant produced only 150 barrels a year. Remnants of the plant are still visible.

Gus Pugh, RD No. 44

Sam Ewalt built this plant in 1858 and sold it to Gus Pugh in 1870. It was located just east of Shawhan in Bourbon County. Gus Pugh remodeled the distillery and by 1882 he was making 250 barrels a year of handmade sweet mash. However, by 1902 R. S. Stroder contracted to bottle and distribute Old Pugh sour mash whiskey.

Joshua Barton, RD No. 160

J. B. Barton, who was born in 1835 at Blocks Crossroad, later operated a distillery above Steel Ford on Hinkston Creek. He was a successful farmer as well and developed a herd of short horn cattle and expanded to buy the Alexander Miller farm south of Millersburg. In 1902, R. S. Strader and Son of Lexington owned the Old Barton brand, which was then being distilled and bottled by James E. Pepper.

J. T. Redmon

John T. Redmon operated a farm and distillery on Flat Run, a tributary of Stoner Creek north of Paris. He also built another distillery on Gray's Run near Cynthiana in Harrison County, which he sold, but he continued operation of the Bourbon County plant. On March 7, 1873, the *Paris True Kentuckian* reported that he produced 2,775 gallons, about 56 barrels in that season.

Boyd County
9th District

John Mock Distillery, RD No. 59

Established in 1880 just seven miles southwest of Ashland just off the present I-64 exit 181 at Coalton, this distillery was operated by John Mock and later by his son, John Jr., and distributed throughout eastern and central Kentucky. During Prohibition, A.

Ph. Stitzel of Louisville bottled the Old Mock brand for medicinal purposes using various distillations.

Bullitt County
5th District

A. B. Chapeze & Co. RD No. 18

Located on the Bardstown-Springfield branch of the L&N Railroad, this distillery was operated by A. B. Chapeze prior to 1874. Ben Chapeze peddled the whiskey over a large part of the country but later contracted with Wright and Taylor, a Louisville wholesaler, to distribute it. In 1892, the plant and Old Charter brand were purchased by Wright and Taylor, who also owned the brands Pride of Louisville, Cane Spring, Kentucky Taylor, and Old Logan. In 1913, mashing capacity was increased from 600 bushels to 1,000 bushels. Marion Taylor had purchased John Wright's interest prior to 1895 and continued operations until 1918 and also distributed medicinal whiskey during prohibition. After repeal, Schenley bought the Old Charter brand. After prohibition was repealed in 1933, the plant was rebuilt by Kentucky Valley Distilling Co. as RD No. 18, using brands Old Stave and Kentucky Valley. Old Tyme Distillers bought the plant later in the 1930s and added the Green River label. Schenley bought the plant during World War II and used it mostly for storage. Charlie Bullock was manager for a period and was replaced by Dan Shacklette.

In 1954, Jimmy (Pinch) Simms helped to open the distillery

for a six-month operation while Schenley was building the George Dickel plant in Coffee County near Tullahoma and Normandy in Tennessee. This was the site of the Old Cascade plant before Tennessee went dry. Jim Beam bought the plant about 1970 for warehousing and it was joined to RD No. 230 as contiguous property by an easement from the L&N Railroad. They have a warehouse capacity of 60,000 barrels. R. J. Corman later bought the branch railroad and operated it mainly for his Old Kentucky dinner train.

Murphy, Barber & Co., RD No. 230

Located on the L&N Railroad's Bardstown-Springfield branch at Clermont, the Murphy Barber Co. was formed in 1880 by Squire Murphy, a local native; A. M. Barber, a transplanted eastern schoolteacher; and Calvin Brown, a whiskey salesman. Mashing capacity was 197 bushels and 1,800 barrels annually and was produced as Cane Spring. In 1893, Murphy died and Brown retired, but the Murphy estate contracted with S. Grabfelder & Co. of Louisville to handle sales. In 1903, Grabfelder purchased the plant and increased capacity to 500 bushels, using it in brands Cane Spring, Echo Spring, Old Mill Valley, and Clermont.

During Prohibition the property was purchased by Jim Beam and son Jeremiah for a rock quarry and all the buildings were razed except for one warehouse. After prohibition Jim Beam reincorporated and rebuilt on this property and established it as Jim Beam RD No. 230, which was the original number of his plant in Nelson County. He started mashing in March 1934 and developed the Old

Tub brand as well as the Jim Beam and Bonded Beam brands.

Beam was also associated with Dave Karp with Loretto distillery RD No. 41. In 1948 they sold to National Distillers, and the Beam interests bought back the No. 230 plant, less any barrel inventory. It was necessary for Beam to repurchase from warehouse receipt holders all the Beam production they could find for their Bonded Beam brand, and they also purchased quantities of Heaven Hill two-year-old for Jim Beam 90 proof.

American Brands bought both the No. 230 plant at Clermont and the No. 13 plant at Boston, Nelson County, in 1966. Jere Beam stayed with the plant until he retired, as did his cousin Carl "Shucks," who was distiller.

In the 1970s the distillery was enlarged to 8,200 bushels per day, and at the present time the Clermont plant has 20 warehouses of 400,000 barrels total capacity.

The warehouse storage of the Beam plants in Nelson and Bullitt are as follows:

Boston plant	Nelson County, No. 13	(4)	42,000 barrels
		(22)	20,000 barrels
Clermont	Bullitt County, No. 230	(20)	20,000 barrels
Chapeze	Bullitt County, No. 79	(3)	20,000 barrels
Waterfill	Nelson County, No. 28	(5)	20,000 barrels
Glencoe	Nelson County, No. 4	(4)	20,000 barrels

(Sold to Heaven Hill in 1997)

The total storage at the above warehouses is in excess of 1,240,000 barrels, which does not include the facilities recently acquired from National Distillers of Old Crow, Old Grandad, and Old Taylor and another facility in Cincinnati. The latter were bought in 1985, and storage continues at all locations as well as extensive bottling at the Old Grandad plant near Frankfort.

R.B. Hayden & Co.,
Barber Ferriell,
Old Granddad, RD No. 420

R. B. Hayden originally started a distillery on his farm at what later was to be Greenbrier Station in Nelson County in 1790. This distillery later became Greenbrier, Wathen, and then Double Springs. Currently it is the site of American Greetings (greeting card producers). Through a series of three generations, Hayden established the Old Grandad brand about 1840. In 1885, together with F. L. Ferriell, he built a new plant at Hobbs Station on the Bardstown-Springfield branch of the L&N Railroad about 12 miles west of Bardstown.

The Greenbrier plant was sold to Brown & Bro. R. B. Hayden, apparently the son of the original owner, died in 1885, and his part was bought by R. S. Barber. The name was changed to Barber, Ferriell & Co. The plant had a mashing capacity of 100 bushels and storage of 7,000 barrels.

Mr. Barber died in 1894 and was succeeded by his son-in-law, A. B. Baldwin. R. E. Wathen bought the plant in 1899 and changed the name to Old Granddad with Nace Wathen distiller and manager. The distillery was destroyed by fire in 1900 and was rebuilt to 400-bushel capacity. Nace Wathen was born at Rolling Fork in 1857 and died in 1912. He was a storekeeper gauger with the U.S. Internal Revenue Department and then joined the J. B. Wathen & Bro. in Louisville, until that company was sold to the trust. When R. E. Wathen bought the plant at Hobbs Station he took a position there.

The plant operated up to Prohibition, when all whiskey was removed to concentration houses of R. E. Wathen in Louisville and bottled as medicinal whiskey. The distillery fell into disrepair, and no remnants remain.

Campbell County
6th District

Old 76 Distillery, RD No. 33

Located near Licking River south of Newport at Finchtown, the distillery was managed by Albert V. Stegeman in 1904 and was closed in 1918 by Prohibition. Brand names were Medallion and Woodruff.

Cave Spring Distillery, RD No. 34

This distillery was built shortly after repeal with a capacity of 850 bushels and bottled Kentucky Banner under contract with George T. Stagg of Frankfort. Schenley acquired the plant and closed it down in the early 1950s.

The Winchester Distillery, RD No. 3

Located at Dayton on the Ohio River and purchased by the trust. It was closed for a period about 1893 for an overhaul of the boiler plant, after which it continued to operate until Prohibition. It was then closed for good and dismantled.

Carroll County
6th District

Whitehead & Company,
Old Darling Distillery, RD No. 4

The State Gazeteer for the state of Kentucky in 1879 listed the Whitehead & Company Distillery as the only one located in Carroll County. It was built across the Kentucky River near Prestonville, directly west of the location selected by the Jett Brothers in 1881. Andrew Darling bought the plant in 1880 and established the brand Old Darling. He also operated under the name of North American Distilling Company, with brands Carroll County Rye and Carroll County Club Bourbon.

Elias Block of Cincinnati controlled all these brands from 1891 to 1908, at which time the operation was sold to the trust. Thomas D. Murphy became the manager, and the company continued operations until closed by Prohibition.

According to Jean Yeager of Carrollton, her father Arthur Dunn was the supervisor for all the men, and Lucinda Cole was the bottling forelady. Arthur and Lucinda married in 1917, and when prohibition was enacted, they moved to Pennsylvania.

They later returned to Milton in Trimble County, where he became a meat cutter for City Meat Market, Pearl Packing Company, and the Kroger Company before he retired in 1962. Mr. Dunn was also associated with Paul C. Dant, Guy Beam, and others in an aborted attempt to revive the Richwood Distillery at Milton in 1948.

The buildings of Old Darling Distillery remained somewhat intact until 1936, when they were gradually razed and the premises were converted to other uses.

Jett Brothers Distillery, RD No. 15
Richland Distillery,
Kentucky Senate, RD No. 36

Captain Albert N. Jett served with the Union Army during the Civil War, and after being mustered out of service he returned to his home in Carrollton. However, in 1867 he moved to Harrison County, where he was employed as a distiller until 1872, at which time he accepted a commission as a U.S. storekeeper-gauger and served in that capacity until 1881.

In the year 1881 Captain Jett returned to Carrollton, and along with his brothers James F., Joseph S., and George W., built the Jett Brothers Distillery just east of the Kentucky River in Carrollton. At this time they established the brands Jett Best, Jett Special, Jett Bourbon, and Jett Rye, as well as a number of other labels.

Albert and George sold their interest to the other two brothers in 1888, and Albert became deputy collector for one year, then transferred as a storekeeper-gauger until 1893, when he returned to the Jett Distillery. There he remained until 1898 when he again became a storekeeper-gauger until 1905.

James F. Jett was the manager of the Jett Distillery. His brother Joseph F., while maintaining an interest in the operation, lived in Peoria, Illinois, where he was also head distiller for the Feeders and Distillers Trust. There is no reference to the acquisition of the Jett Brothers Distillery by the trust, and apparently the Jetts owned and operated it until it was closed by Prohibition.

Mrs. Jennie Jett, widow of George W. Jett, inherited the property during prohibition. On April 6, 1936, she sold the Jett brands and distillery to Oscar G. Kipping and Dora Lee Browning of Carrollton. There must have been a pre-arrangement on this agreement because on April 7, 1936, this agreement was further assigned to the Kentucky Senate Distillery, a name owned by a Cincinnati group. Mrs. Sara Harris of Frankfort, widow of Tom Harris, a former state senator, natural resources commissioner, and commissioner of agriculture during the Ford and Carroll administrations, was the granddaughter of Captain Albert N. Jett and daughter of Luther and Kathryn Jett Fothergill, who furnished me with a copy of this agreement. She couldn't, however, elaborate on the details of the transfer.

The new owners of the distillery refurbished the plant and increased the capacity from 200 to 410 bushels per day, with a warehouse capacity of 40,000 barrels.

The flood of 1937 that devastated the entire Ohio Valley flooded the plant, but the only crucial damage was to their records. A new 15,000-barrel warehouse had just been erected, and none of the whiskey was affected.

Schenley bought the distillery during World War II and operated it for several years, but since it was in the floodplain of the Kentucky and Ohio rivers, they removed all the whiskey and abandoned the plant.

Jim Fothergill of Carrollton, a brother of Mrs. Harris, has a photograph taken during the 1964 flood, and the plant appeared intact except for the high water, but no remnants are visible today.

Some whiskey had been produced there in the 1950s under the name of Blue Ribbon Distillery RD No. 105, which was the brand name used by Fible and Crabb at RD No. 107 at Eminence in Henry County. The registration number was assigned to Buffalo Springs Distillery at Stamping Grounds in Scott County.

Clark County
7th District

A. A. Clay, RD No. 27

Little is known about this distillery except that it operated under the name of A. A. Clay with the brand A. A. Clay Sour Mash. It was located near Kiddville in Clark County, and records show that in 1880 it had only 44 barrels of whiskey in storage.

Crittenden County
2nd District

Old Hickory Distillery, RD No. 49

On a visit to western Kentucky, on October 5, 2002, I stopped by the Wheeler Museum in the town of Marion. They had a display of the Old Hickory Distillery, which was started in 1896 by Fred Hopple, Jr., on the site of the Marion Machine Works. The capacity was listed as 25 bushels, which would only produce three to four barrels at that time. Checking my records further, I find an Old Hickory Brand made by E. E. Robertson at RD No. 49 in Marion. Doss & Robertson apparently operated the distillery around 1910.

An Old Hickory label was registered with the U.S. government by James Walsh of Cincinnati in 1907, and an Old Hickory Rye was patented by P. Goldberg on June 4, 1901. Unregistered labels also appear, but the connection is not shown.

Old Hickory Club—J. P. Ripy Dist., Lawrenceburg, Ky.

Old Hickory Ridge—Morris M. Hagederon, Cincinnati, Ohio

Old Hickory Springs—J. P. Ripy Dist., Lawrenceburg, Ky.

Daviess County
2nd District

Old Stanley Distillery, RD No. 76

In 1960, Ben Medley and his brother Tom having disassociated themselves from the Medley Distilling Co. RD No. 49, built a new distillery at Stanley. It consisted of the still house, dryer house, boiler room, and bottling house, all under one roof. The 5,000-barrel warehouse was close by. The bottling house was equipped for three lines to accommodate one size each to avoid delay in making changes from the various sizes.

I visited the distillery in the early 1970s, and at that time they were not operating but had produced about 2,000 barrels of whiskey. In the Liberty National Bank report of December 31, 1977, they had 147 barrels in storage, 111 of which were more than 8 years old and the remainder produced in 1970 and 1971. The December 31, 1996, report shows 95 barrels of 1990 production, but it is not known who produced it. Their bottling consisted of "Tom Simms," which was their own label, as well as some custom bottling for retailers in Florida and also for Holiday Inns.

Apparently the venture had not been successful, and the plant was sold at public auction in the late 1970s to a Florida company. Harry Hastings, owner of Moon Distributors in Little Rock, had an interest in the company.

The Daviess County Distilling Co., RD No. 2

This distillery was built in 1874 near the bend of the Ohio River and was operated by R. Monarch, president, and John Callaghan, vice president and treasurer. By 1888, they had established a well-known brand, Kentucky Club.

In 1901, George E. Medley, formerly of Springfield, Kentucky, and one-time associate of the Mattingly & Moore plant near Bardstown, purchased an interest in this company from the estate of R. Monarch. In 1904, Mr. Dick Meschendorf of Louisville joined him, and they assumed full control. Mashing capacity at this time was 50 bushels per day. Mr. George Medley died in 1910 and his son Tom succeeded him. In 1911, fire destroyed two warehouses, which were soon rebuilt, and they increased their mashing operations to 750 bushels.

The distillery operated up to Prohibition when it was closed. Inventory was sold to Wathen Bros. and moved to concentration warehouses in Louisville, where it was bottled by American Medicinal Spirits. In 1928 the Daviess County Distillery was sold to the Field Packing Co. directly east of this location, which was the site of the J. W. McCulloch Distillery operating as Green River RD No. 9. The Green River plant burned in 1918, and the only portion of it that was saved was the lower parts of A, B, and C warehouses.

R. Monarch–Glenmore Distilling Co., RD No. 24

The Glenmore Distillery was built in 1869 by Richard and Will Monarch as the R. Monarch Distillery. They also bought a plant around 1890 from E. P. Millett, its location not exactly known.

Millett moved to Louisville, formed the Thixton-Millett Co., and purchased Boone & Bros. Distillery near Bardstown. They closed the Nelson County plant and then bought the Blair plant in Marion County after which they both returned to Louisville.

Brand names of Monarch Distillery were R. Monarch and Kentucky Standard, and in 1888 they advertised the Glenmore brand claiming it was made with the same formula as Hermitage, which was owned by W. A. Gaines. A lawsuit followed, but since most distillery operations were essentially the same at that time, nothing came of it.

During the period up to 1900, when Monarch died, he was operating the Glenmore, R. Monarch, and Daviess County distilleries. Upon his death, the Glenmore plant was sold to James Thompson & Co., a Louisville wholesaler. H. S. Barton, a brother-in-law of the Thompsons, became manager of the distillery, until it was shut down by Prohibition. The plant had been expanded to 5,500 bushels, no doubt the largest in the state.

Glenmore remained a concentration house during prohibition and bottled and distributed whiskey for medicinal purposes. Also, from 1928 through 1930, they received permits to make 6,500 barrels of whiskey to replace depleted stock.

Full production was resumed after prohibition, and they continued to mash until about 1960, except for the war years of 1942 to 1945, when they produced high proof spirits for defense. After the mashing ceased, they produced all their whiskey at the Yellowstone plant in Louisville but maintained their bottling in Owensboro. Their bottling plant was one of the most up-to-date operations in the whiskey business.

Glenmore acquired the Medley Distilling Co., RD No. 49, from Abe Schaecter in 1988, but they sold all their facilities in Daviess and Jefferson counties to United Distillers, a subsidiary of Guinness, in 1991.

The headquarters of Glenmore had been maintained in Louisville, with Colonel Frank Thompson as chairman and Joe Engle-hard as president. When Colonel Thompson retired from the distillery, he devoted his time to the Old South Insurance Co., which was organized mainly to insure whiskey warehouses. Englehard retired a few years later, and Frank Jr. took control. However, he held the post for only about eight years, and when he died, his brother Buddy took over.

During World War II, Glenmore bought the Burks Spring Distillery RD No. 44 in Loretto, Marion County, and then bought the Yellowstone Distillery in Louisville from the Dants in 1944. They sold the Burks Spring Distillery to Dave Karp shortly after the war.

Recently, United Distillers sold the bottling facilities to Canandaigua Wine, and Barton is utilizing it for a large portion of their bottling. The Medley portion that they had acquired was sold by United to Charles W. Medley and his son Sam Wathen Medley, who has continued with the Medley name but changed the registration to No. 10, which was the number used by his grandfather at the original Daviess County Distillery. Charles Medley is leasing part of the plant facilities and is engaged in bottling a single barrel bourbon in a special mold bottle under the name of Wathen.

The Eagle Distillery, RD No. 8

Built in 1869 by T. J. Monarch as a 50-bushel house, it was sold in 1890 for $110,000 to R. Monarch to settle the former estate. It had been increased to 400 bushels by that time and its brands were T. J. Monarch and Imperial. R. Monarch died in 1900, and the plant was sold to Tom Moore of Bardstown and T. E. O'Keefe of Oswego, New York. In 1908, the name was changed to Imperial and the brands were Imperial, Beaver Run, Monteagle, Hazelwood, and Chippewa. The plant was dismantled during Prohibition and the brand name Imperial was acquired by Russell Brown of American Distilling Co. of Pekin, Illinois.

Hill & Perkins, Rock Spring Distilling Co., RD No. 10

Prior to 1881, Alexander Hill and W. H. Perkins operated this plant on the Ohio River about one mile downstream from Owensboro. They sold the plant to J. T. Welch in 1881.

In 1889, the proprietors were recorded as A. Rosenfield and Abe Hirsch with brands Hill & Hill, Tip Top, J.T. Welch, and J.T. Welch McLean County from another Welch Distillery. Silas Rosenfield leased the plant for ten years in 1906 under the name Rock Spring.

The premises were purchased by Wathen Bros. at the beginning of prohibition, and the whiskey was bottled by American Medicinal Spirits using the brand name Hill & Hill. The brand was acquired by National Distillers after prohibition.

Tom Medley acquired the plant from Wathen Bros. in 1933 and after some renovation, began mashing in the fall of 1934. When Tom Medley died in 1940, the distillery was sold to Fleischmann Distillery Co. They operated the plant up until the 1970s, during which time they fully automated the grinding, mashing, and distilling. The bottling was performed at their other plants outside the state.

The M. V. Monarch Co., RD No. 12

On September 2, 1889, Mr. M. V. Monarch, owner of Hanning, Barry, Cliff Falls, Baltimore and Payne Distillery and the Sour Mash Distilling Co., all in Daviess County, consolidated them under the M. V. Monarch Co. Officers were M. V. Monarch as president, P. E. Payne vice president, R. W. Slack secretary and F. W. Clarke treasurer.

Sour Mash Distilling Co., RD No. 12, Medley Distilling Co., RD No. 49

This distillery was owned by M. V. Monarch and incorporated into the plant of that name and bottled M.V. Monarch, Kentucky Tip, Sovereign, and Jockey Club.

A new plant was built on this site in 1937, but it lasted for only about two years and was liquidated. It was bought by bond holders, who sold it to the Medley Bros. in 1940. They operated until 1959, when they sold to Renfield, but Wathen and John stayed on to run the operation. Charles Medley, son of Wathen, took over in 1967. Renfield sold out in 1978 to Abraham Schaecter, who consolidated his entire operations including the operations in Frankfort that he purchased from Sid Flashman. In 1988, Glenmore bought the facilities and retained Charles in charge of distilling.

This operation was short-lived, however; in 1991, United Distillers bought all the Glenmore operations, and again Charles W. and son, Sam W., bought the distillery and renamed it the Medley

Distilling Co. RD No. 10, which was the number used by Tom Medley, grandfather of Charles, at the Daviess County Distilling Co.

J. F. Hanning Distillery

This distillery was built at Yelvington by John Hanning. Mashing capacity was 100 bushels. It burned down within the same year and was rebuilt. Hanning sold to M. V. Monarch Co., referred to in the M. V. Monarch Co. of Owensboro, in 1889. The distillery was sold to the trust in 1899.

J. F. Hanning Distillery

J. F. Hanning built another distillery in Yelvington about 1903 after he had disposed of the other one to M. V. Monarch. This plant had a mashing capacity of only 4 bushels, and Hanning's annual output was 16 barrels, just enough to keep him in his own personal drinking whiskey.

Applegate & Sons, RD No. 7

C. L. Applegate built a distillery in Yelvington in 1868. By 1891 he had established the brands of Rosebud and Beechwood. He was also a breeder of thoroughbreds, and one of his horses bearing the name of Rosebud won the 1914 Kentucky Derby. He operated a wholesale liquor business in Louisville, and in 1910, when

Van Cleve and Hardesty Distillery of Raywick went bankrupt, he bought that plant.

J. W. M. Field, RD No. 3

This distillery was built in 1873 near Owensboro with a mashing capacity of only 2.5 bushels. However, over the years up to enactment of national prohibition, it had been increased to 250 bushels, a 100-fold increase. A few of their white porcelain miniatures shaped like a jug were floating around at one time as well as some of their larger advertising posters. The distillery never reopened after repeal.

M. P. Mattingly, RD No. 13

W. S. Stone built this plant in 1855 near the Ohio River in the town of Mattingly, just west of Owensboro. M. P. Mattingly bought the 60-bushel house in 1863 and by 1891 had increased it to 275 bushels. The brands were W. S. Stone and Daviess Country Club.

M. P. Mattingly, Jr., was operating the plant at the time of prohibition, and he had added the brand Little Tub.

W. L. Barry, George D. Mattingly & Co.

Built by W. L. Barry in Lewisport when it was part of Daviess County but it is now in Hancock. He sold it to a Mr. Reiley, who operated as Reiley Distilling Co. then sold it to George D. Mattingly & Co.

In 1891, their brands were W. L. Barry and Kentucky Sunshine, the latter being used by American Medicinal Spirits for prescription bottling.

J. W. McCullough, RD No. 9, Green River Distilling Co.

John W. McCullough, a former Internal Revenue Officer, had worked as a gauger at this distillery on the Green River below Owensboro, and he purchased it in 1888. He established the brands Green River, Mountain Dew, and Kentucky Moonshine, all advertised as handmade sour mash.

The company was incorporated in 1900, and the name was changed to Green River Distilling Co. Just prior to Prohibition in 1916, J. W. McCullough was president; John L. Layne, secretary and treasurer. Sales were contracted with E. A. Montague of New York, the elite and socially prominent bootleggers during prohibition. The distillery burned in 1918 and only portions of A, B, and C warehouses were saved. The whiskey that was left at the time of prohibition was sent to concentration warehouses of Old Taylor in Woodford County, and as late as 1925 bottling was still being done by American Medicinal Spirits using the Green River label.

The plant was demolished during prohibition but was rebuilt in 1937 and lasted only a short time. The Green River label was acquired by Old Tyme Distillery of New York and produced at the A. B. Chapeze plant RD No. 18 in Bullitt County.

McCullough had advertised his product as "the Whiskey Without a Headache," but with repeal of prohibition many new, more restrictive rules were passed and the Alcohol & Tobacco Tax Division made them drop the slogan. They compromised with "the Whiskey Without Regrets," but it soon lost its popularity.

Fayette County
7th District

Stoll, Clay & Co.,
The Commonwealth Distillery Co., RD No. 12

Originally a Mr. Sanders had erected a cotton mill in 1800 on 12 acres of land at Sandersville, 3 miles north of Lexington. The railroad was eventually run near this mill and in 1880 R. P. Stoll, H. C. Clay, and James S. Stoll converted the brick building to a distillery and operated as Stoll, Clay & Co. with an additional investment of $60,000 for warehouses. Their brands were Owl Club, Elkhorn, and Commonwealth.

They sold out to the trust in 1908 and operated as Commonwealth Distillery Co., with M. A. Goodman as president and manager and offices in Louisville. J. S. Stoll, president of Stoll & Co., died on March 4, 1908. The land was purchased after 1920 by Hillenmeyer & Sons for a nursery. All buildings were removed except one brick warehouse, which is still in use.

Siver Springs Distillery, RD No. 46

This plant was built on 40 acres of land at Yarnells Depot just northwest of Lexington in 1867 and operated by G. W. West & Bro. In 1871, West sold to Younger Stone, who dismantled the distillery. Nat Harris of Versailles bought the property in 1881 and rebuilt the distillery producing 2,000 barrels a year. Mr. and Mrs. James E. Pepper bought the plant in 1895; it was then known as the Nat Harris & Little Pepper Distillery. By 1907, it was operated by James E. Pepper & Co. as the Henry Clay Pure Rye Distilling Co. After 1918 the plant was dismantled.

Headley & Peck, RD No. 54

Erected on the property of Robert L. Crigler of Cincinnati under lease by John A. Headley and C. Y. Peck and located on the Harrodsburg Pike 1.5 miles from Lexington. Built in 1872, it consisted of the distillery, one brick, and three metal-clad frame warehouses with a valuation of $30,000. Production was set at 4,000 barrels annually, and the brand was Woodland. In 1894, a scandal unfolded as warehouse receipts in Texas and Mexico turned out to be fraudulent. No record of the outcome has been found.

Lexington Distillery, RD No. 93

This plant was located adjacent to the Wm. Tarr plant on the Frankfort Turnpike. Before 1833, it was operated by a Mr. Bosworth and later by Daniel and Henry McCourt. By 1882, it had been idled for several years, and the property was purchased by Wm. Tarr & Co. It was acquired by the trust, which built a new bottling house on the premises in 1910. Prior to the time that Wm. Tarr bought the distillery they had gone into receivership and among their assets were more than 10,000 barrels of whiskey in inventory.

The Ashland Distillery Co., Wm. Tarr & Co., RD No. 1

Turner Clay & Co. established a distillery in 1866 on eleven acres of land, on Leestown Pike just beyond the city limits of Lexington. In 1871, it was sold to Wm. Tarr of Bourbon County and T. J. Megibben of Harrison County. The plant burned in 1879, and a new distillery called William Tarr & Co. was built on the site at a cost of $115,000. Principals in the new company were Tarr, Megibben, Sam Clay, Jr., and J. M. Kimbaugh. The plant had a mashing capacity of 984 bushels, an annual production of 5,500 barrels, and produced under the name of Ashland and Old Wm. Tarr.

In 1902, Stoll & Co., part of the trust, purchased the Wm. Tarr Distillery along with the Lexington Distillery adjacent to it. The distillery was dismantled, but they retained the warehouses and in 1909 built a new bottling house. In 1913, KD&W sold the premises to the L&N Railroad and further operations were moved to the Nelson Distillery in Louisville. The warehouses were used continuously for storage until 1923, when everything was all moved to concentration houses in Louisville. It was not until 1966 that the warehouses were remodeled for other use, and the old bottling house burned in 1986.

The Henry Clay Distillery Co., James E. Pepper & Co., RD No. 5

Henry Clay Distillery was built in 1858 by Headley & Farra. The plant burned in 1873, and from 1875 to 1879 the property was used as a pork processing plant. James E. Pepper purchased the property and built a new distillery in 1880, mashing 500 bushels with an annual production of 11,000 barrels. It was reported that the value of the property was $125,000.

Brands were Old Henry Clay and James E. Pepper. In 1882, A. Starkweather of New York was handling sales. However, in 1896 the company became bankrupt with $350,000 in liabilities. Pepper died December 24, 1906, while visiting New York.

A Chicago group reincorporated the distillery as James E. Pepper Distillery Co. in 1908, and in 1911 mashing was increased to 1,000 bushels. During Prohibition, from 1920 to 1933, the warehouses were used as concentration houses and bottling of prescription whiskey continued. Schenley bought the operation in July 1933 for about $1,000,000, razed all the frame buildings, and built a completely modern plant of 1,000-bushel capacity. Fire destroyed the four old, brick warehouses in July 1934 and the 8,000 barrels of whiskey inside, with a resultant loss of some $500,000. Schenley continued to use the plant until 1958. The buildings served as warehouses until 1976 when they were converted to other use.

W. W. Grimes, H. C. Clay & Co., RD No. 150

W. W. Grimes operated a distillery on Boones Creek off U.S. 421 prior to 1880. H. C. Clay & Co., which sold its interest in the Peacock Distillery in Bourbon County, bought this plant in 1880 and operated it for a number of years. Later it was sold to the Iroquois Hunt Club, and the brick distillery was converted to a club house.

H. D. Owings Distillery, RD No. 8

In 1879, Robert F. Johnson built a new distillery on his farm 3.5 miles from Lexington on the Russell Springs Pike (Centerville Road), and in 1882 H. D. Owings was operating the plant, making 800 barrels annually under his own brand name.

Franklin County
7th District

E. H. Taylor Jr. & Co.,
The George T. Stagg Co.,
Kentucky River,
O.F.C., RD No. 2, Carlisle RD No. 113
Ancient Age Distilling Co., The Straight Whiskey Dist. Co. of America, Albert P. Blanton

Edmond Taylor purchased a distillery in Franklin County that had been advertised for sale in the *Western Citizen* of October 8,

1858. By 1869 he had also completed the O.F.C. and Carlisle distilleries, and he began operating as E. H. Taylor, Jr. Co. The O.F.C. was torn down in 1873 and replaced with a modern plant, but it burned in 1882. The modern plant was rebuilt, this time of brick and stone. The Carlisle was not harmed.

Owing to the cost of rebuilding and following the economic slump of 1884, Taylor borrowed heavily from a friend, George T. Stagg of Richmond, who was part owner of a distillery at Silver Creek in Madison County No. 54, originally the W. S. Hume Co. Stagg turned out to be a not-too-trustworthy friend, won foreclosure on Taylor, and continued to use E. H. Taylor's brand name. After considerable litigation Stagg retained the brand E. H. Taylor and left Taylor with the Old Taylor, which he had previously used at the J. S. Taylor plant on Glenns Creek in Woodford County RD No. 53. Stagg prospered in the operation but died in May 1893. Albert P. Blanton, who had started out as office boy, had progressed to manager, and he then became president and manager and later became principal owner.

In 1910, the Carlisle output was leased to Einstein & Palfrey of Chicago. At this time the distillery operated as the Kentucky River Distilling Co., and brands of Carlisle and Cove Spring were made.

When Prohibition was enacted, Blanton purchased the property and obtained a permit to operate a concentration warehouse, bottling house, and distributor of medicinal spirits. In 1929, O.F.C. Distillery was reactivated as one of four Kentucky plants to replenish medicinal stock. In 1933, the Geo. T. Stagg Co., brands and property were leased to Schenley for 99 years. Blanton continued as manager, and Frank Stagg remained in the organization.

Schenley eventually made two districts out of their operations, with Orville Schupp living in Frankfort in charge of the Frankfort area plants and Wathen Knebelkamp in the Louisville district. Orville Schupp's experience began as maintenance engineer at the No. 113 plant in 1939, after which he became plant engineer and then plant manager. When Colonel Albert P. Blanton retired, Schupp became regional manager until 1957.

At this time he moved to Cincinnati as production manager for the district and when Ed Monahan died, Schupp took his place as production manager for all Schenley Industries. He remained in this position after Rapid American bought out Schenley. However, in 1969, he had a confrontation with Rapid American's president during a visit to the Lawrenceburg, Indiana, plant, which led to a separation contract. Sometime later, Riklis, the chairman, abandoned ship with all the cash, leaving several employees, including Schupp, with worthless debentures and monthly contractual payments.

During the Korean crisis in 1950-51, Schenley, as well as all the other distilleries in the state, anticipating another government mandated shut-down similar to that of World War II, produced whiskey to the limits of their capacity. However, the curtailment did not occur, and the overproduction left most of the distilleries with a glut of inventory that they would be hard pressed to dispose of. This was particularly true for the fact that whiskey was required to be moved from bond and the tax paid at eight years. The tax had risen to $10.50 per gallon by this time, and it threatened some distilleries with bankruptcy. Lew Rosenstiel, head of the Schenley empire, began a move to get an extension to 20 years, but it took some time to get the law changed. As an example of what the overproduction caused, whiskey at four years old in 1954-55 was selling for about $1.30 to $1.35 per O.P.G. and warehouse receipt holders had a cost of about $1.50 to $1.55 per gallon invested, including warehouse storage. In the meantime, with the vast amount of whiskey in storage at the Stagg plant it was imperative that something be done. Hence the purchase of the J. W. Dant plant at Gethsemane, owned by Armand Hammer. (More on this venture under J. W. Dant RD No. 47 in Nelson County.)

By 1972 production ceased and bottling was minimal. In 1982, Schenley sold the 152-acre property and Ancient Age brand to Robert Baranaska and Ferdie Falk of New York, retaining 83 percent of the inventory. Ferdie Falk embarked on a program of a single barrel premium priced brand under the name Albert P. Blanton but later sold out in the 1980s to Japanese investor Takara Shuzo. The plant has since been sold to Sazerac of New Orleans and the name changed to Buffalo Trace.

The Frankfort Distillery,
The K. Taylor Dist. Co.,
National Distillers (Old Grand Dad), RD No. 14

W. J. Baker operated this distillery at Forks of Elkhorn shortly after the Civil War and in 1869 was bottling Old Baker and Old

Cabinet brands. He also had Swastika brand, but Hitler and World War II climaxed that. In 1911, the firm was represented by W. J. Baker, Jr. In 1922, the plant was designated a concentration warehouse and bottling was for medicinal purposes. They bottled Old Blue Ribbon and Queen of Nelson for Thos. S. Jones & Co., and Old Baker, Paul Jones, Four Roses, Antique, Kentucky Triumph, and Honey Dew for Paul Jones & Co. By 1928, all the whiskey was sold and the property sold to J. C. Noel of Frankfort.

Paul Jones & Co. bought the name and brands and the Frankfort Distillery Inc. was organized in Louisville and was acquired by Bill Veeneman. (See Paul Jones Dist. Shively.)

By 1930, all but two of the warehouses had been razed and the remains of the property had seriously deteriorated. In 1933, Noel sold the property to parties organizing the K. Taylor Dist. Co. Kenner Taylor, the son of E. H. Taylor, was president but took no actual part and died shortly afterward.

Brands were Kenner Taylor, Golden Bantam, Old John, and Forks of Elkhorn. According to George Koeing, a retired employee, National Distillers purchased the plant on October 1, 1940, and renamed it "Old Grandad." About 1960 the plant was purchased by National Distillers and operated as "Old Grand Dad." It was gradually improved over the next several years to become a most modern and up-to-date operation. Production and bottling were done here for Old Taylor and Old Crow five miles away.

American Brands DBA James B. Beam bought the plant in 1986 and continues storage and bottling there.

John E. Fitzgerald, RD No. 11

This plant was located on Benson Creek outside Frankfort and was built by John Fitzgerald. Brands were Old Fitzgerald, Old Judge, and Benson Springs, distributed by S. C. Herbst of Milwaukee. About 1900, Fitzgerald sold the brands to Herbst and moved to Hammond, Indiana, where he became superintendent of another distillery. The plant continued until Prohibition closed it down.

The brand Old Fitzgerald was purchased and used by W. L. Weller Co. for medicinal whiskey and became the leading brand of Stitzel-Weller Dist. when the Julian P. Van Winkle and Alex Farnsley families organized that plant in 1933. This plant was operated under the names of Sam Clay, Benson Creek, Rocky Ford, and 21 Brands.

Harry Beam became distiller at Sam Clay in 1946, when he left Heaven Hill. He was succeeded later by his older brother, Roy, after he left the Frankfort Distillery in Louisville. Roy died in the 1950s, and another brother, Otis, who had been operating a Bills Auto Supply Store in Leitchfield, Kentucky, took his place. They were all sons of Joe Beam of Bardstown.

Sid Flashman moved his Double Springs operations there from the Old General Plant in Louisville in the late 1960s and then sold it to Abe Schacter, who closed it down and moved everything to Owensboro, where he had acquired the Medley plant.

J. N. Blakemore, RD No. 96

John Neville Blakemore (1837–1898), a very wealthy farmer, operated a small distillery on the Franklin-Anderson County line between Alton Station and Farmdale. In 1880 he was producing the brand Arnold Springs. When he died in 1898, the distillery was sold to the trust and then torn down. "J. N. Blakemore" brand was later made at the trust's "36" plant in Athertonville.

Cedar Run Distillery, J. & J. M. Saffell, Prop., RD No. 91

This distillery was located on the Kentucky River at the mouth of Cedar Run Creek. The Saffells sold to the trust in 1905 and retired from distilling. The trust, however, continued to operate the plant until Prohibition, when it was dismantled. The brand Cedar Run was used during prohibition for medicinal whiskey.

R. P. Pepper

The Ross Pepper Distillery was located west of Frankfort near Benson on Benson Creek in 1870. About 1880 the brand R.P. Pepper was acquired by Paris, Allen & Co., an English group which controlled W. A. Gaines & Co. and the Newcomb-Buchanan Co. No. 368. The brand was later transferred to that plant.

John Cochran & Co.,
Springhill Dist., RD No. 37

This distillery, known as Daniel Boone in 1870, was located south of Frankfort on the west side of the Kentucky River. In 1880 it was registered as John Cochran & Co. Brands were Spring Hill and Franklin. It was sold to the trust in 1899 and then to a Cincinnati Rectifying house in 1910. After 1919, the property was purchased by Charles Irion of Frankfort and Eli H. Brown of Louisville, who set up a chair factory across the river at the Hermitage house. The warehouses were razed for lumber for the chairs. By 1970, most of the remnants were gone.

Hermitage Distillery,
W. A. Gaines & Co., RD No. 4

The Hermitage Distillery, organized in 1862 by Gaines, Barry & Co., stood on the east side of the Kentucky River south of Frankfort and was operated by E. H. Taylor, Jr., George Barry, and W. A. Gaines, all Frankfort residents. Barry was the principal owner and president.

In 1868, the company was reorganized as W. A. Gaines & Co., and it included the purchase of the Crow Distillery from the Oscar Pepper estate. The company was incorporated in 1887, and Marshall J. Allen was named president. In 1922, the company was liquidated and all assets sold. The property was purchased by Eli H. Brown of Louisville in 1926 and converted to a chair factory.

In 1933, the Allied Brewing and Distilling Co. of New York bought the plant for $200,000. Plans to rebuild the distillery did not materialize and in 1945 all the buildings were razed and the land was subdivided. The Gaines Building in downtown Frankfort was purchased by the city in 1981.

Old Kennebec Dist., RD No. 32

J. M. Perkins, a Frankfort banker and owner of the Frankfort & Cincinnati Railroad, built this distillery in the late 1930s. In 1942, the granary and still house burned, but no damage was incurred by the warehouses and bottling house. Brands were Old Kennebec, Jim Perkins, and Sam Clay for Hirsch Bros. The plant's last known use was by a Frankfort wholesaler.

Garrard County
8th District

King & King,
Wm. Berkle, RD No. 15

King & King ran a mill and distillery at what was then known as Kings Mill near Dix River prior to 1880. The Kings were succeeded by Wm. Berkle, who purchased the plant about that time and operated it for a number of years. He produced the Wm. Berkle brand and had H. Rosenthal of Cincinnati as his distributor. The plant ceased to operate about 1907 and Rosenthal purchased the

W. H. Head Distillery RD No. 9 near Raywick in Marion County and continued to produce the Wm. Berkle brand there.

I have a pint (amber) bottle of Wm. Berkle, produced at W. H. Head Dist. Co. Bonded Warehouse No. 329 Marion County, that is labeled for medicinal purposes. There is no prescription label attached but it was produced in the spring of 1914 and bottled in the spring of 1925 at General Bonded Warehouse No. 1, 5th District.

J. W. Miller

Miller operated a small distillery near Dix River during 1880-95 and produced a brand called Dix River Rock Bass, so-called from his interest in fishing in the river nearby. The plant was unused for a number of years and may have been submerged in the area of Herrington Lake when it was built in 1929.

E. H. Chase & Co., RD No. 28

Located on Canoe Creek near Bryantville and operated between 1882 and 1884, this plant produced the brand E. H. Chase. Supposedly they operated another plant in nearby Boyle County, but records are not available.

Harrison County
6th District

Harrison County had 30 distilleries in 1882, but apparently most of them were very small and records are not available. These usually ran from 2 to 10 bushels per day, provided a very limited amount of liquor, and did not affect the commercial market. Nine of the better known or most prominent distilleries established are listed here.

Edgewater Distillery, RD No. 1

Shawhan and Brandon built a 100-bushel distillery a short distance from Lair in 1837, which was one of the earliest in the county. Brandon failed in 1841, and Shawhan continued producing until 1850 and sold out to John Lair, Sr., who then operated it until 1854. Lair leased the plant to Shawhan, Snell, and Megibben for three years, after which Megibben purchased the plant and developed a larger stock farm as well. He increased the capacity in 1882 to 500 bushels. Megibben died in 1890, and his brands Edgewater Bourbon and Edgewater Rye ceased to exist.

Crescent Distillery, RD No. 6

This distillery was purchased in 1868 by C. B. Cook, who operated as "C. B. Cook & Co." Wm. Adams joined him in 1874 as a junior partner. By 1882, the plant had a capacity of 150 bushels and an output of 2,500 barrels annually. At this time they had 6,000 barrels in storage out of a total storage of 8,000 barrels. The plant ceased to operate in the early 1900s, and the brand name disappeared.

L. L. Van Hook & Co., RD No. 35

Built in 1865 by Trimble & Peck and sold to a banker by the name of Luther Van Hook in 1868, the distillery burned in 1869 but was rebuilt immediately and continued as L. Van Hook & Co. By 1882 their mashing capacity was 300 bushels daily with an output of 3,000 barrels annually. Three warehouses on the premises had a capacity of only 7,500 barrels thus making it imperative to move whiskey at a young age. T. J. Megibben bought the operation in the early 1880s but sold out in 1888 to his son-in-law Felix S. Ashbrook, who operated under that name.

Ashbrook died November 18, 1910, at the age of 48. He had been mayor of Cynthiana for seventeen years.

After Ashbrook's death, R. V. Bishop was appointed president and general manager; T. M. Clay, treasurer; and Reed Ashbrook, assistant treasurer.

By 1920 the plant had grown considerably but was shut down by Prohibition. In 1924, the whiskey was removed to a concentration warehouse, and the buildings were converted to other uses. The brands Van Hook and Babbling Brook produced by this company were used by American Medicinal Spirits during prohibition.

Makemson Mill & Distillery,
G. W. Taylor, RD No. 13

David Makemson settled in Mill Creek near Poindexter about 1795. Later on, his sons, John and Andy, operated a mill and distillery on the farm, but eventually they sold to G. W. Taylor, who operated as Mill Creek Dist. with the brand Old G.W. Taylor. This brand was sold to Wigglesworth Bros. in 1905.

John M. January,
T. G. Craig, RD No. 17

This plant was built near Berry Station on the South Fork of Licking River in 1853 by John January. After a few years he sold to a Mr. Davis, who subsequently sold to S. B. Cook in 1860. Cook sold it to his son, C. B. Cook, in 1867; and after a very short period of eight months he sold to Lair, Redmon & Co. In 1871, Lair & Kern bought it; after operating only one season, they sold to John Pugh, who ran the plant for one year, after which it remained idle until 1880, when it was purchased by T. G. Craig. Craig operated the plant at 200-bushel capacity for a number of years, producing about 2,500 barrels annually under the name T. G. Craig.

A. Keller,
Ashbrook Bros., RD No. 9

Built on the South Fork of Licking River just north of Cynthiana in 1840 by Abraham Keller, this plant operated as Keller and Shawhan. Keller sold to J. A. Cook in 1861 and in 1863 T. V. Ashbrook acquired one-half interest. Cook died that year; his half interest was taken over by F. G. and S. J. Ashbrook, and the name was changed to Ashbrook Bros. By 1882 the capacity was 300 bushels daily and about 2,500 barrels annually. Total warehouse capacity was 9,000 barrels, 5,000 of which were stored in stone warehouses. The brand produced was A. Keller Bourbon.

Ashbrook Bros. employed ten hands at the rate of $1.50 per day. T. V. Ashbrook died in 1874, and his interest went to his two brothers. T. J. died in 1884 and S. J. continued with the operation. In 1891, Ashbrook claimed a continuous operation of a crop of whiskey every year since 1840.

The distillery was sold in 1902 to KD&W (the trust), who operated as A. Keller with the brand Old A. Keller. In 1914, the trust started producing as G. G. White & Co., preparatory to phasing out the Geo. White plant in Bourbon County. The last superintendent was Clifton Atherton, a grandson of J. M. Atherton. The plant closed in 1920, and all the whiskey was moved to the Wathen concentration warehouses in Louisville. The property was sold to Frazier LeBus of Cynthiana.

John Poindexter,
Wigglesworth Bros., RD No. 10

John Poindexter purchased a mill on the Licking River from Phil Keath in 1850 and converted it to a distillery. He operated for 30 years under the brand Poindexter Bourbon. The Wigglesworth Bros. bought it in 1880 and increased capacity to 100 bushels and an annual output of 1,500 barrels. Brands were Poindexter Bourbon and "Wigglesworth Bros., Sweet Mash." One of the brothers died in 1889, and on October 12 of that year, the property was sold at the courthouse.

The sale included 3.5 acres of land, a three-story distillery of 100-bushel capacity, a granary, a nice dwelling with a supply of water from a well adjacent to the distillery, four warehouses with a capacity of 6,000 to 8,000 barrels, and the brand name Poindexter. W. T. Wigglesworth, the surviving brother, bought the company. In 1905, it was incorporated as Wigglesworth Bros. Inc. Shortly after, Wigglesworth bought the brand "Old G.W. Taylor" from Mill Creek Dist., and, using both brands, he continued operations until Prohibition. In 1924, all whiskey in storage was transferred to the Pepper concentration warehouses in Lexington and bottled for medicinal spirits.

Redmon Distilling Co., RD No. 15

John T. Redmon had operated a small farm distillery in Bourbon County, but in 1859 he built a larger plant on Leesburg Pike, across the Licking River from Cynthiana. He sold the distillery and moved back to his farm operation. It passed through a number of hands in the intervening years, and in 1880 the owners were listed as Thomas Hinkston, president; L. Van Hook, treasurer; J. A. Wolford, secretary; with S. J. Ashbrook and W. A. Cook, directors.

The company had two large, brick warehouses for storage, and the brands produced were Redmon Distilling Co. and H.C.K., both sweet mash whiskeys.

Megibben, Bramble & Co., RD No. 38,
G. R. Sharpe, RD No. 19,
Julius Kessler & Co., RD No. 9
Old Lewis Hunter

T. J. Megibben built the Megibben & Bramble Distillery about 1850 near Lair on the Licking River and used the brand "Excelsior." Megibben's nephew bought it and operated as T. J. Megibben and Co., beginning in 1868 and continuing until he died in 1891. It was then purchased by G. S. Sharpe of nearby Ruddles Mill, who produced the Excelsior and G.R. Sharpe brands until he was killed in a boat explosion on the Pacific Coast in 1902. The trust bought it at that time. Kessler introduced the "Old Lewis Hunter" brand but was sued for infringement by the "Hunters Rye" brand of Baltimore. Kessler claimed the name originated from an early settler who made whiskey nearby, but his claim was never substantiated. However, he continued to use the name.

In 1913, the mashing capacity was increased to 700 bushels from 600, and a new 16,000-barrel warehouse was constructed and the cattle feeding pens were rebuilt. Since Kessler also owned the Paris Distillery in Bourbon County, which had been damaged considerably by fire in that year, his plans were to produce the Sam Clay and Paris Club brands, along with the G.B. Sharpe and Old Lewis Hunter brands, at this plant.

The plant was closed during prohibition, and by 1932 the idle plant had deteriorated considerably. Reorganized in 1932 with Sam B. Walton as president, a complete new plant of 950 bushels and six new warehouses was built by the mid to late 1930s and a new Registration No. 15 was assigned.

Seagrams bought the distillery in 1942 and operated under the War Production Board for high proof spirits and then continued with bourbon production until 1947 after which they shut it down. They resumed operations again in 1958 and finally closed completely in 1974.

Desmond Beam, who had been employed at the Woodford County Distillery RD No. 40 in Midway, moved to this plant and was distiller until it closed. Charles Beam, his nephew, was assistant until he left to run the Four Roses Distillery RD No. 8 in Anderson County.

At the time the distillery closed they had a mashing capacity of 1,200 bushels and storage of some 60,000 barrels. An attempt was made to convert the plant to fuel alcohol production by a group who bought it about 1980, but the venture was never completed. The warehouses were dismantled by Gerald Greene of Loretto, Kentucky.

Henderson County
2nd District

Kentucky Peerless Dist. Co., RD No. 50

W. W. Worsham & Co. was built about 1881 near the Ohio River in Henderson, using the brand name "Peerless," a handmade sour mash. In 1894, the name was changed to the Worsham Distilling Co., and in 1915 the company was known as Kentucky Peerless

Dist. Co. Henry Kraver was president and manager; C. M. Bullitt, vice president; and A. E. Kraver, secretary.

Withers, Dade & Co., RD No. 32

Withers Dade & Co. operated a distillery near Henderson in 1880, producing a brand by that name, and calling it a "Hand Made Sour Mash." Annual production was only 300 to 400 barrels and distributed by Templet & Washburn of Louisville. The distillery burned in 1888, and the firm dissolved.

Henry County
5th District

Fible & Crabb, RD No. 107

This plant was built in 1872 by D. M. Fible and W. L. Crabb near Eminence on the L&N Railroad and operated as Fible & Crabb Distillery, with the brand by that name, as well as Kentucky Poteen, taken from the Irish name for moonshine or illicit spirits. Fible died in 1891 and the company reorganized as Fible and Crabb Distilling Co. Crabb contracted with Geo. Benz & Co. of St. Paul, Minnesota, to finance production and sales and, after building a new bottling plant, enter into one of the first ventures of fancy packaging. The Old Crabb brand had a blue ribbon stamped in gold with Fible & Crabb printed over the cork. They also bottled the Dew Drops brand.

The plant sold in 1900 to Geo. Benz & Son, and Old Blue Ribbon became their main brand—sold only to high-class bars and clubs. Nicholas Miller, who was a former part owner of the Nelson County Kentucky Distillery Co. No. 294 at New Hope and the Coon Hollow brand, had offices in Louisville and handled sales for many years prior to Prohibition.

The plant was operated as the Eminence Distillery Co. from 1905 to 1918 and was then abandoned after 1922, when all the whiskey was removed to Louisville Public Warehouse and bottled and sold for medicinal spirits. Mr. Miller maintained an office in the Keller building at 5th and Main streets in Louisville until 1929. The bricks in the buildings were salvaged, and after about 1940 the remaining buildings were converted to other uses.

Jefferson County
5th District

Park and Tilford Distillery, RD No. 6

This distillery located at 35th and Tyler in Louisville was the original Bonnie Brothers and was owned by John and Arthur Schulte of New York, who were also engaged in the perfume and essential oil business. The plant was sold to Schenley in 1953; they operated it until 1957, when they closed the distillery but continued bottling and warehousing until the early 1960s. The premises were then sold to Harshaw Chemical Company.

Oliver McGowan was the distiller, and, according to an article in the *Kentucky Beverage Journal* of March 1956, Jack McGaughey was made manager of the P & T Distilleries for Schenley in Louisville, Midway, and Tell City, Indiana. The article went on to say that the distillery was 116 years old, which would place its origin in 1840, a date I cannot substantiate.

Yellowstone Distillery, RD No. 240

J. Bernard Dant, who had started the Cold Springs Distillery at Gethsemane in 1865 and later merged it with Taylor & Williams under the name of Yellowstone, moved to Louisville with his family. Shortly after prohibition was repealed, he and his sons Mike, Walter, and Sam, and a nephew, James Patrick Kearns, Jr., built a new plant at 3000 7th Street Road. The original plant area was taken over by Will Dant and Joe B. Head, who established the Dant & Head Distillery RD No. 47. The original registration number 240 was transferred to the new Yellowstone plant. Wilmer Beam was the distiller, and Ray Pfeiffer sales manager, while Jimmy Kearns became president.

Glenmore bought the distillery in 1944 but made no drastic changes until 1954, when Kearns became a vice-president in the corporate headquarters. Ray Pfeiffer took over sales as general sales manager; C. A. "Gus" Silliman handled sales for Yellowstone.

Paul Kirn succeeded Jimmy Kearns as plant manager, and when Wilmer Beam retired, Poss Greenwell took his place. Poss followed in retirement soon after and Jack Beam, Wilmer's nephew, became distiller. Joe Ruttle, who had been employed at T. W. Samuels after

Westerman took over, became distiller after Jack Beam left, and he was followed by Bill Creel. Paul Kirn retired in 1985, and Bill Creel joined Barton Brands at Bardstown. The plant ceased all operations in 1991.

The distillery had a capacity of 1,000 bushels per day, and they had built seven 20,000-barrel warehouses. Everything was painted yellow to denote the Yellowstone brand. The plant provided all the production for Glenmore products from the early 1970s on, since the production facilities at Owensboro had discontinued distillation for quite a number of years and only performed the bottling operations.

John P. Dant,
Old Boone, RD No. 39

John P. Dant, Sr., the third son of J. W. Dant, built the John P. Dant Distillery at Meadowlawn in Jefferson County shortly after prohibition was repealed. He also leased the Grosscurth Distillery RD No. 26 at Anchorage in Jefferson County during World War II and operated as Meadowlawn Distillery Company.

John P. Sr.'s son John P. Jr. succeeded him after he died, and on May 1, 1945, Marvin Padgett, who had been connected with Tom Moore, bought controlling interest. They also ran a bottling operation on Main Street in Louisville. In December 1950, Marvin bought the remaining interest in the distillery, and John P. Jr. retired to Florida, where he died in 1978. Marvin Padgett bought the name Old Boone from Seagrams in 1954, according to Bill Padgett, son of Marvin, who was plant manager until 1977, when it was closed.

Mashing capacity was 750 bushels per day, or about 75 barrels, and they had six warehouses of a total capacity of approximately 95,000 barrels. Their main brands were Old Boone, Distiller's Choice, and Old 1889. The latter was bought from Tom Pendergast of Kansas City and was sold mainly in the Kansas City area. Volume on this brand amounted to about 50,000 cases annually.

Pat Buse, a son of Ray Buse, a Cincinnati broker, bought the distillery in 1959 and operated it for a number of years. However, a series of disasters hit the plant. In November 1966, a fire destroyed the bottling house and case storage room, which were rebuilt a short time later. In January 1971, a boiler blew up and caused considerable damage when the explosion ruptured a gas line, which burned the distillery. The distillery was rebuilt and new mashing and distillation equipment was installed, but following this, a water tank was installed on top of the distillery building and apparently was not structurally sound. The tank shifted and crashed through a portion of the distillery and office.

Buse had leased warehouse facilities from D. W. Karp at the St. Francis plant RD No. 21 from 1969 to 1977, but in 1977 he decided to cease operations completely and sold the Old Boone equipment at public auction and abandoned the property. Arthur Ball of Lebanon, who had been associated with the Loretto Distillery RD No. 41, was hired to oversee the warehouse operations at St. Francis. Henry Cooper was comptroller and Oscar Cravens distiller when the plant closed.

During the Dant regime, Thad Dant, a son of Jim Dant, was employed at the distillery, as was Phil Dant, son of Harry Dant and a grandson of Jim Dant. Thus as shown, a long line of Dants were associated with distilleries, not only in Marion County, their original homestead, but in Nelson County and Jefferson County as well.

Marion County Distillery Co., RD No. 372

J. G. Mattingly of Marion County built this distillery in 1866 at 3105 Rudd Lane; he also owned the West End Distillery nearby. The brand name was Marion. On December 7, 1887, the plant and brand were purchased by Wm. Patterson, who produced 5,000 barrels in 1888. In 1905, the plant and brands were sold to the trust of KD&W, who operated it until prohibition. It was dismantled about 1924.

Bernheim Bros. & Uri,
United American Co., RD No. 9

This plant was built in 1897 by Bernheim Bros. and Uri on Bernheim Lane in Louisville. They had been operating a WLD business in Paducah since 1872. Bernard and Isaac W. Bernheim and N. M. Uri were the principals. Uri sold out in 1903 to form his own company, and that same year Bernheim Distilling Co. was organized. On February 7, 1909, the still house burned to the ground, but it was quickly replaced by a new 1,200-bushel house. In 1911, the property was changed to the United American Co., which also bought the Warwich Dist. No. 1 at Silver Creek in Madison County. Bernheim bought this plant from Burnam, Bennett &

Co. Capacity was increased to 1,600 bushels. Officers were Albert S. Roth as president and Milton W. Barkhouse as vice president.

During 1920-33, both plants, one in Jefferson and the other in Madison County, were partially dismantled and the property sold, but Bernheim operated as a medicinal spirits distributor, and Gabe Felsenthal was manager.

Loe Gerngross and Emil Schwarzhaupt bought the plant in 1933 with the plans to produce the I.W. Harper brand at the Selliger plant RD No. 412 when it was rebuilt at 17th and Breckinridge streets.

The Newcomb Buchanan Co., RD No. 4 (Nelson), The Anderson & Nelson Dist. Co., RD No. 97 (Anderson), RD No. 368 (Elk Run).

In 1872, the Newcomb-Buchanan Co. was the largest distilling company in Kentucky. Geo. C. Buchanan, the president, built the Anderson, Nelson, Buchanan, and Graystone distilleries. In 1879, the company reorganized, and in 1880 they took over the R. P. (Ross) Pepper plant of Frankfort. The company reorganized again in 1885, and the name was changed to Anderson-Nelson Distilling Co., with Fred W. Adams as secretary and manager and Herman Becurts as president. Buchanan remained to handle sales. The warehouses of the company held whiskey brands and owners in 1885 were as follows: Warehouse No. 4: owner Newcomb-Buchanan, brand Nelson; No. 97: owner Anderson Distillery Co., brand Anderson; No. 352: owner Jacob Amber & Co., brand

Woodcock; No. 353: owner Geo. C. Buchanan, brand Buchanan; No. 353: owner John Endress & Co., brand Grape Creek; No. 368: owner R. P. Pepper & Co., brand Old R.P. Pepper; No. 368: owner J. A. Monks & Sons, brand Graystone; No. 369: owner J. A. Monks & Sons, brand Monks.

Financial backing was secured through Paris, Allen & Co., an English firm, and in 1885 they gained control and incorporated W. A. Gaines Co. and the Anderson & Nelson Distillery Co. The Graystone Distillery, operating under the name of Allen Bradley Co., was producing great quantities of whiskey, which they were able to sell for 23 cents a gallon while the competition, like Crow & Hermitage in Frankfort, were asking 60 to 65 cents per gallon. In July 1890 the Graystone Distillery burned and was replaced as Elk Run, but above the floodplain of Bear Grass Creek. Mr. Becurts died in 1891, and the Jesse-Moore Hunt Co. of California acquired an interest. Mr. Moore of this company was president of Moore & Selliger No. 412 at 17th and Breckinridge streets. The company sold out to the trust in 1905, and by 1911 the Elk Run Dist. No. 368 was the largest of all KD&W plants, mashing 5,000 bushels. Harry Wilkin was manager and distiller.

At this time they built the largest bonded warehouses for storage on record, erected in two sections of 150,000 barrels each. The house was twelve stories tall and cost an estimated $400,000. This is today's "Distillery Commons" on Lexington Road. Fred W. Adams died at his home in eastern Louisville on December 12, 1912, at the age of 66. A native of England, he had been responsible for the financial backing of the company from 1885 to 1905.

Brands bottled by the Elk Run Dist. in 1912 were Anderson, Nelson, Buchanan, Slocum, Jefferson, Jackson, U.S. Club, and Elk Run; they also produced for other distilleries in the trust as "Regan and Imorde."

In 1918, a large alcohol plant was built adjacent to the Nelson plant on Hamilton Avenue, operated by U.S. Industrial Alcohol. They were using steel tanks for alcohol storage and had not kept them full. As a result, a flood at Bear Grass Creek broke them loose, floating them into the warehouses and destroying them.

The warehouses were used for concentration houses during Prohibition. The Elk Run plant was left intact, and the others were razed. Elk Run started back after repeal.

Amil Klempner bought the lower property adjoining Spring Street for a scrap metal yard, and it is still run as Klempner Bros. Sometime in the 1960s, National Distillers renovated the large brick warehouses, but one proved unsafe and was razed. National Distillers had vacated all the property by the mid-1980s, and the building was converted to other uses.

The Mellwood Distillery Co., RD No. 34,
General Distillers of Kentucky, RD No. 30

Mr. George W. Swearingen, a Bullitt County native, after graduating from college shortly after the Civil War, built the Mellwood Distillery on Mellwood Avenue between Frankfort Avenue and Brownsboro Road. He was president and principal owner, and Rudolph Balke of Cincinnati was vice president. Swearingen sold to

Balke in 1889, and Jacob Schmidlapp, also of Cincinnati, joined the company.

In 1893, the distillery was replaced with a six-story building constructed of brick, stone, steel, and concrete with a slate roof. It was sold to the trust in 1896, and D. K. Weiskopf was named president; Henry Imorde, vice president; and Henry Wilken, former distiller for Elk Run RD No. 368, secretary and treasurer. Imorde left in 1908 to form the Regan and Imorde Distilling Co., another satellite of the trust.

In 1909, fire destroyed the cattle pens along Bear Grass Creek and threatened the Nelson and Anderson distilleries. Production ceased in 1918, but the office continued in use until 1924 when it was moved to Hamilton Avenue, site of Elk Run Dist. The distillery was renovated by Karl Nussbaum in 1935 with Walter Borgerding as president and Selby Hahn as distiller; it operated as General Distillers of Kentucky. Sid Flashman of the Double Springs plant in Nelson County, took over the bottling house in the early 1960s. He was bottling for Mellwood of Cincinnati, Double Springs of Greenbrier, Nelson County, and Old Farmers.

D. L. Graves & Co.,
The Mayflowers Distillery Co.,
Old Kentucky Distillery, RD No. 354

The distillery, located at 242 Transit in Louisville, was operated by D. L. Graves in 1880 with brands Ashton and Mayflower.

In 1882, H. A. Thierman, Sr., bought the plant and changed it to Mayflower. D. Meschendorf bought an interest shortly after, and in 1892 he became sole proprietor, changing the name to Old Kentucky Distillery. However, Thierman retained the Mayflower brand and produced it at his Rugby plant RD No. 360. Brands of Old Kentucky Distillery were Kentucky Dew, Cherokee Spring, and Old Kentucky, later adding Old Watermill, Normandy Rye, Old Jefferson County, and Dew Drops Malt. Blends were "Woodbury," "Old Stony Fort," and "Royal Velvet." In 1885, H. A. Thiermen, Sr., bought the plant. The company incorporated in 1900 with Meschendorf as president, O. H. Irvine as vice president, and Dan Schlegal as secretary.

Meschendorff died at the age of 53 on November 11, 1911, having been the president of Daviess County Distillery Co. at Owensboro. He was also associated with Pleasure Ridge Park Distillery, Old Times Distillery, Eminence Distillery, and others.

Officers in Old Kentucky Distillery between 1912 and 1920 were O. H. Irvine as president, Dan Schlegal as vice president, and J. J. Sass as secretary and treasurer. Whiskey was removed from the warehouses by 1923, and the warehouses were razed. The brick bottling house was kept unused during Prohibition, but was renovated and re-equipped in 1933 pending completion of a new plant near Shively. The distillery building was partially destroyed by fire in 1925 except for a brick portion that was used by George Howell as a riding school. In 1960, all the remaining buildings were removed to make way for the new Interstate highway. I have a bottle of Normandy Rye with a strip seal across the top stating that if broken the guarantee of purity no longer applies.

J. G. Mattingly & Sons, West End Distillery, RD No. 2

J. G. Mattingly built what was reported to be the first registered distillery in Kentucky. In 1845, at 40th and High streets, he produced "J.G. Mattingly & Sons" brand.

In 1888, he installed a columnar, or "coffee" still, which it was hoped could compete against the trust. The trust was selling whiskey below cost in order to force the competition into bankruptcy. In spite of his efforts, Mattingly became insolvent in 1890 and reorganized as J. G. Mattingly Co., with Paul Jones as president, S. P. Jones as secretary-treasurer, and James Cunningham as general manager. However, by 1900 the company fell on hard times and was ordered sold. The trust bought the plant and brands in 1902.

In 1903, the still house was destroyed by fire at a loss of $50,000, but the warehouses containing 60,000 barrels were spared. Mattingly had retired in 1900 and returned to St. Marys in Marion County, where he died on January 7, 1910, at age 68.

F. G. Paine & Co., RD No. 29

Paine built this distillery on Dixie Highway at Pleasure Ridge Park in the early 1870s and produced a brand called Kentucky Comfort. He was quite successful until the panic in the early 1890s when he was forced to sell. In 1891, the distillery was renamed Pleasure Ridge Park Distillery with G. W. Stockhoff as president, D. Meschendorf as vice president, and A. W. Bierbaum as secretary-treasurer. Mr. Paine retired but continued to live near the distillery.

In 1892, the company built two new warehouses of 10,000 barrels each. Again in 1903, the company built a very large brick warehouse with 18-inch-thick walls. The plant changed hands in the period 1903 to 1909, having operated as the Combined Distillery of Kentucky that made a quantity of whiskey called "Corn Flower" for wholesale dealer Nathan F. Block. In 1916, the plant was operating as the Kentucky Comfort Distilling Co., owned by the Associated Distilleries of Kentucky and operated by Rosenfield Bros. Brands were Kentucky Comfort and Gladstone.

Old Times Distillery Co., No. 1 S.M. Dist., RD No. 1

This distillery, located at 2725 W. Broadway, was established in 1869 by John G. Roach with the brand Old Times, which he sold to Anderson Biggs in 1878. Biggs died in 1889, and his widow, who was opposed to the liquor industry, sold to the first bidder for $17,000. The new owners had been associated with F. G. Paine Distillery RD No. 29. Charles Lemon became president; D. Meschendorf, vice president; and A. W. Bierbaum, secretary and treasurer. Brand names were Old Times and Gladstone. Bierbaum died in 1890, and in 1897 Meschendorf withdrew after he purchased the Mayflower Distillery RD No. 354. Lemon died December 11, 1908, at age 50 and was succeeded by J. J. Beck and then D. H. Russell.

After Meschendorf withdrew in 1897 his share was bought by Ferdinand Westheimer, who operated a distributing house in Cincinnati. He died in 1913, having acquired complete interest and changed the name to No. 1 S.M. Distillery, which continued to operate until 1918.

The Sunny Brook Distillery Co., RD No. 5 and No. 297

Located at 28th and Broadway, this plant operated as Associated Distilleries of Kentucky in 1882 and was producing for John G. Roach, originally with Old Time Distillery RD No. 1. Also he was with the Belle of Nelson and Bartley & Johnson distilleries, both of Nelson County. In 1892, the Rosenfield family of Chicago purchased the plant and operated as Rosenfield Bros. & Co. with brands Old Sunny Brook and Willow Creek. In 1914, the distillery was sold to Sunny Brook Distillery for $1 million, and Morris Rosenfield became president and Joseph Sampson Rosenfield secretary. In 1917, Louis Rosenfield bought the plant at auction for salvage, paying $35,000 for the property and $20,000 for the name and brands. The widow of Louis Rosenfield sold the property to American Medicinal Spirits in 1933 for some $600,000 to $700,000 with a plan to renovate the distillery at an additional cost of $300,000. The warehouses were maintained during Prohibition and used as concentration warehouses. National Distillers bought the plant and operated it for a number of years but then discontinued and razed all the buildings by 1975.

J. B. Wathen & Bro. Co., RD No. 263

J. B. and M. A. Wathen built the J. B. Wathen & Bro. Co. in 1880 at 26th and Broadway. They had previously been in business with their father at the No. 270 plant in Lebanon, and when he died they moved to Louisville. Their production consisted of 10,000 barrels a year of "Wathen Bourbon" and "Wathen Rye" until 1885. At this time they introduced the Criterion brand and produced 3,500 barrels of each. They fell on hard times in 1887, but with an arrangement with creditors, retained control, and after three years they paid off all debts and continued in business.

In 1899, the company was sold to the trust, and the name was changed to Big Spring Dist. Co. W. J. O'Hearn was distiller. M. A. (Nace) went with the Old Granddad Dist. as president, which had been purchased by R. E. Wathen & Co. The trust operated this distillery until 1916, when it was sold to other interests.

Ferncliff Dist. Co., RD No. 409

This plant was located at Logan and Lampton streets, next to the Shafer-Myer Brewery. No record is available of mashing capacity or annual production, but they were apparently successful in their small operation. Records of 1892 list Joseph Schwab as president and George Gutig as secretary and treasurer. Their brand was Ferncliff. By 1910, "Schwab Bros." was added, and Joseph Schwab, Jr., was president and distiller.

Shut down by prohibition, all property remained intact until 1924 and the whiskey was moved to a concentration warehouse. The warehouses, granary, and office were later occupied by Ferncliff Feed & Grain Co.

Kentucky Distilling Co., Beargrass Distillery, RD No. 1

Dorn & Barkhouse Distillery was operated by Louis Barkhouse in 1864 at 238-300 Story Avenue. His brother Julius replaced Dorn in 1875 and then changed the name to Kentucky Distilling Co. They produced under the name of "Beargrass" and "Kentucky Pride" and later in 1880 added the Carlisle brand. During the 1880s they were producing about 6,200 barrels annually, but the plant burned in 1890 and was never rebuilt.

John G. Roach & Co.,
Old Log Cabin Distillery,
Julius Kessler & Co., RD No. 8

John Roach owned the Uniontown Dist. in Union County having purchased it with the Old Log Cabin brand from J. M. Lancaster in 1878. The stillhouse burned in 1890, and he sold the remainder of the property to the trust. He built the John G. Roach Distillery in west Louisville in 1892 at 30th and Garland streets and continued with the brand Old Log Cabin. He retired in 1900 and sold out to the trust, which operated the distillery up to Prohibition as Julius Kessler & Co. National Distillers obtained the brand and used it for a number of years after repeal.

Moore & Selliger,
Max Selliger & Co., RD No. 1-2

George Moore and Max Selliger operated this plant at 17th and Breckinridge streets in 1870. Their brands were Astor, a sweet mash, and Belmont and Nutwood, both sour mashes.

Mr. Moore died in 1896 and Selliger continued as Max Selliger & Co. He built another distillery on the premises in 1905 and in 1911 built a new eight-story brick warehouse at a cost of $15,000. The plant was shut down during Prohibition, but the property continued to be maintained. In 1933, Bernheim of RD No. 9 sold the I.W. Harper brand to Leo Gerngross and Emil Schwarzhaupt, who had purchased the Moore & Selliger plant RD No. 412 from the Selliger estate. They demolished the oldest distillery and boiler plant and replaced them with new buildings and equipment. The operations were redesignated as RD No. 1, I. W. Harper and RD No. 2, Old Charter. They departed from the usual practice of installing cypress fermenters and constructed them from tile, which were used for many years.

In June 1933, Lambert Willett was superintendent of the new construction along with his son Thompson, until Thompson left in 1936 to build the Willett Distillery RD No. 43 on the site of the Boone Bros. Distillery near Bardstown. Schenley bought the distilleries in 1937 and Lambert continued until 1942, when he left to run his farm in Nelson County. Wathen Knebelkamp was named superintendent and became district manager of all Schenley distilleries in the Louisville area. He later left to become president of

Churchill Downs. Greg Schweri was plant manager and Dick Miller distiller. Dick died and Jim "Pinch" Simms replaced him. Veith Herre became plant manager after Schweri left and was succeeded by Dick Jefferson. Ralph Dupps was chief engineer, and he left about 1955 to become president of the George Dickel plant, which Schenley had rebuilt in Coffee County, Tennessee, on the site of the Old Cascade Distillery. Meshulam Riklis of Rapid American Conglomerate bought out Schenley while Lewis Rosentiel was living and then sold to Guinness of London. The plant has been consolidated with Stitzel Weller and all the Glenmore operations and is now producing under the name United Distillers. Bernheim Distillery, as this plant is known, went through extensive renovations after it was acquired by United, and on April 28, 1999, it was sold to Heaven Hill of Bardstown at an undisclosed price to replace their facilities that burned in November 1996. They also acquired seven brick warehouses with a capacity of about 400,000 barrels and are presently mashing 2,250 bushels per day.

The H. A. Thierman Co., Rugby Distillery, RD No. 360

H. A. Thierman, having been a wholesale liquor dealer, purchased this plant at 36th and Missouri streets in 1864, which had been operated by John G. Roach and others as American Distilling Co. Brands were "Belle of Louisville," "Belair," and Rugby Distillery Co. "White Corn." In 1886, he changed the name to H. A. Thierman Co. He bought the Mayflower Distillery RD No. 354 in 1882 from D. L. Graves, but sold an interest in that plant to D. Meschendorf soon after. In 1892, he sold his entire interest to Meschendorf. Thierman died February 15, 1900, still owning the H. A. Thierman Co. He was also a major stockholder in John T. Barbee Co. RD No. 32 in Woodford County.

The company incorporated in 1906, and Wm. Ruedeman became president; Thomas Thierman, vice president; and Ed Bobbitt, secretary and manager. The Belle of Louisville brand was dropped and the "Bel Air" label was being used by John G. Roach of the trust. They substituted "Belle of Jefferson," "Mayflower" and "Indian Hill."

The Ohio River flooded this area of West Louisville in 1913, and a warehouse containing 3,460 barrels capsized, losing 200 completely. The property was vacated after 1920 and a few years later was in complete disrepair.

Hope Distilling Co.

In 1817, New England parties built one of the largest distilleries at the time in Kentucky at Main Street and Portland Avenue at a cost of $100,000. A 45 H.P. steam engine, two English stills of 1,500-gallon capacity, and a 750-gallon doubler were installed. In 1819, they produced only 1,200 gallons per day and by 1821 had increased to 1,500 gallons. Slop was fed in nearby cattle pens.

The venture failed shortly after and the plant was idled for a number of years and it eventually burned.

Crystal Springs Distillery Co., RD No. 3, RD No. 78

John Callaghan operated this distillery at 1st and Magnolia streets in the 1870s, making only a sweet mash whiskey. Brands were Crystal Springs and Garland.

He also produced "Kentucky Dew" for Wallwork and Harris and "White Frost" for Thierman Bros. Production was sold also to F. Stitzel, Woodford County Distillery, and F. Jaeger.

Callaghan left the company in 1880 and joined the newly organized distillery Belle of Marion Distillery Co., with proprietors Boldrick and Callaghan. This plant was located at Calvary in Marion County RD No. 370. Crystal Springs continued to operate making the brand Crystal Springs for F. Jaeger. The plant sold to KD&W (the trust) in 1908 and continued to operate until Prohibition, when it was closed down.

The Hoffheimer Bros.,
Proprietors of the White Mills Dist. Co., RD No. 414,
Lynndale Distillery Co., RD No. 470

Prior to 1890 the White Mills Distillery Co. at 18th and Howard streets was owned and operated by Hoffheimer Bros., a wholesale firm in Cincinnati which also controlled the production of T.B. Ripy in Anderson County. Nathan Hoffheimer was president, and his brands were White Mills Bourbon and Hoffheimer Bros. Pure Rye.

A few years later the Lynndale Distillery was built adjacent making "Lynndale Bourbon." Hoffheimer sold the property in 1919 to G. Lee Redmon Co., which used the warehouses as concentration houses and the bottling house for bottling medicinal spirits. Bottling was done for Taylor & Williams (Yellowstone), Max Selliger & Co. (Belmont), Friedman, Keiler & Co. (Brook Hill), as well as Brown Forman and others.

Brown Forman bought the property in 1924, including the whiskey inventory, and continued bottling medicinal whiskey. Brown Forman built a 6,000-bushel plant on this site in 1933 in anticipation of repeal. It is the present site of B. F. Corporate Headquarters and Old Forester Dist.

Jacob Stitzel Distillery, Glencoe Distillery Co., RD No. 106

Jacob Stitzel built this plant at 26th and Broadway in 1872 with a mashing capacity of 160 bushels. The distillery and warehouses were completely destroyed in 1883. The distillery was rebuilt and in 1890 Stitzel won a Medal of Honor at the Paris Exhibition for his "Mondamin Sour Mash." Other brands were Merryland Rye and a contract operation for Phil Hollenback & Co., "Glencoe" brand.

Stitzel's sons, Phil and Fred, left the firm in 1906 and built the Stitzel Bros. Distillery No. 17 on Story Avenue. Jacob Stitzel sold his distillery in 1908 to Phil Hollenback and W. L. Weller and they changed the name to Glencoe Distilling Co. Jacob Stitzel remained as manager but died November 20, 1913, at age 65 and was succeeded by his son, Frank H. Stitzel. The Hollenback brands Fortuna, Glencoe, and Pride of the West were being produced, but the brands Mondamin and Merryland Rye were being used by the Stitzel Bros. Distillery RD No. 17. All the whiskey was removed by 1924 to a concentration warehouse, and the distillery was dismantled. The remaining buildings were used by Martin Broom and Mop Co. and a fruit preserving company.

The distillery was reestablished in 1934 by the Hollenbacks on Cane Run and Campground roads in Jefferson County. Hollenback sold to National Distillers in 1943, who continued to produce high proof spirits for defense purposes in World War II. In 1946, National moved the name of Glencoe to their No. 4 plant near Bardstown and continued to produce the Fortuna brand until 1950, when they sold this operation and the brand ceased to exist.

Walter Doerting, Sr., was an officer in the company for many years, and his son, Walter, Jr., was associated with them until World War II. After the war, Walter, Jr., was employed by AT&T until his retirement.

Stitzel Bros. Distillery, RD No. 17

This plant was built in 1906 at Story and Johnson streets by Phil and Fred Stitzel, sons of Jacob Stitzel. They kept the Mondamin Sour Mash and Merryland Rye brands established by their father.

Tennessee went dry in 1909, and they contracted to make the Cascade brand for George Dickel Co. of Coffee County in Tennessee and in 1910 added the Mammoth Cave brand for W. L. Weller and Sons. They were designated as a concentration warehouse during Prohibition and bottled whiskey for many bulk holders for medicinal purposes. In 1930, permits were issued to produce medicinal whiskey to replace depleted stocks, and they re-opened the plant to produce whiskey for Frankfort Distillery, W. L. Weller, and others. Phil Stitzel was distiller and manager as was a nephew, Pete J. Stitzel.

In 1933, the plant was readied for use, and as soon as prohibition was repealed they operated as Stitzel-Weller, while a new, more modern plant was being built at Shively. It operated for several years but was discontinued, and eventually all the buildings were razed.

W. L. Weller & Sons,
Stitzel Weller Distillery, Old Fitzgerald, RD No. 16

William Larue Weller established a wholesale liquor business in Louisville called W. L. Weller & Sons. Julian P. Van Winkle and Alex T. Farnsley joined the company, and after Mr. Weller's death they purchased the company. They bought whiskey on warehouse receipts from a number of distillers, including Stitzel Bros. in Louisville and Old Joe in Anderson County, and had it bottled under the brand names Old W.L. Weller, Mammoth Cave, and Cabin Still. They also distributed a brand of gin called Stone Root.

Old Joe Distillery burned in 1912, and the Hawkins Bros. rebuilt the plant; most of their output was made for W. L. Weller & Sons. Phil Stitzel of Stitzel Bros. produced medicinal whiskey for them during Prohibition. Weller also obtained the Old Fitzgerald brand from A. C. Herbst and also bottled it during prohibition. After repeal and continuing for a few years, the Stitzel Bros. Distillery RD No. 17 operated as the Stitzel-Weller Distillery under control of the Van Winkle and Farnsley families. Work was started on a new Stitzel Weller Distillery in 1933, and after it was completed they transferred all production to that plant. They added a private brand called Rebel Yell for Charlie Farnsley, which was designed to sell south of the Mason-Dixon Line, but some of it infiltrated to wholesalers north of the line. In this event, the cases were branded "Contraband."

Charlie Farnsley had the company apply for a label approval on another brand called Damn Yankee, but the Alcohol Bureau in Washington denied it, saying it was in bad taste. He then countered, submitting another request for label approval of "Old Bad Taste."

Charlie was quite a politician, having been mayor of Louisville, and he used "Rebel Yell" for lobbying whiskey for state legislators in Frankfort. Stitzel Weller sold a lot of whiskey on warehouse receipts to help finance their operation, and among them was Oscar J. Conrad of Conrad Grocery in St. Louis, for which they bottled "Nicholson 1849." The distillery operated for years with Julian P. "Pappy" Van Winkle at the helm and his son Julian and son-in-law King McClure. King later became chairman of the board.

Will McGill, a brother-in-law of Joe Beam of Bardstown, was their distiller. He was succeeded by Andy Corcoran, who was also general manager. Following him were Johnny Holzknecht and, after his death, Ham Goff and then Norm Hayden, who worked himself up from a minor position in the bottling house. Also following Andy Corcoran's death in 1959, Roy Hawes became distiller; on his retirement, his assistant, Woody Wilson, took over. Pappy liked to point out to visitors the large bronze plaque he had installed at the entrance, stating, "No chemists allowed. This is a whiskey distillery, not a factory," implying of course that the process of making whiskey is an art and not an exact science that could be controlled strictly by formulas and test tubes.

He even joked that some of the blenders used deodorant in their products. In June 1972, the company was sold to Norton Simon for a sum of $20 million after all the principals had died. It then operated as Old Fitzgerald under the subsidiary Somerset Importers. At this time Norton Simon closed out their operations at Camp Nelson in Jessamine County, which was the plant they bought from Bill Thompson called Kentucky River RD No. 45 and which Norton Simon had operated as Canada Dry. Norton Simon eventually sold to Guinness of London, and the plant closed. Production was moved to the Bernheim plant, operating as United Distillers.

King McClure, Pappy Van Winkle's son-in-law, attended most of the meetings of Kentucky Distillers Association and the Distilled Spirits Institute. He tells of a humorous story about attending a meeting in New York City while he was staying at the Waldorf Astoria. King called for room service and identified himself as King McClure, and the attendant, being accustomed to royalty, replied, "Yes, your majesty." Of course, King got a great kick out of this.

Andy Corcoran, who joined Stitzel Weller in 1942 as assistant distiller to Will McGill, succeeded him in 1952 and was also appointed superintendent. Andy's maternal grandfather was James A. Wathen, and his father was a distiller as well as a partner in Matt Corcoran & Co., makers of distilling equipment.

Thixton Millet & Co., RD No. 11

John Thixton took over his father's wholesale liquor business in Owensboro in 1889. E. P. Millett, who owned an Owensboro distillery, sold it to Richard Monarch of Glenmore, after which he joined Thixton and formed the Thixton Millett Co., wholesale dealers and distillers agents. They moved to Louisville in 1901 and owned a brand named Thixton's V.O. In 1903, they purchased the Boone Bros. Distillery RD No. 11 including the Old Boone brand. They closed this plant in 1912 and purchased the Old Saxon Distillery in Chicago, now St. Francis, in Marion County, operated by Blair, Ballard, and Osbourne. The RD number remained the same. They operated this plant until Prohibition and then closed out. Mr. Millett later went into the lumber business in Louisville.

Applegate & Sons

C. L. Applegate & Co. was established in 1868. In 1891, they were operating under the name Applegate & Sons Distillers, with offices at 130 S. 2nd Street in Louisville and distillery RD No. 7 at Yelvington in Daviess County. Their brands were Rosebud and Beechwood, distributed by Gust, Haye & Co. in Galveston, Texas, and J. F. Daugherty & Co., Keokuk, Illinois. Tom Moore of Bardstown produced and bottled most of their whiskey from 1900 to 1912.

The Van Cleve and Hardesty Distillery RD No. 15, having gone broke, was purchased at public auction by Applegate. They rebuilt the plant and operated it with brands Old Rosebud, Old Applegate, and Beechwood. Mr. H. C. Applegate, a member of the firm, owned the 1914 winner of the Kentucky Derby, "Old Rosebud" by name.

Brown Forman Co., RD No. 414

George Garvin Brown was born in Munfordville in Hart County in 1863. At the age of 17, he moved to Louisville to complete his high school education. However, in 1864 before completing high school, he quit and took a job with a drug firm, where he worked for about six years. In 1870, he organized a wholesale liquor business with his older half-brother, John Thompson Street Brown, Jr., the company being known as J. T. S. Brown & Bro. Their offices were established on Main Street in Louisville, and they purchased whiskey from J. M. Atherton Co. Mellwood Distillery, and J. B. Mattingly at St. Marys in Marion County. These were blended and sold as barrel goods under the names "Sidros Bourbon," "Atherton Bourbon," and "Mellwood Bourbon." Later they marketed "Major Paul's," "Widow McBee," and "Larue's Best." Since whiskey was dispensed in barrels to the various saloons, it soon became apparent that some unscrupulous vendors were adulterating the product by watering down or introducing cheaper products in the same barrel. In order to prevent this outcome, the Browns introduced bottled goods under the name "Old Forrester," after the name of Nathan Bedford Forrest, a famous Civil War general.

Contrary to the statement that Old Forrester was named for Nathan Bedford Forrest, a famous Confederate General in the Civil War, Mike Veach, a historian with United Distillers, but now with the Filson Club, states that it is more likely named for Dr. William Forrester, a prominent Louisville physician, with the possibility of appealing to doctors who prescribed whiskey for medicine. The name was later changed to "Old Forester."

This venture was years ahead of the eventual adoption of the "Bottled in Bond" Act passed by Congress in 1897 under President Grover Cleveland's administration. This was promoted by John G. Carlisle, a Kentuckian serving as secretary of the treasury. Carlisle was also connected with the Carlisle Allowance setting up a maximum loss of whiskey stored in bond during the aging process. Any excessive loss over the allowance was taxable, which prompted considerable leak hunting and loss by theft. This allowance was repealed in 1951, and a system of bulk gauging was adopted. Prior to that barrels were gauged individually or by an average gauge of a number of barrels, which was time-consuming and very expensive.

George Forman of Paris, Kentucky, was hired as a salesman and later a bookkeeper. In 1873, Henry Chambers, who had given George Brown his first job in the drug business, became a major stockholder, and the name was changed to Brown, Chambers & Co. J. T. S. Brown, Jr., retired.

In 1876, James Thompson, a native of Ireland, was hired, and three years later in 1879 he and George Brown formed a sales agency to represent Brown and Chambers. In 1881 Henry Chambers retired, selling his interest to George Brown, James Thompson, and George Forman. The name was then changed to Brown, Thompson & Co., with Forman being a junior partner. The panic of 1887 caused George Brown to lose his accumulated personal wealth from his investment in the Giant Tobacco Co., which went under.

Thompson sold his interest to Brown and Forman in 1890 after he bought the Glenmore Distillery RD No. 24 in Daviess County from the Monarch estate. At that time the name was changed to Brown, Forman & Co., with Brown owning 90 percent of the company and Forman the other 10 percent. Forman died on November 19, 1901, and Brown bought out his interest and retained the name. Brown-Forman was incorporated in December 1901 with a capital of $100,000, and the next year they bought into the Ben Mattingly Dist. RD No. 14 at St. Marys in Marion County and their barrel inventory that they had been buying for the past twenty-five years.

B. F. Mattingly retained the controlling interest and Geo. Brown, Fontaine Kremer, W. B. Penick, and P. B. Mattingly the remainder. The whiskey was produced at the Mattingly plant, and since they had no warehouses or bottling facilities, it was transferred to the Brown-Forman plant in Louisville. George Brown suffered a heart attack in 1904 and he had his son Owsley join the firm and eventually take over the operation. In 1907, they built warehouses and a bottling house at St. Marys at a cost of $75,000.

George Garvin Brown died in 1917, and Owsley became president. When Prohibition was enacted the distillery at St. Marys was dismantled and the remaining whiskey was shipped to the concentration warehouses of G. Lee Redmon in Louisville, where stocks of Taylor & Williams, Max Selliger, and Friedman-Keiler (Brook Hill) were stored. In 1924, Brown-Forman bought out the G. Lee Redmon Company and most of the barrel goods, which they bottled during prohibition for medicinal spirits.

After prohibition they rebuilt the distillery and bottling plant and added more warehouses to make it the main Old Forester distillery. They tapped Dr. Frank Shipman, a chemical engineer from Speed Scientific School of the University of Louisville, as production manager, and later Dr. Bill Spanyer, also a Speed graduate. The succession of presidents after Owsley Brown were Dan Street, who had been their chief legal counsel; Bill Lucas, a Speed School mechanical engineer; and then Owsley Brown III, their present chairman. In 1955, they built the Early Times plant RD No. 354 in Shively, and Austin Reed was production manager. In 1956, they bought out the Jack Daniels plant in Lynchburg, Moore County, Tennessee, from the Motlows for $18 million. Prior to this they had bought the Labrot & Graham Distillery RD No. 82 in 1940 located in Woodford County mainly for their barrel inventory. It was maintained as an experimental farm. They bought Canadian Mist owned by Barton and located in Canada for $32 million and also Southern Comfort, a cordial, located in St. Louis. In recent years, Brown-Forman has diversified further in buying Hartmann luggage and business cases, Lenox crystal, and Gorham silver, stainless and crystal.

Cane Run Distillery

This plant was built in 1891 by J. S. Hackett and G. McGowan of the Greenbrier Distillery in Nelson County.

Joseph E. Seagram Distillery, RD No. 37, Julius Kessler

Seagrams built a very large distillery operation on 7th Street Road in Louisville in 1936, with a mashing capacity of 5,500 bushels. This plant was state-of-the-art for equipment and construction and dwarfed everything in the state at that time. However, it was not designed to produce bourbon whiskey but was confined to producing a whiskey and high proof grain neutral spirits for use in their popular spirit blends of Five Crown and Seven Crown. The Five Crown consisted of 25 percent whiskey and the Seven Crown of 37.5 percent, the balance being grain neutral spirits and blending agents for flavor and color. The purpose was to produce a distilled spirit of absolute uniformity and accustom the public by education to adapt their tastes to this product.

The theory was good and no one can deny the success of their operations in the U.S. and especially in Canada. In fact, Seagrams can be credited as being one of the greatest training areas in the field of distillation as well as management. Many bourbon distillers throughout the state have acquired personnel from Seagrams plants, and they have been quite successful.

It was strictly by chance that Seagrams entered the bourbon whiskey market. With the onset of World War II, they entered into the production of high proof spirits for defense, and since the distillation of whiskey was discontinued, they bought up and leased a number of distilleries to extend their alcohol production but also acquired bourbon whiskey inventory that they could use in their blended products.

After the war ended, they continued with the production of bourbon whiskey and entered the market with a large number of popular brands that they had acquired and adopted some others. The names "Henry McKenna," "Mattingly & Moore," "Old Baker," "Bench Mark," and "Eagle Rare" come to mind, as well as "Four Roses" and "Paul Jones," which were spirit blends for a period.

The distilleries that they bought consisted of H. McKenna, Cummins-Collins, Old Lewis Hunter, and Old Prentice, and they leased the Blair Distillery and Old Colonel. Seagrams has since disposed of those plants except the Old Prentice, now called Four Roses RD No. 8, in Anderson County. And with this disposition, they have completely forsaken the bourbon business domestically and operate the Lawrenceburg, Kentucky, plant strictly for export.

In 1958, Mickey McGuire built twenty warehouses off KY 245 near the Nelson-Bullitt county line for D. W. Karp, who had agreed to lease them to Seagrams. These houses were all one-floor plans, seven tiers high, containing 21,300 barrels each. Karp suffered a heart attack shortly after, and Seagrams purchased the complex.

The operation originally called Lotus and now Four Roses BW No. 64 has been equipped with a cistern room for receiving bulk whiskey from their Lawrenceburg, Kentucky, and Lawrenceburg, Indiana, plants for entry. In addition, they have a dump room installed and a bottling line for bottling a single barrel "Four Roses" bourbon whiskey for export. Shortly after Seagrams closed their small plants, they closed the 7th Street operation in 1983, and by 1985 all whiskey was removed from those warehouses.

Fred Wilkie, brother of Wendell Wilkie, was overall manager of the Seagrams operation in Kentucky, Joe Prochaska was production manager, and Paul Kolochov was chief chemist. A mammoth shake-up took place in the 1950s and a large number of the Wilkie crowd left. Wilkie was with the Kingan Packing Company in Indianapolis for a while, and Prochaska joined Heublein in Hartford, Connecticut. Armand Bouchet followed as manager of the plant, and Bill Rheindollar succeeded him.

On December 21, 2001, Seagrams went out of the whiskey business. Their Four Roses Plant, RD No. 8 in Anderson County, along with the Four Roses or Lotus operation in Bullitt County, went to Kirin Brewing of Japan. Penrod Ricard, owners of Wild Turkey, bought the Lawrenceburg, Indiana, plant and their Scotch holdings plus Seagrams Gin. Diageo of London bought the remainder of their products. Most of their bourbon labels acquired during World War II had already been sold to other distilleries.

Grosscurth Distillery, RD No. 26

This distillery was built in 1933 near Anchorage with a mashing capacity of 400 bushels warehousing 35,000 barrels. Mr. C.

A. Grosscurth owned and operated the plant assisted by his son Charles. At one time they were also involved in the Old Prentice Distillery RD No. 8 in Anderson County, and for a period during World War II had leased the John P. Dant Distillery RD No. 39 at Meadowlawn in Jefferson County.

A quantity of Grosscurth whiskey showed up in the bulk market through brokers as late as 1954, but the distillery eventually shut down, and it was demolished in 1976. For a period it operated as Waterfill & Frazier before Joe Makler moved that name to the Shawhan or Independent Distillery RD No. 28 near Bardstown. In 1947, Mr. Grosscurth Sr. was factoring grain accounts for H. P. Rardin, a grain dealer and elevator operator in Kansas, Illinois, and his son was operating the distillery.

The Louisville Distillery

Mr. George C. Collins, Jr., a partner of Arthur J. Cummins at the Cummins-Collins Distillery RD No. 20 at Athertonville in Larue County, died in 1945, and Cummins incorporated the business. However, the enterprise was apparently too large an undertaking or the price may have been attractive, and the plant was sold to Seagrams in 1946.

Arthur J. Cummins then proceeded to build a new distillery on the property of the Old Frankenmuth Brewery at 15th and Hill streets in Louisville, with a capacity of 900 bushels. No warehouses were constructed, but storage was utilized at General Distillery on Mellwood Avenue, owned by Nussbaum. The general office and bottling house was located in Louisville at 1514 S. Brook Street in Louisville, which was formerly occupied by Cummins-Collins.

The first entry of new whiskey was entered in March 1947, but after less than two years Arthur died, on January 15, 1949. The plant was sold soon after to Barton of Bardstown, who made corn whiskey there for a period. Barton acquired the brand Kentucky Gentleman, which was successfully distributed as well as the brands Heart of Kentucky, Four Score, and Gift of Kentucky. Barton dismantled the distillery in the late 1950s and the property is now occupied by Kelley Technical Coatings.

Paul Jones & Co., Wholesale Liquor Dealer, RD No. 7

Paul Jones moved his family from Virginia to Atlanta, Georgia, and began a very successful career as a whiskey salesman for R. M. Rose & Co., peddling it mostly in Tennessee and Georgia. He moved to Louisville after the Civil War and established the Paul Jones & Co., buying the Four Roses brand from R. M. Rose. From Louisville he traveled throughout the country selling whiskey in barrels as "Jones Four Star Whiskey."

In 1890, he formed a company with himself as president, his son, Saunders P. Jones, as secretary and treasurer, and James Cunningham as general manager. They operated the J. G. Mattingly & Sons plant RD No. 2, which was bankrupt. This venture was not successful, and they sold to the trust in 1902.

The wholesale company, however, continued successfully, and when Prohibition was enacted they owned thousands of barrels of whiskey in a large number of Kentucky, Maryland, and Pennsylvania distilleries. At the same time they were involved in other businesses, including Jefferson Island Salt, the same lake that was sucked dry years later by a hole that developed from underground oil exploration in Louisiana.

By 1925, the theft of whiskey in rural warehouses had become so rampant that the Bureau of Internal Revenue ordered all whiskey removed and taken to warehouses in the metropolitan areas. Paul Jones moved their whiskey to Frankfort Distillery in Frankfort, where it was bottled for medicinal purposes as "Four Roses," "Paul Jones," and "Antique."

By 1928, all whiskey was gone from Frankfort Distillery, and Paul Jones bought the Frankfort name and, with T. W. Hinde of Chicago as president, reorganized in Louisville as Frankfort Distillery. S. C. Miller and W. H. Veeneman were also involved in this transaction. In addition they purchased two rye distilleries in Maryland and an interest in A. Ph. Stitzel. In 1937, they completed building a 3,100-bushel plant in Shively, and they were involved in producing a blend of straight whiskeys under the names of "Paul Jones," "Four Roses," "Old Oscar Pepper," and "Mattingly & Moore." Roy Beam, a son of Joe Beam, became distiller.

There was at this time a German immigrant by the name of Dr. Lenz, who was a chemist and operated a school for distillers in the Louisville area. Apparently he had some knowledge of fermentation, distillation, and blending, whether from his knowledge of chemistry or by association with European brandy operations, but he acted as consultant to a number of distillers. This work included the formulation of blends for Frankfort Distillery. Dr. Lenz later fell on hard times possibly owing to his German name and heritage and ended up completely broke in New York, where he died.

Bill Veeneman sold his plant early in World War II to Seagrams, and they continued using the same brands for years until they discontinued their straight whiskey operations. The Frankfort Distillery was shut down after the war, and Seagrams is now operating the Old Prentice Distillery RD No. 8 in Anderson County as Four Roses. The warehousing complex, formerly known as Lotus in Bullitt County, also bears the name Four Roses. The warehouses were constructed by Mickey McGuire in 1958 for Dave Karp, who leased them to Seagrams and later sold to them. The Lotus plant later built a dump room and cistern room, and they are presently bottling a single barrel whiskey and also receiving whiskey in bulk from their Lawrenceburg plant for entry in their warehouses.

Jessamine County
8th District

Jessamine County had a record of a large number of distilleries in the early 1800s. These distilleries were run mostly in conjunction with water-powered mills by the enterprising farmers along Hickman Creek, a tributary of the Kentucky River. They were strictly seasonal, there was no widespread distribution of their products, and eventually they became extinct. There were as many as fifty of these distilleries in 1825, but by 1882 records show only two.

E. J. Curley & Company, RD No. 15,
Kentucky River, RD No. 45,
Canada Dry

Built in 1880 by E. J. Curley, the distillery was located near the mouth of Hickman Creek where it flowed into the Kentucky River. His brands were Boone's Knoll, Royal Bourbon, and Blue Grass Bourbon and Rye. The operation was not successful because in 1889 his horses and wagons were impounded for nonpayment of taxes, but somehow he was able to stay in operation until Prohibition. At that time American Medicinal Spirits took over the remaining whiskey and brands.

The stone distillery was a magnificent structure, and the inside was constructed of some of the most beautiful timber available. Around 1923 it was converted into a resort hotel, with a commanding view of the Kentucky River and Palisades. After the repeal of prohibition, the property was bought by Gratz Hawkins and others, who renovated the distillery and built new warehouses. They began producing whiskey under the name of Kentucky River RD No. 45.

The plant was later bought by Bill Thompson, and, under the management of F. B. Mitchell, they added the brand Old Lazy Days. Thompson sold to Norton Simon sometime in the 1960s. Norton Simon continued to operate the plant as Canada Dry until the late 1970s, when they bought the Stitzel-Weller Distillery RD No. 16 in Shively, Jefferson County.

At one time Ed Kimmins was manager, and Mel Hawkins, a nephew of Gratz Hawkins, was distiller. Longtime employees included Plug Johnson, maintenance supervisor, and Ray Clark, warehouse superintendent. Mike Sotak became overall manager under Norton Simon, Ed Ziegler was the chemist, and Gene Stratton was office manager.

The distillery building burned, and the warehouses were leased for a time to Seagrams to house production from their Anderson County plant. Since then, they have leased to Boulevard of Anderson County for their "Wild Turkey" whiskey.

Old Lexington Club Distilling Company, RD No. 86

Records show that in 1890 this company was sold to a Cincinnati concern for $10,000. Their brand was Old Lexington Club. Before this date, around 1880, the company was called Almond Distillery. Since it was built in the floodplain of Hickman Creek and the Kentucky River, it was flooded periodically; and shortly after prohibition the entire plant was dismantled and razed. Apparently the stone buildings from two other distilleries still exist; one in Union Mills on East Hickman Creek and the other on Jessamine Creek near Glass Mill.

Kenton County
6th District

James Walsh & Company

This company, with offices in Cincinnati, operated a rectifying house in Covington near the suspension bridge that spanned the Ohio River. Their brands were Ned White and Golden Pheasant, which were straight whiskeys, as well as a number of other bourbons and rye whiskey blends. They operated the Rossville Distillery at Rossville, Indiana, and controlled the production of the Paris Distillery RD No. 77 (Sam Clay, Jr., Company) in Bourbon County.

In 1892, N. J. Walsh leased the Sam Clay plant and began operations as the Paris Distillery Company, with H. D. Haynes as manager. On March 18, 1893, the Covington operation burned to the ground. Walsh sold the Paris Distillery Company to the trust in 1902.

About 1907, the Walsh Company was purchased by W. P., E. A., and V. M. O'Shaughnessy, who operated the Rossville plant, making "James Walsh Bourbon and Rye." The plant continued production of grain alcohol for medicinal and commercial purposes during Prohibition under the name of U.S. Industrial Alcohol and continued after prohibition. It was then sold to Schenley.

New England Distilling Company, RD No. 11

Since 1885 this plant was a rectifying house as well as general offices for Crigler & Crigler. It was located at 215 Pike Street near

Central Covington Station. It was purchased later by the New England Distilling Company, which produced a brand of rum that was used mainly for flavoring in tobacco and food products. It was the only rum plant in Kentucky before and after Prohibition. The New England Company produced between 5,000 and 10,000 gallons of rum daily.

New England was operated during prohibition by Henry E. Pogue and Herbert Hoffheimer of Cincinnati for rum used by the American Tobacco Company from 1920 to 1933. The company was sold to Schenley in 1933, but Pogue continued with them until 1938 when he suffered a heart attack. After about two years he went to work for J. T. S. Brown Company.

The Willow Run Distillery,
The Latonia Distillery

Charles L. Miller operated this plant on the L&N Railroad near Latonia Station as the Willow Run Distillery. In 1891, it was operated as the Latonia Distillery by Cincinnati wholesalers Crigler & Crigler. It was sold to the trust in 1893 and later dismantled.

Larue County
5th District

J. M. Atherton & Company
Atherton Distillery, RD No. 87
Mayfield Distillery, RD No. 229
Windsor Distillery, RD No. 36

Cummins Collins, RD No. 20
Old Farmer Distillery

The location of the original distillery seems to be in some dispute. According to Samuel Elliott writing for the *Nelson County Record* in 1896, he claims the J. M. Atherton Distillery was in Nelson County, but still places it south of the Rolling Fork River, the dividing line at this point between Nelson and Larue. However, Mr. Elliott must have been a frequent visitor to the distilleries and wrote so prolifically and complimentarily of their products that he may have imbibed too freely and did not know exactly what county he was in.

More recent information places the J. M. Atherton plant just south of Athertonville in Larue County. In 1879, J. M. Atherton purchased another site where John Boone had operated a distillery and built not one, but two distilleries on this property. It was reported that Boone had employed both Thomas Lincoln and his son Abe at this location before they moved to Indiana.

Atherton built the J. M. Atherton plant RD No. 87 and the Mayfield Distillery RD No. 229 and then added a third distillery called Windsor Distillery RD No. 36, which had a combined capacity of 2,200 bushels by 1893 and employed about 200 men. Their brands were Atherton, Mayfield, Clifton, Windsor, Howard, Carter, Kenwood, Brownfield, and Baker. Atherton's son, Peter Lee, joined him and they moved their offices to Louisville, where they had other business property and investments. The companies were sold to the trust in 1899.

Atherton's brother-in-law, Alex Mayfield, superintendent of the Mayfield plant, Mayfields' son-in-law, John Knox Daugherty, Clifton Atherton, son of Peter Lee, and John Carter, another relative, remained with the trust when the plant changed hands.

Clifton Atherton became superintendent of two other distilleries bought out by the trust: the S. P. Lancaster RD No. 86 and No. 415 in Nelson County and A. Keller RD No. 9 in Franklin County.

The Windsor No. 36 house under the trust fell heir to the brands Belle of Marion, Coon Hollow, W. T. Snyder, J. N. Blakemore, M. V. Monarch, and others.

According to George Barry, a native of New Haven and former mayor and civic leader, the L&N Railroad ran a spur from New Haven to Athertonville and furnished a steam engine to transport their box cars to and from the distillery to ship their whiskey. He said that the spur was kept quite busy with frequent trips and that the business was a thriving industry. George Barry died September 12, 1998. He would have been 95 on December 27, 1998.

When Prohibition was enacted, all of the whiskey was removed to concentration warehouses, and the distilleries were abandoned.

In 1933, the distillery was rebuilt as a modern plant by A. J. Cummins and Hunt Collins and renamed Cummins-Collins RD No. 20. Their brand was "A. J. Cummins."

Seagrams bought the plant in 1946. They operated alternately with H. McKenna, Fairfield, Hunter-Wilson or Old Lewis Hunter, Cynthiana, and Old Prentice of Lawrenceburg. Sometime in the late 1970s and early 1980s, the distillery and warehouses were razed. The property is now occupied by a stave mill owned by Leonard Kennedy and Bert Zimlick, who are furnishing the staves to Bluegrass Cooperage owned by Brown-Forman.

According to an article in the *Lebanon Enterprise* dated October 15, 1948, George Dant had shares in the Cummins Distillery at the time of his death in 1943. He was president of the Farmer's National Bank of Lebanon, which was also the executor of his will. His stock amounted to about 10 percent of the outstanding shares from which $3 million was derived from the sale of 51,694 barrels of whiskey. No mention is made that this included the distillery premises, but apparently it must have been the case because the amount would represent about $58.30 per barrel, or roughly $1.20 per original proof gallon based on forty-eight gallons per barrel. Also no mention is made of the ages of the whiskey involved, but this would be a very high price for whiskey produced before 1943 and certainly in excess of the O.P.A. ceiling price, which was in effect at that time.

Lincoln County
8th District

Edgewood Distillery Company, RD No. 236
Paxton Brothers and Company

Adam G. Diehl organized and operated this company on Gilbert's Creek, a tributary of the Dix River northeast of Stanford and produced "Edgewood Bourbon" and "Edgewood Rye." About 1895 he turned the business over to his brother-in-law Thomas W. Paxton, who changed the name to Paxton Brothers.

Paxton died in 1905, and about 1910 the plant was purchased by G. W. Traylor, who operated another distillery near Stanford called Traylor Distillery (no further information is available on this operation). Traylor died in 1911, but his company continued to operate until Prohibition. The brand names were continued during prohibition by American Medicinal Spirits.

J. H. Hutchings & Company, RD No. 81
Crab Orchard Distillery Company

J. H. Hutchings operated a 65-bushel house near the L&N Railroad station in Crab Orchard producing a brand by that name. He sold out to the trust in 1902. In 1907, the trust advertised the plant for sale and it is recorded that in 1912 it was sold to parties in Chicago for $1,500.

Madison County
8th District

Burnam, Bennett and Company, RD No. 1

Thompson S. Burnam of Winchester and John G. Bennett operated a distillery in 1885 located near Silver Creek on Kentucky Highway 52. They produced the Warwick and Old Burnam brands.

The plant was sold to Bernheim of Louisville in 1907 and operated up to prohibition.

W. S. Hume and Company, RD No. 54
The Silver Creek Distillery

Another distillery located on Silver Creek near the community by that name was operated by W. S. Collins in 1871, producing the brand Governor's Choice. By 1884, the plant was operating as W. S. Hume and Company, with brands Hume Bourbon and Hume Rye. George T. Stagg, who had been a former store-keeper gauger, managed the plant and had a share in the company.

Mr. Hume died in a boat wreck on the West Coast in 1906, and at this time the operations were controlled by Hume and Lancaster Distillery Companies RD No. 68 and No. 415 near Bardstown. This latter operation was controlled by the trust. They were bottling "Hume," "Belle of Nelson," and "Old Lancaster," but by the year 1910 they were owned outright by the trust (Kentucky Distilleries and Warehouse Company).

Marion County
5th District

J. W. Dant, RD No. 169

In 1836, J. W. Dant started his distillery on his farm, Walnut Ridge, a few miles west of Loretto in Marion County, about a mile from the Nelson County line. The L&N Railroad eventually ran past the distillery, and it was established as Dant Station. In 1891, J. W.'s son Wallace succeeded him, and operations continued until Prohibition, but by that time Wallace's younger brother George had taken over. George Dant, believing that prohibition would be short-lived, merely boarded up the doors and windows and said, "I'll be back." Sure enough, after fourteen lean years capped by a crippling depression, prohibition was repealed, and it was only necessary to rip off the boards, make some minor improvements and repairs, as crude as they were, and he was off and running.

Jesse Moore Hunt built a warehouse for J. W. Dant, and they made whiskey for Hunt under the name of "West Point." The Dant plant was incorporated in 1897, and in 1908 there were 100 shares of J. W. Dant stock. George owned 51 shares, his brother Sid held 39, and another brother Wallace owned 10.

One unique thing about Mr. Dant's operation was it was built to take advantage of gravity. The mash tub was considerably higher than the fermenters and with the aid of a very large outlet pipe, he was able to fill the tubs in a short time without pumping. Some said the initial flow was almost enough to knock out the bottom of the fermenters.

Empty cases were unloaded to a case storage room above the bottling house, since it was located against a hillside, and they slid down a chute to the bottling line. Whiskey in the warehouses was moved to a hoist in "A" warehouse, which was nearest the dump room, and taken to the third floor, where it was run across a ramp and dumped in the dump room. From there it was filtered by gravity to a bottling tank and further to the bottling line. Time was not important, and they simply took advantage of what they had. I would think, too, that the filtration was not the clearest, since it was run across a fine screen to remove the heavier char and a felt blanket took care of the remainder.

The plant was reorganized in 1934 with George W. Dant as president; T. S. Dant, vice president; J. E. "Shorty" Dant, secretary and treasurer; and A. F. Dant, distiller. Their mashing capacity was 425 bushels per day, and the two warehouses of about 12,000 barrels total, built before prohibition, were still utilized.

Armand Hammer of Occidental Petroleum purchased the plant along with the Dant and Head Distillery RD No. 47 at Gethsemane in Nelson County and operated as United Distillers of America. The last production in the distillery was in the spring of 1948, and Coleman Bixler was distiller. He had been distiller at H. McKenna RD No. 111 and H. E. Pogue RD No. 22—the first was located at Fairfield in Nelson County and the latter at Maysville in Mason County.

Sometime after Hammer bought Dant RD No. 169 they continued mashing for a while. The distillery had never been modernized, and it was nothing more than a shell, with large holes in the clapboard and sheet-metal siding. Hammer made an inspection of the distillery on a cold and windy winter's day and found Jim Devine huddled next to the beer still he was running, bundled up in an overcoat and using the heat of the still to keep off the chill. Making conversation, Hammer said to Jim, "Cold in here, isn't it?"

Jim replied, while spitting a stream of tobacco at a crack in the wall, "Aw, I don't pay much attention to it. The wind comes in these cracks here and goes out those over yonder."

Schenley bought the plant on March 4, 1953, and continued bottling for a while, until they could complete constructing and equipping a new bottling house at the Dant RD No. 47 plant at Gethsemane. By the end of May 1953 all operations had ceased and the plant was abandoned, after all the whiskey was removed from the warehouses. Any equipment of any value was removed. The warehouses were burned by vandals about 1966. Maker's Mark purchased an old barrel hoist and rails that were used in "A" warehouse from Schenley, which they used for several years in their "D" warehouse, until it was replaced by a new one required by OSHA.

J. E. "Shorty" Dant, a nephew of George Dant, was an officer in the company when Hammer bought it. After he was let out, he became a storekeeper gauger. He was assigned to the Dant No. 169 and also No. 47 alternately, and he related a story to me in 1952 about the use of a Dant label by the Dant and Head Distillery. After prohibition, Shorty's brother Will Dant and Joe B. Head established the distillery of Dant and Head and were bottling whiskey as "W. W. Dant." Uncle George felt that this was an encroachment on the "J. W. Dant" brand, and he sued to stop them and also asked for damages. George won the suit, and Dant and Head sent him a check for the judgment. On top of the check was the slogan "Fine Dant Whiskies."

About the end of World War II and shortly thereafter, cooperage was in short supply, and whiskey was being entered in used barrels, usually for two years, and then being transferred to new barrels. The O.P.A. ceiling price during the war was $12.04, but beginning in December 1946, O.P.A. was abandoned, grain allocations were lifted, and distilleries began to run at maximum capacity. As a result, the price of barrels shot as high as $28. Also during the Korean War, 1950 to 1953, barrels were at a premium and in very short supply. New companies sprang up to produce barrels, and staves were being used that had not been dried properly. Barrels were brought in from as far away as London, Ontario, from the London Petrolia Barrel Company. They held liquid, but their quality was questionable.

A lot of experimentation went on, beginning immediately after the war. The use of used cooperage for a two-year period and then exchanging it for new cooperage was an interim solution. As long as the whiskey was stored in new barrels for a two-year period it could be called straight whiskey, and then after a total of four years it could be Bottled-in-Bond without actually claiming a four-year age, but by reference to the strip stamp it implied as much. Some pressure was put on Congress to approve aging in used cooperage and claiming the full age, but the approval never happened. However, in 1968, a new class of whiskey was established called American light whiskey. This was distilled over 160 proof and entered in used cooperage. Of course, the aging in used barrels did not produce the same effect, and additional chips were added to supplement the depleted char in the used barrels.

George Dant, before his death in 1943, came up with a charred oak section or X brace that he inserted in a number of barrels to enhance the aging. However, as this did not produce the same results either, it was finally abandoned, and the use of the traditional new barrel was resumed by all.

George Dant, at the time of his death at 71 years on April 25, 1943, owned most of the farm at Dant Station, was president of the Farmer's National Bank of Lebanon, president of the J. W. Dant Distillery, chairman-of-the-board of Cummins-Collins Distillery RD No. 20 in Larue County where he was a stockholder, and also held stock in the John P. Dant Distillery RD No. 39 at Meadow-lawn. Mr. George Dant was a very frugal and rather eccentric person. He lived in a house on the distillery premises that was far from luxurious, considering his financial condition. The house was rather shabbily kept, and the inside was papered with newspapers. He heated the house with a pot-bellied stove, and he lacked many amenities he could have afforded. Mr. Charles C. Boldrick of Lebanon was his attorney, and on one occasion he took his son Sam with him to discuss some legal matters. After finishing up, Sam mentioned to his father that he felt sorry for Mr. Dant. "No need for that son," said Mr. Boldrick. "George Dant can afford anything he wants." George Dant married at a late age to Georgia Ferriell and it wasn't long before they constructed a beautiful, up-to-date house just west of the distillery where they lived until George died.

Phil Dant, a son of Harry Dant and a grandson of Jim Dant, started employment in the Dant RD No. 169 in 1936 and stayed until 1942, when he was employed at Shawhan near Bardstown. This plant was still owned by Tom Pendergast of Kansas City at the time and was under the direction of Frank Schutte. Phil was appointed plant manager in May 1943, but he left for service in World War II shortly after. On his return he joined John P. Dant at Meadowlawn and also ran a bottling operation on Main Street in Louisville. Schenley bought the bottling plant, and Phil continued to run it as Vostok Vodka. After this he held a number of other positions with Schenley, including plant manager of Park and Tilford at 35th and Tyler streets in Louisville and the George T. Stagg plant in Bardstown. Phil retired from the whiskey business in August 1980.

According to Phil, his Uncle George related a number of stories about J. W. when he established the distillery in 1836. Apparently he produced a quantity of whiskey in excess of local requirements, and after accumulating this inventory, he decided to extend his territory. J. W. would hire a wagon headed to Bardstown to transport several barrels of whiskey over the Gilkey Run Road to the Beech Fork River. Here he would have a raft built and would send the whiskey by water all the way to New Orleans. The raft had to travel from the Beech Fork to the Rolling Fork, to the Salt and Ohio rivers, and on to the Mississippi. Apparently J. W. made three such shipments, and after the first two he walked back home. However, by the third trip he was able to afford a mule, and he rode back. No information was furnished on the net profit resulting from this venture.

It seems that a number of the Dant family were employed at Dant RD No. 169 from time to time, according to the genealogy records of Lorene Dant Goepper. Beginning with Wallace, George, Albert, Harry, Edwin, and Phil, they spread out to a number of plants in Marion, Nelson, and Jefferson counties. Thad, a son of

Jim Dant, was distiller for Blair-Osborn-Ballard, Blair Distillery, Thixton Millett, and later John P. Dant.

Wallace Dant, son of J. W., ran the Dant RD No. 169 plant and was replaced by his brother George. Will, a son of Wallace, started the Dant and Head Distillery RD No. 47 with Joe B. Head. After selling this plant he built the Dant and Dant of Kentucky in Louisville, and he retired from National Distillers.

Will's son Wallace, was working at RD No. 47 with his father and stayed on with Armand Hammer and Schenley when the distillery was sold. When Schenley shut down in 1961, he moved to Bernheim, and he died in 1976. Sidney and Jim, sons of J. W., were also connected with the Dant RD No. 169, but Bernard established the Cold Springs Distillery at Gethsemane and later changed the name to Yellowstone. Bernard and his sons Mike, Walter, and Sam, and a nephew, James Patrick Kearns, built the new Yellowstone Distillery on 7th Street in Louisville, which they later sold to Glenmore. Jimmy Kearns became president of Yellowstone, and after the acquisition he became a vice president of Glenmore. Will's son Wallace died in 1976.

Van Cleve and Hardesty,
W. J. Hardesty,
Applegate and Sons, RD No. 15

Built sometime prior to 1900 on Kentucky Highway 84, this distillery was a short distance from Raywick. Mr. M. J. Hardesty bought the distillery in 1906 but became insolvent by 1910. The plant had a mashing capacity of 50 bushels per day, with one 1,600-barrel warehouse and another of about 900 barrels. The property was sold to Applegate and Sons at the Marion County Courthouse in Lebanon. Applegate had been producing his brands Old Applegate and Old Rosebud at Yelvington RD No. 7 in Daviess County.

Loretto Distilling Company, RD No. 41
Maker's Mark

In March 1936, D. W. Karp and Associates bought the J. W. Thompson farm on the west side of Loretto and built a distillery of 1,200-bushel capacity. They operated until World War II, when they installed a rectifying column and produced high proof spirits for the war effort. Philip Blum, who was also associated with James B. Beam, was a principal owner. They engaged mostly in rectified products under the name "David Springs" and bottled blended whiskey as well as cordials and other products.

The company was sold on March 10, 1948, to National Distillers, which used the three warehouses of approximately 47,000 barrels. Burnett "Bud" Ryan supervised the warehousing. In September 1955, National Distillers had moved all their whiskey, and they then sold to J. T. S. Brown, which was owned by Bob Gould. Gould had fronted for Schenley on a number of other transactions, and Schenley actually assumed control. They moved a quantity of whiskey into the warehouses and transferred Dick Hamilton from the RD No. 9 plant in Lebanon to supervise.

In May 1969, when Schenley had no further use of the warehouses, they were offered to Star Hill, now Maker's Mark. Although Maker's Mark had no immediate need for the warehouses, it was an appealing offer and the deed was transferred on June 10, 1969. The only value of the plant, besides the real estate of 135 acres, was the three warehouses, along with some salvageable material that was utilized by Maker's Mark. The distillery building was falling down and represented a hazard, so it was demolished in 1975. Maker's Mark continues to use the warehouses for storage and added another 20,000-barrel house, built by Buzick in 1987. Four additional 20,000-barrel warehouses were constructed in 2001, and several more are under construction in 2002.

W. H. Head, RD No. 9
H. Rosenthal and Sons, RD No. 329

W. H. Head was operating a distillery near Raywick on the Rolling Fork River in 1880. His brand was "W. H. Head and Company." H. Rosenthal and Sons of Cincinnati bought the plant in 1907. He discontinued his operation at RD No. 15 in Bryantsville, Garrard County, at this time and moved his brands Fern Hill and Wm. Birkle to this location. The name of the plant was changed to Wm. Birkle Distillery.

I have a bottle of Wm. Birkle Bottled-in-Bond made at RD No. 329. The strip stamp bears a production date of spring 1914 with bottling in spring 1925 at General Bonded Warehouse No. 1, 5th District, which was obviously for medicinal purposes but bears no prescription label.

J. B. Mattingly, RD No. 14
Brown Forman Company

Immediately after the War Between the States, J. B. Mattingly operated a small distillery just out of St. Mary's. He had no warehouses and sold his output directly to wholesale dealers and local saloons. Whiskey was transported to Louisville for aging at the Brown-Forman Distillery operations, where they were involved in the G. Lee Redmond Company. This was the former Hoffheimer Brothers or White Mills Distillery RD No. 414 at the present Brown-Forman site at 18th and Howard.

In 1870 a wholesale firm, J. T. S. Brown and Brothers, began buying the production for distributors, and this arrangement continued until 1901. In 1901, the Brown-Forman Company was formed and they bought into the J. B. Mattingly Company. Ben Mattingly retained controlling interest, but George Brown, Fontaine Kremer, W. B. Penick, and P. B. Mattingly held the remaining interest. In 1907, they built warehouses and a bottling house on the premises at a cost of $75,000.

Production of whiskey discontinued around 1918, and the barrel inventory was moved to the White Mills plant RD No. 414 in Jefferson County, where it was stored and bottled for medicinal purposes.

In 1919, the entire facility in Marion County was destroyed by fire, and the only reference to this operation is a road bearing the name Brown-Forman. It connects the Blandford-Frogtown Road and Kentucky Highway 84 just west of St. Mary's.

Smith and Smith, RD No. 11
Blair-Ballard and Osborne
Thixton-Millett Company
Blair Distilling Company, RD No. 21

J. R. and J. P. Smith operated this plant before 1855, and it was located in downtown Chicago, now St. Francis, Marion County. Their brand, Smith and Smith, handmade sour mash, consisted of about 100 to 200 barrels a year, a minuscule quantity by today's standards. This whiskey was distributed by Templet and Washburn, brokers of Louisville.

John Proctor Dant, Sr., bought the distillery on December 4, 1855, and operated it until 1891. After selling he moved to Louisville. Thad Dant, son of Jim Dant and nephew of John Proctor, was employed as distiller.

In 1891, the plant was acquired by Blair and Ballard, and the name changed to Blair-Ballard and Osborn. It was sold again to Thixton and Millett, who started out in Daviess County, moved to Louisville in 1901, and then bought out Boone Brothers in Nelson County in 1903—after selling that plant in 1912, they took over this plant the same year. They operated until prohibition and then shut down. Mr. Millett went into the lumber business sometime after prohibition.

Nick Blair rebuilt the distillery in 1935 with a capacity of 500 bushels, and his brands were Colonel Blair, Nick Blair, and Blair's Old Club. Walter Blair was the last member of the Blair family to be associated with the plant before selling out to a Mr. Lehr. D. W. Karp bought the distillery from Lehr.

In 1943, Karp leased the distillery to Seagrams on a ten-year renewable basis. They operated during World War II for the government program of high proof spirits but held the plant only for storage afterward. They renewed their ten-year lease in 1953, and when this expired they renewed only on an annual basis. Seagrams emptied the warehouses by 1965 and vacated the premises. Early in 1970 Old Boone RD No. 39 at Meadowlawn needed additional storage, and they leased the warehouses. Mr. Arthur Ball, who had been a stockholder in the Loretto Distillery RD No. 41, was hired to oversee the storage. This lasted until 1977, when Pat Buse discontinued his operation at Meadowlawn. After the whiskey was removed, the Karps hired Gerald Green, a local salvage operator, to remove the warehouses. The premises have lain fallow ever since.

Boldrick and Callaghan, RD No. 370
The Belle of Marion Distillery

Richard Wathen operated this distillery on the Rolling Fork River near Calvary from 1852 to 1875 along with his sons R. N. "Nace" and J. B. Wathen. In 1875, his sons left to buy the Moore and Grigsby Distillery RD No. 270 in Lebanon. In 1880 the plant was sold to Ralph L. Spalding and Charles D. Boldrick of Lebanon and Frank Callaghan of Louisville. Callaghan had been associated with the Crystal Springs Distillery RD No. 3 and RD No. 78 at 1st and Magnolia streets in Louisville. The name was changed to Belle of Marion.

Spalding was killed in a machinery accident at the distillery a short time later and his brother C. C. Spalding succeeded him; the name changed again to Spalding, Boldrick and Company. C. C. Spalding retired, and it became Boldrick and Callaghan. Callaghan died in 1889, and Mr. Boldrick assumed full ownership. Plant capacity at this time was 300 bushels per day, with brands Belle of Marion and Callaghan.

The distillery was sold to the trust in 1900, and they continued operations until just before prohibition. The plant was closed, and production was moved to the "36" house in Athertonville, still using the company name and brands. The distillery eventually fell into disrepair, but some of the buildings were being used for a farm operation.

Burks Spring Distillery, RD No. 440
John C. Weller Company
Old Samuels Distillery, RD No. 44
Maker's Mark Distillery

Charles Burks built a grist mill and distillery on Hardin's Creek 3.5 miles southeast of Loretto in 1805, drawing water from a mill race built on the creek. He died in 1831, and his heirs continued the operation. George R. Burks joined the company in 1878 and rebuilt the distillery, adding a bottling house and a manager's residence. The distillery was called Burks Spring, and their main brands were Burks Spring and Old Happy Hollow. In 1906, John C. Weller, a Louisville wholesaler, contracted for their entire output, adding the brands Faymus and J. C. W. The Burks family moved to Louisville at the beginning of Prohibition, and Ernest Bickett bought the farm of 202 acres with the distillery.

I was told that during prohibition George Remus of Erlanger entered the picture and, without approval of the Internal Revenue Service, removed most of the barrels from "A" warehouse. Bill Shockency, a tenant on the farm, was told to get lost while this took place. The old "A" warehouse, which held approximately 5,000 barrels, was used as a hay barn during prohibition. The dunnage rails were removed, and a number of them were used to add a room to Shockency's house. An old hay hook was still in place a few years ago.

At the repeal of prohibition some members of Mr. Bickett's family renovated the plant and revived the operation. Among them were Frank and Orris Bickett and their brothers-in-law, Hood Hamilton and Alton Thompson. Henry O'Neal was distiller just prior to prohibition and was followed by Ken Mills, after prohibition was repealed.

Brown Kaiser operated the distillery for a short period, and in 1943 Glenmore bought the plant mainly for inventory, but they also continued to produce high-proof spirits for defense purposes. During their stay, Glenmore built a beautiful eight-acre lake, spring fed, high on the hill above the distillery. A 6-inch line, running about three-quarters of a mile, delivered water at 20 pounds pressure, giving a sufficient static pressure to operate the cooling coils on the mash tub and condensers. The entire plant, including the mash tub rakes, the mill, and all the elevators and conveyors, was run by an old 75 H.P. Murray steam engine. A series of line shafts and jack shafts was connected by belts to the main drive pulley. Everything has since been electrified. Since there was no power source prior to rural electrification, this was necessary after the old water wheel was abandoned. I was told that prior to R.E.A. it was not uncommon to hang a coal oil lantern on the tail box when it was dark in order to check the proof of distillation. Fortunately they never had a fire, but many distilleries did.

D. W. Karp bought the plant after World War II and operated it for a period during the Korean War in 1950 and 1951. After that it was shut down and idled for more than two years, except for some whiskey stored in the warehouses belonging mostly to Bob Gould at Ripy RD No. 27 in Anderson County.

On October 1, 1953, T. W. "Bill" Samuels bought the farm, including the lake and distillery, for $50,000. He immediately began an extensive renovation of the distillery, changing pipelines and adding tanks for his planned operation. He installed a sophisticated water system for both boiler water use and reducing water that was probably second to none in the state. Production was begun in February 1954, and the first entry was barreled on February 20,

1954, of some 18 barrels. The intention was to produce about 2,000 barrels annually until the market could be tested. However, the first year brought the operation a little short due to warm weather, and the season ended with 1,527 barrels.

The next season got started a little earlier in late 1954 and by April 1955, 2,550 barrels were filled. Elmo Beam, the oldest son of Joe Beam, was distiller for the first two seasons. He had been assistant to Mr. Morgan Edelen at the T. W. Samuels Distillery RD No. 145 and came out of retirement to get the plant started. However, Elmo died on April 5, 1955.

Late in 1954 Bill had an idea to enter the bottling business in order to get reacquainted with various wholesalers and to work the kinks out of the bottling house. He bought a number of barrels of Barton whiskey stored at County Line Distillery RD No. 13 at Boston, Kentucky, through Art Williams, a broker. He was to use this in a Burks Spring bottling. He also bought a number of barrels of "Old Happy Hollow" from Bob Gould that were stored at Ripy RD No. 27 and were to be used in bonded brand. This venture was only partially successful, and in the spring of 1957 the remaining whiskey was sold and bottling ceased to await the aging of the "Old Samuels" production. In the meantime, T. W. Samuels Distillery, owned by Foster Trading Corporation, sued to prevent the use of the Old Samuels brand, and the name was dropped, substituted with the name Star Hill Distilling Company, which was an old label that Bill Samuels owned and which was also the name of his farm in Bardstown.

In the spring of 1957, a meeting was held at the University

Club in St. Louis consisting of George Shields and Dick Winkler of French and Shields Advertising Agency; Hubbard Buckner, vice-president of First National Bank of Louisville and a board member of the company; Ed Budde and Pat Quinn, old associates of Bill's in the T. W. Samuel's operation; Buford Penland of Penland Distributors of Dallas; Bill Samuels; and Sam K. Cecil. Prior to this time, George Shields had made numerous trips to the distillery to study the operation, and at the meeting he presented the entire advertising program, including the name "Maker's Mark" and the packaging.

In the next year everything was readied to procure bottles, wax, labels, and all the other material needed for bottling, and on May 7, 1958, one barrel was dumped and bottled. From this bottling, samples were distributed, and a regular bottling schedule was begun in August 1958 to make the debut to the wholesalers that had been lined up.

The company experienced some difficulties in the early years, and a number of strategies were employed. Munson Shaw, an import agent, was hired for about three years to promote the brand, but this effort was not effective. In 1963, Parrott and Company was retained as a sales agent on the West Coast, and this failed to produce sufficient results.

However, over the years, relations were established with wholesalers, especially Crane Distributing Company in Kentucky and the McKesson Liquor Companies outside of Kentucky. The brand gradually took root and it built its firmest base in Kentucky and Tennessee. In December 1981, the company was sold to Hiram Walker, whose main operations were in Peoria, Illinois, and Walkerville, Ontario. Hiram Walker retained Maker's Mark for a while but then sold their entire operation to Allied Lyons of London, having already abandoned their plant in Peoria.

I was able to procure a quart of Bottled-in-Bond "Happy Hollow" whiskey, which was some of the last bottled before Prohibition. The strip stamp shows that it was made in spring 1911 and bottled at Burks Spring Distillery in the fall of 1918.

Maker's Mark has added to their production facilities by the installation of an additional beer still and Mash tub along with fermenters to accommodate the increase. A new cistern room and dumping room have also been added to keep pace with the ever increasing production.

W. Q. Emison and Company
R. B. Lancaster

This distillery originated in Lebanon and was operated by Emison and Bob Lancaster for a number of years and produced the Maple Grove and Falcon brands. Bob Lancaster, who was a brother of Sam Lancaster, owner of S. P. Lancaster Distillery RD No. 415 near Bardstown, bought out Emison's share and made whiskey for a time using the "R. B. Lancaster" brand. No further information is available on this plant.

Moore and Grigsby, RD No. 270
J. B. Wathen and Brothers
Mueller, Wathen and Kobert
Charles Kobert and Company, RD No. 299
John A. Wathen, RD No. 9

Moore and Grigsby operated this plant just outside the city limits of Lebanon prior to 1875. In 1875, J. B. Wathen and R. N. (Nace), who had worked with their father at Distillery RD No. 370 near Calvary on the Rolling Fork River (later the Boldrick-Callaghan distillery) bought this plant and increased the capacity to 100 bushels. They operated under the name J. B. Wathen and Brothers. In 1879, they took on H. Mueller and Charles Kobert of Cincinnati as partners and added a second distillery RD No. 299.

The original plant, now operating as Mueller, Wathen and Company, was refitted with a three-chambered wood still and produced a sweet mash named "Rolling Fork." The second plant produced a sour mash called "Cumberland" in a three-chambered still, and the mashing capacity of this one was 300 bushels.

In 1880, J. B. Wathen sold his interest and moved to Louisville where he established the J. B. Wathen and Brothers Distillery RD No. 263 at 26th and Broadway.

Mueller, Wathen, and Kobert built one of the first bottling houses on distillery property and increased their business of Rolling Fork and Cumberland brands. The company dropped the

"Moore and Grigsby" brands and by 1905 were making only sour mash whiskey, but they were still using the wood stills.

Operations continued until Prohibition, but after that the property deteriorated considerably. In 1931, the brick still house was destroyed by fire. John A. Wathen acquired the premises and in 1934 built a much larger, more modern distillery of 2,100 bushels, producing and bottling as "John A. Wathen." Schenley purchased the distillery in the early 1940s and produced high proof spirits for defense purposes during World War II. They operated for a period after the war under the name of Pebbleford and Poindexter, but they made their last run in the spring of 1949. For a short time they experimented with using the slop dryers to produce a whey from surplus milk, but this was short-lived. They eventually sold the property, and the buildings were dismantled sometime in the early 1970s.

Ballard and Lancaster
R. Cummins and Company, RD No. 357

An atlas of the Balltown precinct of Nelson County dated 1882 shows the Ballard and Lancaster Distillery on the Beech Fork River southeast of Bardstown near a ford, which is now bridged on the Botland-Manton Road, Kentucky Highway 605. No record is available on when it was moved.

Richard Cummins sold his two farm distilleries at Coon Hollow on the Nelson-Marion line near the L&N Railroad and just off Kentucky Highway 52 in 1880 and bought the Ballard and Lancaster plant, which was located at that time directly behind the old J. H. Lyon General Store in Loretto, some two years later. Brands were "Ballard and Lancaster" and R. Cummins. Mr. Cummins turned the operation over to his son J. P. Cummins in 1891, and he died in 1903.

J. P. Cummins sold this plant to the trust, and in 1911 the distillery was operating under the name Winston Drug Company, but still using the brand R. Cummins. There is no record of operations after 1911, but the distillery apparently was razed at prohibition and never rebuilt.

Mason County
6th District

H. E. Pogue, RD No. 22

According to a booklet published by the Pogue Distillery shortly after repeal of Prohibition, the first distillery was established at a junction of the old "Buffalo Trace," the overland trail to the south and west. This was originally Bourbon County, still a part of Virginia. It is now Mason County, and the settlement of Limestone Landing was later to be called Maysville.

The H. E. Pogue Distillery was set up on or near the same location in 1869, and in 1876 it became Pogue and Thomas. The Pogue family reacquired the operation later and over time produced the Old Pogue and Old Time brands of bourbon; Old Maysville Club, a rye; and Royal Club, a rye and wheat whiskey.

The original Pogues, father and son, were killed in separate machinery accidents, becoming entangled in belts operating the machinery. Henry E. Pogue III succeeded his grandfather and father until 1925, when he moved to Covington to join the New England Distillery, producers of rum. They bottled whiskey until 1925 for American Medicinal Spirits and remained a bonded whiskey warehouse for that time; the remaining stocks were moved to concentration warehouses in Louisville. During this period their brands were Old Jordan and Old Time. (Jack Pogue, a retired veterinarian living in Danville, and a son of H. E. Pogue III, has bottles of the above brands, but the dates on the strip stamp are illegible.)

In 1933 the plant was sold to Rose of Chicago, who renovated the plant with many modern improvements, including a refrigeration system for summertime operation. There were also three, 10,000-barrel warehouses.

Rose sold in 1942 to Schenley, who operated the distillery producing high proof spirits during World War II for defense purposes. The Parkers, who were wholesalers in Covington, operated the bottling plant and apparently used whiskeys produced at other plants as well. Orene Parker was associated with the T. J. Pottinger Distillery No. 405 in 1883, and he rejoined the wholesale house in Covington. Schenley operated the distillery for a period after the war, and it is now abandoned. Both Frankie Smith and Donald Parrish of Bardstown own ceramic jugs emblazoned with R. A. Parker, Nelson County Whiskey, and it is assumed that these were the products of the T. J. Pottinger Distillery.

Alfred C. Parker, who married Marguerite Pogue, was accountant for the distillery, and his wife was a supervisor of the bottling plant until it closed. When F. M. Head and M. C. Beam acquired the T. J. Pottinger Distillery at Gethsemane Station, Pottinger joined the Parkers at their wholesale house in Covington.

Meade County
5th District

Five distilleries were reported to be in existence in Meade County in 1882. No information is available on these plants, however, except that there were, presumably, some brandy operations included. The five were J. P. Benham & Co., Crecelius & Bro., George Greenwell, Joseph Montreal, and G. D. Richardson.

John A. Barry Dist., RD No. 160
Old Poindexter, RD No. 33

John A. Barry Distillery was built about 1934 on the site of a former brandy distillery. The firm went into bankruptcy in 1937 and was sold to E. H. Shelman, a treasurer of the company and former banker. Located near the town of Ekron, it was renamed the Poindexter Distillery.

Poindexter whiskey was a little unusual in that they used 60 percent corn and 40 percent small grain in their formula as opposed to the 70 percent to 72 percent corn used by others. I was told that the additional small grain making up this formula was unmalted barley.

The distillery was bought by Schenley about 1948, and the name was transferred to the RD No. 9 at Lebanon, formerly John A. Wathen.

Mercer County
8th District

John B. Thompson & Co., RD No. 163
Old Jordan Distillery

Phil Jordan built this distillery on Town Creek at Oregon, and after his death it was sold to John B. Thompson in 1878 and moved to Harrodsburg on the Southern Railroad. The distillery operated as Old Jordan. By the year 1900, Thompson was also producing "Runnymeade Rye." In 1905, John B., O. M., and Phil Thompson incorporated the business. By 1909, the Live Oak Distillery Co. of Cincinnati contracted for their entire production. R. F. Balke was sole owner of Live Oak and by 1917 he became owner of Old Jordan.

When Prohibition was enacted, all the whiskey was removed to concentration warehouses, and the buildings were converted to a furniture manufacturing plant.

Shortly after repeal, the brand Old Jordan was bottled by T. W. Samuels Dist. RD No. 145 at Deatsville in Nelson County.

The D. L. Moore Distillery, RD No. 23

Hon. D. L. Moore built this distillery in 1871 on Shawnee Run near Burgin. He produced the "Moore and Rebstock" brand for

Charles Rebstock of St. Louis and his own Stonewall brand until 1889. On February 6, 1889, he sold the distillery and 36 acres of real estate to J. S. and M. Dowling of Lawrenceburg for $35,000. Moore was the executor of the estate of Judge W. H. McBrayer, who left the Cedar Run Distillery RD No. 44 in Anderson County to Moore's children, who were all minors and grandchildren of McBrayer. For this reason, he left to manage the Cedar Run plant. The Dowlings were also part owners of Waterfill & Dowling Distillery, formerly Waterfill & Frazier RD No. 41 as well as a cooperage plant in Anderson County. They continued this operation until prohibition, when it was closed and dismantled.

In 1934, the distillery was rebuilt near the original site on the Southern Railroad and operated as Dowling Bros. until the 1950s. Since then it has been owned alternately by Schenley and Bob Gould. In July 1972, when Gould sold the J. T. S. Brown or Ripy plant RD No. 27 at Tyrone in Anderson County to Austin-Nicholas, he moved his bulk whiskey to the Mercer County plant and part to the Old Joe Distillery RD No. 35 in Anderson County. In the early 1960s, Gould was bottling a fourteen-year-old whiskey called "Dowling's DeLuxe" (94.6 proof) at the Ripy plant.

This distillery has since been vacated and is in very bad condition. Weeds and bushes have grown up, and windows are broken. The warehouse still has the name Dowling Distillery painted on the side. According to Shirlie B. Isaacs, who owns adjoining property, Alvin Gould's widow still owns the property and has posted it for sale at $125,000. Mrs. Isaacs's father, Henry Bradford, worked at the distillery for many years and was well known for his expertise in the construction and maintenance field.

According to George Chinn in his *History of Harrodsburg and the Great Settlement Area of Kentucky, 1774–1900,* 125,000 gallons of "Old Bourbon" were shipped from Burgin annually, the product of Messrs. D. L. Moore and J. A. and Cabbell Huguely. Chinn further states that they consumed about 45,000 bushels of grain and employed 15 laborers at a rate of $20 to $100 per month. This was apparently a period between 1875 and 1894, because he mentions that the federal excise tax was 90 cents per gallon, the only period of time where this was true.

J. Vanarsdall,
D. L. Moore Jr.,
D. L. Moore Dist., RD No. 118

J. Vanarsdall operated a water-powered mill and distillery on the Salt River in 1865 near what is now called Vanarsdell. He produced a brand under his name until 1885, when he leased the property to Mullins and Crigler of Covington.

D. L. Moore, Jr., purchased the distillery in 1892 and made the brands D. L. Moore Jr. and Vanarsdall. When his father died he changed the name to D. L. Moore Distilling Co. Operations continued until Prohibition, at which time the whiskey in storage was moved to the concentration warehouses of James E. Pepper in Lexington and the plant was dismantled.

C. M. Dedman, Ky. Owl Dist. Co., RD No. 16

Charles M. Dedman operated a distillery at Oregon, Kentucky, near the ferry landing on the Kentucky River prior to 1880. This site is a few miles east of Salvisa off U.S. Hwy. 127. The distillery was known as Kentucky Owl Distilling Co.; C. M. Dedman, Prop., and their main brand was Kentucky Owl. The distillery operated until 1916 and then closed. Mr. Dedman died in 1918, and since his in-laws were opposed to liquor for religious reasons, it was never re-opened. In addition, he was a pharmacist, owned a drugstore in Harrodsburg, and was succeeded by his son Thomas Curry Dedman, also a pharmacist. In deference to their in-laws, they declined to sell whiskey on prescription during prohibition.

Mr. C. M. Dedman was the son of Dixon Dedman and Mary McBrayer Dedman. Mary McBrayer was the sister of Judge W. H. McBrayer, who owned the Cedar Brook Dist. RD No. 44 in Anderson County.

Thomas Curry Dedman, son of C. M. Dedman, was married to a daughter of Nick Goddard who operated the Goddard College in Harrodsburg, which was later changed to Beaumont College and became Beaumont Inn in 1918. It is currently operated by Thomas Curry (Bud) Dedman, Jr., and his son Charles M. (Chuck) Dedman.

Montgomery County
7th District

Old McBrayer Dist. Co.

Capt. John H. McBrayer operated a grist mill on Lulbegrud Creek in the community of New Market, a short distance out of Mt. Sterling, in 1870. The mill was converted to a distillery and operated as J. H. McBrayer. He sold later to Judge W. H. McBrayer, who, in turn, sold to W. W. Johnson & Co. John H. McBrayer was connected with Geo. A. Edmonson at the David S. Wood Distillery RD No. 19 in Nelson County in 1896-97. Johnson sold in 1885 to E. H. Taylor and a Mr. Mayhair, who operated under the name of Taylor & Mayhair with brands Old McBrayer, Newmarket, W. W. Johnson, and Old Botts.

Johnson repurchased the plant in 1888, ran it until 1907, and then sold to Rosenfield Bros. & Co. of Chicago, who were operating the Sunnybrook Dist. RD No. 5 in Louisville at that time. He retained the Old McBrayer brand. Rosenfield apparently ran this plant until Prohibition, when it was closed and partially dismantled.

The distillery was rebuilt in 1937 as McBrayer Springs Distilling Co., with Frank Gorman as president and G. M. "Fred" Forsythe as superintendent. Gorman had been superintendent prior to 1907, and Forsythe had recently been secretary and treasurer of Old Lewis Hunter RD No. 15 in Harrison County as well as superintendent for several plants in Anderson County and Old Jordan in Mercer County. The distiller was Louis Bond, who had experience with W. W. Johnson prior to 1907 and L. Van Hook RD No. 35 in Harrison County.

The distillery lasted only a few years after prohibition and closed. The buildings were used later as an aggregate processing plant.

Nelson County
5th District

According to Mrs. Guy Ritchie, whose husband was a fifth-generation descendant of John Ritchie, in an article published in the *Kentucky Standard* on December 16, 1965, John Ritchie was born in Scotland in 1752 and migrated to Virginia. Further, according to an article in the *Nelson County Record* of March 16, 1897, he joined a group moving to eastern Kentucky. From there he proceeded by way of the Ohio River to what is now Louisville.

Not satisfied, he moved farther down the Ohio River to Salt River, and then took the Rolling Fork to the Beech Fork, which he followed to Landing Run Creek. Here he settled and built a cabin in 1780. At this same time he set up a distillery on the banks of the Beech Fork and produced his first whiskey. During that year he had produced enough whiskey to load a flatboat, which he proceeded to float to New Orleans where it was quickly disposed of. He and his crew tramped back home, no doubt by way of the Natchez Trace.

The old cabin still stands with a date of 1780 chiseled in a rock of the chimney, but no one is around to locate the old distillery.

T. W. Samuels Distillery Inc., RD No. 145

In 1844, Taylor William Samuels turned his father's farm into a distillery with his son W. I. as T. W. Samuels and Son. The distillery was located in a valley off the Deatsville-Lenore Road, now KY 523, about one mile below Deatsville. Both father and son died the same year in 1898 and Leslie B., son of W. I., took the reins.

On November 9, 1909, the distillery and six warehouses, including 9,000 barrels of whiskey were destroyed by fire at a loss of $100,000. The distillery was rebuilt at the same location and in 1913 the Starr Distillery of Cincinnati purchased controlling interest, with Leslie B. still part owner and manager. The plant closed at Prohibition and all the buildings were razed except for the old government office, which stayed intact for years but has now vanished.

In 1933, the company was reorganized and seeking outside financing. Leslie B. entered into an arrangement with Robert L. Block of Cincinnati, a son-in-law of Isaac W. Benheim. Block became president and Leslie B. vice-president. Bill Samuels (T. W.), fresh out of engineering school at Speed, became manager.

The new plant was to be constructed at a more favorable location about one mile south of the previous one, still on KY 523, but on the Bardstown-Springfield branch of the L&N Railroad. The old location was utilized for cattle pens to feed the surplus slop from the distillation. They had installed a dryer house but did not have evaporators at that time and produced only light grains, the thin going to the cattle pens.

The new distillery started out with 600-bushel capacity and the first production was May 1934. By 1937, the demand was rapidly increasing and the capacity was raised to 1,864 bushels. Eight mashes were made each day of 233 bushels each, with eight fermenters filled and eight emptied. This required three shifts on a 24-hour basis.

Leslie B. died in 1936 and Bill became vice-president and production manager and Charlie DeSpain, chief chemist and assistant manager. Morgan Edelen was distiller and Elmo Beam assistant.

Their main brand was "T. W. Samuels" Bottled-in-Bond black label after May 1938, and before that they marketed a younger whiskey. When whiskey became four years old, they entered into a big business of four-year 90 proof using the same designed label, but in a red background.

T. W. had a contract with Clear Spring Corporation of Chicago bottling "Pebbleford" Bond in 4/5-quart bottles, which was a departure from the standard quart at that time, and "Old Underoof" 93 proof, which was packaged in amber glass.

They also had a contract with Jack Martin of Heublein for all water mash, which was the first three days of operation after a shut down when slop was not available for set back. Howard Bitter, Heublein's chief chemist and rectifier, was probably one of the most astute in the business at that time. His taste buds were fantastic.

"T. W. Samuels" brand developed rapidly in Cincinnati, Texas, and the West Coast, and at one time in the late 1930s they were sorely in need of four-year-old whiskey for their 90 proof tax-paid bottling. At that time a large number of barrels became available at the Labrot & Graham plant RD No. 52 in Woodford County and this filled the gap. A short time later, about 1940, Brown-Forman bought the Labrot & Graham plant and their remaining inventory.

Ed Budde, who came to T. W. from Brown-Forman, became sales manager and Charles F. Miller of Cincinnati had a sales agency. Miller ran into financial difficulties and was bought out by the T. W. Samuels distillery, and the agency had to release some other brands including H. McKenna.

Buford Penland of Southwestern Drug, later Penland Distributors of Dallas, along with Pat Quinn, a sales representative from New Orleans, did a great job of distribution throughout the southwest.

Kentucky sales were handled by M. S. (Mitch) Crane of Crane Distributing of Lexington. Crane later sold out to two of his salesmen, Owen Campbell and Wick Rogers. Wick left later and bought a farm in Boyle County, but Owen continued to improve the distributorship. By the time he died in the early 1970s, he had six wholesale houses; Crane & United in Lexington, Jefferson & State in Louisville, Dixie in Covington, and the latest acquisition, Gateway, from J. Graham Brown in Louisville.

In 1943, the Blocks wanted to sell the distillery because the price was right and some estate problems needed attention. Bill Samuels objected to the sale and made an effort to secure financing, but he was unable to do so, and the sale was finalized. The Foster Trading Corporation of New York took control and changed the name to Country Distillers. Just prior to the sale of the distillery they had also installed a triple-effect evaporator to dry the thin slop and began producing dark grains.

According to a story in the *Cincinnati Enquirer*, immediately after the sale of the distillery, Charles H. Biederman, president of Biederman Motors Company of Cincinnati, filed suit against the former owners for allegedly misrepresenting the value of the stock. His suit was to recover $82,500, which was the amount he lost on 100 shares from the $175 claimed when the fair market value was $1,000 a share. The defendants in the case were Robert L. Block, president of the company, Margaret Thoban, Block's private secretary, Edward M. Budde, vice-president, Charles J. Ritman, assistant secretary, and his assistant, Floyd A. Rickert.

I do not know the outcome of that suit, but about the same time, the *Cincinnati Enquirer* reported that another suit was filed in Nelson Circuit Court by the Office of Price Administration for triple damages of $5,292,375 against the company for allegedly selling whiskey above the O.P.A. ceiling price.

The new company continued to produce high proof spirits for defense, and shortly after the purchase they eliminated the old mash tubs and installed a continuous cooker. While the continuous cooker sped up the mashing operation and probably worked well on the spirit production, it had a different effect when producing bourbon. After they started back making whiskey, they continued with the same procedure of cooking under pressure. In fact, the pressure was so high that the grain developed a burned taste and smell, and this carried over into the distillation. The smell filled the air from quite a distance.

The distillery produced whiskey up to 1952, a large part of their production taking place in 1950-51 during the Korean crisis. When this whiskey entered the market their sales plummeted and it wasn't long before they ceased operations entirely.

On September 15, 1949, they had a fire in "B" warehouse, destroying a large number of barrels, and but for the efforts of the Bardstown Volunteer Fire Department, they would have lost more warehouses and other buildings.

Sometime prior to the fire, the Bardstown Volunteer Fire Department solicited funds to buy a new truck to serve residences and businesses outside the city limits. Sam Westerman, manager of the distillery, declined to participate and, ironically, his was the first fire that needed the equipment. He did make a contribution after the fire.

The distillery facilities remained somewhat intact for a long period and eventually a portion of the plant was bought to bottle spring water from the springs feeding the lakes. The label on the plastic jug of spring water resembles the label used on the "T. W. Samuels" bottled in bond. Heaven Hill, needing additional storage, bought seven of the 20,000-barrel warehouses, and Maker's Mark bought the other two. Both are storing whiskey there at present.

A contractor by the name of Van Winkle constructed "A" warehouse, but apparently it was not properly braced with buck braces and lateral braces, and when it was filled, it began to creel. The house was unloaded and torn down.

Tom and Ray Parrish entered the warehouse construction business, and they built the other ones on the premises.

Cold Springs Distillery,
J. B. Dant Proprietor, RD No. 240
Taylor Williams Inc.

J. Bernard Dant, a son of J. W. Dant, built a distillery about 1880 at Gethsemane Station on the L&N Railroad making "Cold Spring Hand-Made Sour Mash Whiskey" and "Nelson County Club," a rye whiskey. Crittenden Clark was distiller. D. H. Taylor Wholesale Firm was established in Louisville about 1865 known as D. H. Taylor and Company. They controlled the output of Hawkins Brothers RD No. 124 at Ripyville in Anderson County and "Rich Hill" and "Honey Dew" private labels. J. T. Williams joined the firm in 1877, and it became known as Taylor & Williams.

In the 1880s, J. B. Dant contracted with Taylor & Williams to produce whiskey under the "Yellowstone" label, named after the national park which had been established in 1872.

In 1903, Taylor & Williams was incorporated with J. B. Dant, president, W. H. Duane, vice-president, C. J. Cassilly, secretary, and Sam J. Dant, treasurer. In 1910, Taylor & Williams purchased the distillery of M. C. Beam, which was adjacent, and thereafter only the brands of Taylor & Williams were used.

The distillery was shut down and dismantled during Prohibition, and after repeal Will Dant joined with Joe B. Head to rebuild the plant on the same site as the Taylor & Williams and M. C. Beam and became Dant & Head RD No. 47. J. Bernard Dant with sons Mike, Wallace, and Sam, and a nephew, Jimmy Kearns, moved to Louisville to establish the Yellowstone Distillery RD No. 240 at 3000 7th Street Road near Shively. Glenmore bought the Yellowstone plant and it became the main distilling plant for some time.

Sam Dant was distiller and he was succeeded by Wilmer Beam, a son of Joe Beam. When Wilmer retired, Poss Greenwell took over, and he was followed by a nephew of Wilmer, Jack Beam, a son of Roy. When Jack left, Joe Ruddle became distiller. (More on the Yellowstone operation under Jefferson County.)

Coon Hollow Distillery

Joe Eddie Masterson, who spent the last twenty-two years in a genealogical work on the Masterson families, mainly located around New Hope, has found record of deeds in Nelson County of a distillery located at Coon Hollow in 1873. Said distillery was owned by Green and Wash Masterson, brothers. Green sold a portion of this property to his son Stephen, and he, in turn, sold to Richard Cummins. Richard Cummins sold his interest in the property November 30, 1878, to T. J. Miller, but the distillery burned in 1884 and Stephen Masterson left town having been suspect in the burning. In February 1886, Stephen sold his interest in the property to J. L. Cheshire and it is described as the location of a burned distillery. Apparently Richard Cummins, after selling his interest and the distillery burning, moved the entire operation to the Nelson-Marion line and established the new plant as Coon Hollow, and the location assumed the name of Coon Hollow Station.

R. Cummins and Company
The Nelson County Distilling Company
A. Cummins Distillery, RD No. 10

Richard Cummins was born in Carlow County, Ireland, on May 8, 1830. When he was fourteen years old, he was apprenticed as a yeast maker and worked at this until 1848, when he came to America. He first worked at a distillery in New Jersey until 1852, when he and Henry McKenna moved to Illinois and started a distillery, which they operated for only two years, after which they both moved to Kentucky.

Henry McKenna established the H. McKenna plant at Fairfield RD No. 111 in 1855, and Richard Cummins located at Raywick in Marion County, where he was associated with a Dr. Taylor Mitchell in what was then Messengers Mill. This operation continued until sometime after the Civil War, when Mr. Cummins built a distillery of 100-bushel capacity on the Marion-Nelson county line near the L&N Railroad and called it Coon Hollow—and the station assumed that name. This was followed by another distillery he called Big Springs. In 1880, Julius Wanner and Nicholas Miller purchased the distillery and brands and changed the name to Nelson County Distilling Company, with offices in Louisville.

The Nelson County Distillery began a newspaper called the *Coon Hollow Herald,* which was directed mainly to physicians and pharmacists to promote the distillery's whiskey and furnished free of charge. I do not know if the paper was a regular publication, but I imagine it was printed occasionally whenever the *spirit* moved them. According to one edition of the paper dated May 1, 1891, their whiskey was bottled at the George C. Buchanan Distillery at 1725 Hamilton Street in Louisville. It also states that they had entered into a contract with William Figgan, a wholesale liquor dealer in Quincey, Illinois, to produce a brand called "Fern Grove" for a number of years.

The trust bought the operation in 1900, and the buildings were dismantled and abandoned, but the Coon Hollow brand was continued at the No. 36 house in Athertonville and the Big Springs brand at the J. B. Wathen & Brothers plant in Louisville.

Later Arthur Cummins put a 100-bushel distillery at Coon Hollow and produced "Willow Springs." In 1908, the operation was incorporated, with J. P. and Martin J. Cummins as principal owners. Arthur Cummins, a nephew of Richard Cummins, was associated with the plant as was his son Arthur J. The distillery continued until national Prohibition but was never revived afterward.

E. L. Miles, RD No. 146, New Hope Distilling Co., RD No. 101

Henry Miles started a distillery on his farm a little east of New Hope in 1796 with a mashing capacity of only 5 bushels per day. His son Edward L. Miles joined him, and eventually, when the L&N Railroad was built in 1857, he built a 20-bushel plant on the railroad. The plant operated as E. L. Miles & Co., making a sweet mash whiskey by that name. T. L. Sherley of Louisville took over the distribution about 1870 and built a large market in the West.

By 1875, Miles and Sherley joined in partnership and built the New Hope Distilling Co. of 200-bushel capacity adjacent to the smaller distillery. Here they produced a sour mash bourbon and a rye they called "New Hope." By 1895, the plant capacity had been increased to 1,000 bushels. Mr. Sherley died in 1900 and Miles continued to operate but sold to the trust shortly after. The plant was never revived after repeal of prohibition.

Belle of Nelson, RD No. 271

There seems to be some confusion concerning this plant. In the first place, J. G. Mattingly of the original Mattingly & Moore RD No. 277 near Bardstown established this brand in 1877. Mattingly & Moore was reorganized in 1881, and Bartley-Johnson, who had made a success of the brand, bought it.

They moved the operation to a location not far from New Hope on the South Fork of Pottinger Creek about two miles west of the Marion County line.

A reorganization took place in 1891 with Robert J. Tilford as president; Darwin W. Johnson as vice president; and Judge James S. Pirtle, Henry J. Tilford, and Daniel Bartley as directors. The company sold out to the trust in 1900, but by 1905 the brands were being made by Stoll & Co., a part of the trust, in New Hope.

F. G. Walker, RD No. 410

Felix G. Walker built a distillery in 1881 just west of Bardstown on U.S. 62, which is the present location of the Nelson County Road Department. The capacity of the distillery was 240 bushels with warehouse capacity of 8,000 barrels. His brand was Queen of Nelson.

Mr. Morgan Edelen was distiller, and with D. S. Wood as co-partner he later acquired a distillery in Chaplin, which was burned shortly after their production started. Mr. Edelen related that the residents of Chaplin were very much opposed to liquor and he was wrong to operate the plant there in the first place. He later became master distiller for T. W. Samuels Dist. RD No. 145 after repeal.

Mr. Walker retired in 1896, and a group headed by R. H. Edelen, Sr., assumed control; they operated the plant as Mattingly & Moore and also as Simms, Moore and Edelen. In 1916, they were declared bankrupt, and the plant was sold at the courthouse door to James B. Beam for $13,000, with the option to buy 2,347 barrels of 1911 to 1914 crops. The warehouse capacity at this time was 20,000 barrels. The distillery was shut down at Prohibition and most of the equipment was salvaged.

I grew up in the shadow of the distillery, so I was quite familiar with the property. Shortly after prohibition was enacted, a considerable amount of whiskey was stolen from the warehouses before it could be moved to concentration houses. I can vividly recall in 1923 or 1924 standing with my mother at a kitchen window watching one of the warehouses go up in flames, possibly to cover up the theft of whiskey.

Peter Smith, a local farmer, used one of the warehouses to store tobacco for curing, and Hubert Hinkle used the distillery for a hay barn. Johnny Jones rented a portion of the distillery to set up an auto salvage and repair shop, and Reginald Grigsby, Jr., used a portion of it about 1925 to build an airplane. After it was completed, except for the wings, he trucked it to another location, assembled the wings, and took his first flight. Reginald continued to fly that plane for some time, but finally his license was lifted for a number of infractions of safety rules. In one instance in particular, on a beautiful Sunday afternoon he proceeded to run all the golfers off the Shawnee golf course by buzzing them.

A few cockfights were staged in the old dump room pits, and it was the scene of some pretty wild parties in the Roaring Twenties. Mr. Charlie Cusick tore the dunnage rails and some other lumber from one of the warehouses and used the material to raise the roof of his house on South Fourth Street in Bardstown to build a second story. Mr. W. G. Foster operated a laundry in the old bottling house for a short time but later removed it to the Tom Moore bottling house. The state highway department took over the premises in the late 1920s and used the entire distillery building for a maintenance and parts shop, and truck storage and other equipment was stored in the rear.

The old office building for the distillery passed to private hands and was used for many years as a residence. It consisted of only two rooms, but John Rollin, the first tenant, added two rooms. Several tenants lived in it over a period of thirty years, and it was then converted to a grocery store; however, in the late 1970s, it was torn down along with the Cecil residence next door to make room for the new Nelson County Jail.

When the distillery was abandoned, an old safe was left in the office building, which, I am sure, was empty; but as kids, we often wondered if there were some valuable papers left inside. To my knowledge, the safe was never unlocked. No remnants of the old distillery are discernible today, and even the old pond for their water supply is filled in.

S. P. Lancaster, RD No. 415,
Independent, Shawhan, Waterfill & Frazier, RD No. 28

In 1850, Sam P. and J. M. "Matt" Lancaster built a distillery on Plum Run Road about six miles north of Bardstown. Their farm bordered on Coxs Creek, a never-failing stream of water that gave them a plentiful supply for the operation for their 30-bushel capacity.

The Bardstown-Springfield branch of the L&N Railroad was completed on March 19, 1860, and since it was necessary to haul supplies in and finished product out by mule team and wagon, Sam argued that it would be more advantageous to locate the distillery on the railroad. In addition, they knew of a spring called Old Blue Talbott, located directly behind the Talbott family residence, which would provide ample limestone water necessary for the mashing operation. Brother Matt dissented, and it is not known whether it was before or after his death that Sam purchased the acreage, including the spring, and moved in 1881. It is not known either why it took so long. They increased their capacity to 400 bushels by 1895, making the brands Old Lancaster, Marion C, and Burr Oak.

In 1903, the company was sold to the trust and operated under the name of Hume & Lancaster, a subsidiary. Mr. Clifton Atherton was the superintendent in 1916, Tom Byrnes was warehouse supervisor, and a young black man named Tom Blandford, starting out as a mash hand, eventually became distiller. Blandford was a farmhand on the Ben Johnson farm nearby, but having developed his skills as a distiller, he remained in the whiskey business. It was reported that he was illiterate and couldn't even read the figures on the scales, but, by what he called mental measurements, he arrived at the correct amounts and produced a product of excellent quality. The plant was shut down during Prohibition, and the buildings soon deteriorated.

In 1933, Will Stiles owned the property and, with financial assistance of Rupert Pletsch, organized the Independent Distillery. Pletsch was president; W. O. Stiles, vice president; Harry Wolfe, secretary; N. C. Leidgen, sales manager; and Jack Stiles, distiller. They sold the distillery to Tom Pendergast, political boss of Kansas City; in 1938, he changed the name to Shawhan and brought in his own manager, Chester Hecker. The Shawhan name had originated in Bourbon County, later moved to Harrison County, and in 1918 to Weston, Missouri. Pendergast acquired this plant during prohibition and then moved the name to Bardstown.

The distillery at Weston, Missouri, was sold to Cloud Cray, and the name was changed to McCormick. They ran the plant for a number of years, but when I visited them about five years ago, the distillery was shut down, although the security men on duty stated that they were bottling periodically. I could not find out whether it was their production or whiskey they purchased.

Pendergast sold to the states of Washington and Oregon in 1943 under a provision by the federal government to allow them access to whiskey during World War II. This commerce was managed by Sam Farber and Frank Schulte of the Hirsch Distilling Co. of St. Louis. After the war they were required to divest themselves of this arrangement and they sold to Joe Makler of Chicago, who changed the name to Waterfill and Frazier. This name originated in Anderson County and was moved to the location of Grosscurth Distillery RD No. 26 in Jefferson County. Dominic Schuler was manager for Makler, with Mr. Veal in charge of bottling and rectifying. C. M. Ritchie, a longtime employee, took over the bottling, and after Schuler died, Ritchie assumed overall management and stayed on until he died. They produced some American light whiskey in 1968 but closed the plant in 1969.

A near disastrous fire broke out at the distillery on July 4, 1968, burning down a warehouse of about 15,000-barrel capacity, but the Bardstown Volunteer Fire Department miraculously saved the other buildings. The plant had been closed for some time when James B. Beam, having lost several warehouses at the No. 13 plant at Boston due to a tornado on April 3, 1974, bought the premises for storage that same year. A warehouse of about 20,000-barrel capacity was torn down, leaving them with five 20,000-barrel houses. One of these had been leased to the No. 4 plant as BW No. 87. In addition to storage, Beam has carried on a recooperage operation there for used barrels for export, and a security firm monitoring a number of businesses in the Bardstown area is headquartered in the old office building.

H. Sutherland, RD No. 168

John Sutherland operated a distillery in 1780 on his farm south of Bardstown on Sutherland Road. His son William succeeded him in 1824. Their mashing capacity was 20 bushels per day. William died in 1862, and his son Henry operated it until he died on January 12, 1916, at the age of 90. Henry's three sons operated it until closed by Prohibition. The Sutherlands produced a well-known brand, Bardstown Belle, as well as a number of private label brands used by the saloons in the Bardstown area.

When prohibition was enacted, the warehouses of all the distilleries were taken over by the federal government and placed under strict surveillance, with federal guards and sealed locks. However, persons unknown entered the warehouses at Sutherland and removed a large quantity of whiskey. This was not an isolated case. The same thing happened at a large number of other distilleries throughout the state. One tale that has been told is that the legal whiskey was removed and replaced with moonshine. Then when the moonshine aged for a period, the thieves came back and stole the moonshine. The distillery did not survive prohibition and was abandoned soon after.

T. J. Pottinger & Co.,
F. M. Head, Head & Beam,
M. C. Beam & Co., RD No. 405,
Dant & Head, RD No. 47

Francis M. Head of New Hope and Orene Parker of Covington operated a distillery near New Hope on Pottinger Creek in 1872 known as F. M. Head & Co. M. C. Beam, who had been a distiller for Jack Beam, at Early Times RD No. 7 near Woodlawn, succeeded Mr. Parker in 1883, and the name was changed to Head & Beam. They purchased the T. J. Pottinger & Co. plant farther west at Gethsemane Station and continued operating with brands F.M. Head, Head & Beam, Old Trump, and "T.J. Pottinger & Co." M. C. Beam purchased Head's interest about 1900, and the plant then became M. C. Beam & Co. Taylor & Williams bought the M. C. Beam Co. in 1910, and it became part of the Yellowstone plant.

At this stage, it appears there is no regular progression of the above named distilleries because Yellowstone moved to Louisville after repeal and the Dant & Head Distillery was established by Will Dant and Joe B. Head as RD No. 47 at the site of those plants when prohibition was repealed.

The Dant & Head plant went through a number of changes of ownership during and after World War II, including Timken Roller Bearing and National Distillers. National Distillers sold in 1947 to Armand Hammer of Occidental Petroleum, who first operated as United Distillers of America. However, he also bought the J. W. Dant Distillery RD No. 169, and this became his main brand as a bottled in bond. Hammer also operated a tax-paid bottling house and used the brands Olde Bourbon, Jesse Moore, Jim Dant, and many other private labels from wholesalers throughout the country.

Toby Head stayed on as manager for a period and then was replaced by Johnny Beardsley. Stafford Anderson became distiller in 1952 after leaving T. W. Samuels at Deatsville. Harry Barron called all the shots for Hammer, who operated from their office in New York. In August 1952, Hammer had a sales manager by the name of Newt Cook, who was a former Schenley man and may have been the "Man in the Trojan Horse" as events turned out. The floor price on a 4/5-quart bottled-in-bond bourbon was set at $4.40. Hammer had a fair inventory of various distillery productions; he reduced his price to $4.20 and the "J.W. Dant" brand soared. It was obvious, however, that if this situation continued for any length of time, he would be hard pressed to sustain the brand unless he had further access to more whiskey.

Schenley, in the meantime, had a glut of inventory, especially from Straight Whiskey Distilling Co. of America No. 113 made at the Ancient Age plant in 1950 and 1951, plus distillations from previous years. This was due to the overproduction during the Korean War and the anticipated shortage in the whiskey industry that never came about. It was imperative that Schenley acquire a volume brand that would move inventory in view of the eight-year Force Out law. Government regulations required that if whiskey was not bottled or if the taxes were not paid by the time it reached eight years old, then it must be removed from bonded warehouses, regauged, and the federal excise tax paid, which was $10.50 per gallon at that time. This would put Schenley in a financial bind. Rosenstiel, chairman of Schenley, was working on an extension of this period to twenty years, but it was still in the works and had not been approved at this time. The Forand Bill extending the period was not passed until 1958.

Early in 1953, Hammer was running out of whiskey, so Schenley moved in on February 20, 1953, shut down the plant temporarily, and took an inventory of all the property. From there the transaction moved rapidly, and the final acquisition date was March 4, 1953. I stood on the porch of the distillery after the acquisition and discussed the sale with Ed Fine, one of Schenley's attorneys, who had been in on the final closing. He told me that each side had a battery of attorneys and accountants bottled up in a conference room at the Waldorf in New York for several hours haggling over the terms for the Dant No. 169 and No. 47 plants. They finished up sometime after midnight and adjourned and gathered up their papers. Hammer walked out with a check for $6,100,000, and as they passed the Bull and Bear bar, Ed said, "And Hammer, with all that money in his pocket, was too cheap to offer to buy a drink for us."

Schenley officials, including Art Graber, a very knowledgeable engineer, and Ned Drucker, both of the Cincinnati office, made a survey of the facilities and decided to build a new Quonset hut–type bottling house with three high-speed lines as well as retaining the older lines in place. These new lines were 120 bottles per minute, while the older lines were all the old New Jersey Pony semi-automatic lines at 60 per minute. Schenley had surplus property scattered in many plants, and it was only necessary to transfer it to the Dant plant.

I was told that Hammer originally had distribution in only 60 percent of the available marketing territory and Schenley could expand that to 100 percent with their vast network of sales and marketing offices. Soon J. W. Dant was spread across the country, using the production from Frankfort No. 113. They did commit one error that backfired. Half-pints were selling well in Kentucky, and they were using whiskey produced at Dant No. 47. They decided to substitute the No. 113 distillation for this territory, and sales plummeted. This was corrected in short order.

While the inventory was taking place, I was called in to taste some whiskey that Hammer owned, made at Manor No. 9 in Pennsylvania, that was questionable. I suggested that they reject this lot, but since it was such an insignificant quantity they bought it anyway. Sometime later I set up a quality control laboratory in the bottling house, and, according to Schenley policy, established by Don Brandt, chief of quality control in Cincinnati, no whiskey could be bottled without Q.C. approval.

At this point they decided to bottle the "Old Manor" whiskey and when samples were submitted, I turned it down. The manager decided to dump it anyway, but about halfway through, he had second thoughts and called Cincinnati to verify his decision. They turned him down and ordered the whiskey tax paid, and the whiskey rebarreled and placed in tax-paid storage. Wathen Knebelkamp came through the laboratory a few days later and questioned me on the rejection of the Manor whiskey. I told him it had been questionable previously, but he persisted for a better explanation. After some urging, I finally told him the reason was that it tasted as if it had been drunk once before. This seemed to satisfy him; but later on, some brilliant mind got the idea of putting it in a blend, and they produced a standard for me to go by. They planned to bottle it in a pint decanter-type bottle modeled after J. W. Dant's "pinch" or side-board bottle, which was very attractive and called a "Tip" bottle. Since the whiskey met the standard my hands were tied, but the product was pretty bad. Shortly after, Colonel Knebelkamp came back through and asked me how the "Tip" bottle was going.

I couldn't resist, so I told him that we had always had difficulty with employees lifting a bottle occasionally for their own personal use. Likewise, when we started bottling the "Tip" bottle, they carried out a number of bottles. I then told him that our biggest problem now was that they were trying to bring them back.

Schenley operated the distillery and continued bottling until March 1954, when they shut down everything and moved the bottling to Bernheim in Louisville. This was, ostensibly, to rid themselves of some overhead personnel acquired from Hammer, but the move appeared very drastic and expensive. In September 1954, they moved back, opened up all the facilities, and resumed mashing and bottling until some time in 1961, when they closed again, this time permanently. They removed all the equipment worth salvaging and sold the remainder for junk. Nolin Masterson was the last man on the premises, and a few personnel were transferred to the Bernheim plant.

The Quonset hut bottling house was used by the Burk Bros., formerly from Louisiana, as a sawmill to produce logs for prefabricated log houses. This lasted for a few years, but by the early 1970s the entire plant had been abandoned and most of the buildings razed.

The J. W. Dant label was recently sold to Heaven Hill.

D. M. Beam & D. M. Beam & Co., 1860-1894, RD No. 230,
Beam and Hart 1894-1900,
J. B. Beam 1900-1919,
Clear Spring Distilling Co. 1900-1919,
The Bardstown Distillery 1934-1946, RD No. 4,
Glencoe Distilling Co., 1946-1950,
Alfred Hart 1950-1951,
Barton 1951-1974,
J. B. Beam 1974-1997,
Heaven Hill 1997-

Jacob Beam, a native of Maryland, moved to Washington County on a farm near Manton around 1795 and set up a distillery. His son David M. Beam succeeded him and continued operating at the same location. However, the demand for the product outgrew the facilities, and a new and larger plant was built adjoining Nazareth College and Convent, about three miles north of Bardstown in Nelson County. When the Bardstown-Springfield branch of the L&N Railroad was completed March 19, 1860, it ran directly in front of the distillery. The first brand that was established was Old Tub.

Jim Beam, son of David, joined the firm later, and in 1894 he joined with his brother-in-law, Albert J. Hart, as the Beam and Hart Distillery with Jim Beam as distiller and manager. They had a mashing capacity of 150 bushels per day and four warehouses with a total capacity of 10,000 barrels. In January of the next year another reorganization took place, establishing the Clear Springs Distillery Co., with James B. Beam as president and Thomas C. Dennehy and J. S. Kenny of Chicago as co-owners. They continued with the Old Tub brand and added "Clear Springs" and "Pebbleford."

Walter Brown of Chicago acquired the Clear Springs name after Prohibition was repealed and operated as Clear Springs Corp., a tenant lessee of T. W. Samuels RD No. 145. His brands in the 1930s were "Pebbleford," bottled in bond in 4/5-quart bottles, a rarity at the time, and "Old Underoof" 93 proof, which was bottled in amber glass, the quart bottle being square. These brands were produced and bottled at the T. W. Samuels Distillery.

Jim Beam sold the distillery to W. O. Stiles, Garfield Barnes, and Lambert Willett just prior to prohibition, and they continued bottling for a short time. According to records in the Nelson County Courthouse, the property was sold to Joe Downs on December 30, 1924, and then back to W .O. Stiles on October 9, 1926.

Charlie Neumann had moved to Bardstown in 1931 and was somehow associated with Lewis Guthrie, and he bought the property from Stiles. Shortly after repeal, the plant was rebuilt as Bardstown Distillery RD No. 4 with Joe Cravens, son of Henry Cravens, as distiller. Henry Cravens was distiller for Jack Beam at Early Times prior to prohibition and was grandfather of Bob Briney at

Double Springs and Oscar Cravens of Old Boone at Meadowlawn. Bardstown Distillery introduced the fiddle bottle in amber glass in all sizes in recognition of Stephen Collins Foster, the songwriter and composer of "My Old Kentucky Home," "Camptown Races," and many others. Brand names were Bardstown, Bourbon Springs, and Old Anthem.

Jim Beam, having divested himself of the above property, teamed up with Harry Blum, a Chicago rectifier, and his son Philip and built the James B. Beam Distillery on the site of the old Murphy Barber Co. in Bullitt County, retaining the original Registry No. 230. Jim Beam and son Jere operated a rock quarry at this location during prohibition.

Bardstown Distillery was sold to National Distillers in 1941, and in 1950 it was sold to Alfred Hart, a California brokerage firm. Hart held it for a very short time and then sold to Phil Hollenbach, who operated it as Glencoe, using the "Fortuna" label. Glencoe sold to Haas Bros., who, in turn, sold to Barton in 1968. Barton used the warehouses for storage and the railroad sidings for shipping whiskey, since they did not have direct access to a rail heading at their location. Plans were to build a bottling house, but the soil bearing was not adequate and they abandoned this project and sold to James B. Beam in 1971. Thus Beam came full circle in the ownership of the plant. Beam used the four warehouses containing 52,524 barrels space, but the remainder of the buildings are not usable. I have learned just recently that Beam has sold this property to Heaven Hill RD No. 31, which plans to use the storage to replace some of their storage lost in their fire of November 1996.

Part of the property, including the lakes lying on the south side of the access road, KY 332, has been sold to the Filiatreau family for an extension of their golf course Cedar Fil to 18 holes.

Tom Moore Distillery, RD No. 355,
The Barton Distilling Co. RD No. 12,
Barton Brands Inc.

Mr. Thomas S. Moore, having been a member of the firm of Mattingly & Moore, withdrew his interest and purchased the adjoining property of 116 acres from J. W. Muir in 1889. On this property, just half a mile from Bardstown city limits on what was then U.S. 31E or Jackson Highway, he built a modern distillery of 100 bushels. The road was rerouted in 1933 owing to the deterioration of a covered bridge across the Beech Fork River, a short distance away. The bridge fell in 1938, and the road has been closed and is used only by the distillery.

Moore's brands were Tom Moore and Dan'l Boone, and later, about 1899, he acquired the Silas Jones brand from Stoner & McGee at Hunters Depot when they dissolved partnership.

Mr. Moore's financing came from T. E. O'Keefe of Oswego, New York, and they eventually purchased the Eagle Distillery RD No. 8 in Daviess County from the R. Monarch estate. In 1909, fire destroyed two of their three warehouses, with a resultant loss of 14,000 barrels of whiskey. No other property was damaged, and the warehouses were soon rebuilt.

In the years preceding Prohibition, Tom Moore bottled private brands for distributors Hermann Bros. and Hilmar Ehrmann of Louisville, Eitel Bros. of Chicago, and J. E. McNamara of Indianapolis, as well as some bottling for Applegate & Sons RD No. 15 in Raywick, Marion County, for distribution to local saloons. Shortly after prohibition, all whiskey that was not stolen was moved to concentration houses, and the equipment was salvaged. The property was practically abandoned except that Mr. W. G. Foster, a former flour mill operator, moved his laundry from the F. G. Walker plant to the Tom Moore bottling house in the late 1920s and operated it for several years.

In 1934, Con Moore, son of Tom Moore, with financial backing from Detroit, rebuilt the plant to 2,400-bushel capacity, including a dryer house for drying the slop into distillers grain. Harry Tuer, Marvin Padgett, and Abe Schaecter were officers in the company. Gerald Padgett, brother of Marvin, and a Mr. Kendall handled the slop disposal in excess of dry house facilities and fed cattle, as well as selling some to local farmers and feeders.

Harry Tuer renovated the old Ben Hardin home, which had been occupied by the Charlie Pete Rapier family, and resided there for a period, after which Kendall moved in. It was sold at public auction in the late 1950s to Jack Muir, a local banker and historian, and is presently occupied by Dr. Harry Spalding and his wife, Sandy.

Mr. Moore left the company in the late 1930s and moved to Denver, Colorado, where he set up another distillery.

Sometime in 1936, due to a failed dryer house system, a massive slop spill ran into the Beech Fork River and caused a fish kill that contaminated the river for twelve to fourteen miles downstream.

Oscar Getz bought the distillery in 1944 and changed the name to Barton. He continued producing high proof spirits for the war effort and at the end of the war went back to producing bourbon. His brother-in-law, Lester Abelson, ran the operation from their Chicago office. The distillery building caught fire on June 1, 1945, and put them out of action until it was rebuilt later that year.

Dr. Frank Kraus came in as manager in October 1944, when he left the Seagrams operation. In December 1948, he brought in his brother Paul, who had been in service in World War II and was also a former Seagrams man. Paul left in September 1950 to manage their alcohol plant in Omaha but returned in 1953.

The distillery produced the Tom Moore brand, Kentucky Gentleman, Colonel Lee, and Very Old Barton, as well as other brands. It was also engaged in producing whiskey for Brown Forman before the Early Times Distillery was built at Shively and in more recent years, for Hiram Walker after the Peoria, Illinois, plant was shut down. Over the years the distillery was expanded to about 6,500 bushels, and their bottling and warehouse facilities kept pace to accommodate the increase. Some 30 warehouses containing a total of 600,000 barrels have been built. Cliff Buzick built most of them.

Barton built the Canadian Mist Distillery in Collingwood, Ontario, in the 1960s and sent Andy McHaffie there to oversee the construction and operation. The Canadian Mist brand developed so well that Brown Forman purchased it on August 31, 1971, for

$32 million. Barton bought a distillery in Scotland and later built another and imported whiskey in bulk for bottling at Barton as "House of Stuart." In addition, they acquired another plant in Marietta, Georgia, in 1975.

Barton bought the Churchill Dist. RD No. 13 in Boston, Kentucky, in 1951 and operated it as County Line Distillery but sold it to James B. Beam in 1953. They also bought the Glencoe plant RD No. 4 from Haas Bros. in 1968 and sold it to Beam, the original owners, in 1971. It was only used for storage and the rail siding for a shipping point. As reported under description of RD No. 4 in Nelson County, Barton had planned to relocate its bottling facilities at the Glencoe location, but this never materialized.

Herman Bixler was the first distiller at Tom Moore after Prohibition, and he was succeeded in the early 1940s by his nephew Sam Simpson, who had been distiller at H. McKenna RD No. 111 in Fairfield.

Dr. Frank Kraus left Barton and transferred to James B. Beam and was succeeded by his brother, Paul. Paul was moved to the Chicago headquarters and Chuck Brauch became manager. When he retired, Fred McMillen took over, but after Barton bought out the Glenmore operations in Owensboro, McMillen was given the job of overall superintendent; and at present Joe Borders, a long-time manager, is in charge. Lester Abelson died in November 1980 and Oscar Getz two years later. When Getz died and they were no longer associated with the distillery, Mrs. Getz donated their museum to the City of Bardstown on July 12, 1984. It contains a valuable collection of whiskey memorabilia that was accumulated by Mr. Getz over his lifetime.

Amalgamated Dist. Products P.L.C. bought Barton on June 18, 1982, and changed the name to Barton Brands Ltd. On October 21, 1983, they sold to Argyle, and Ellis Goodman became executive vice president and chief executive officer of Barton. Argyle sold to a partnership on February 23, 1987, and then Canandaigua Wine bought the operation on June 21, 1993. Canandaigua Wine of Canandaigua, New York, are the owners of Paul Masson Brandy, Invernook, Taylor, and Almaden wines, along with many other well-known products. Since the acquisition they have bought out most of the former Glenmore operations in Owensboro, Daviess County, along with the Viking Distillery in Albany, Georgia, in 1995. The Viking plant has been in operation for many years, being known as Paramount and also as Johnston. At one time they bottled a new whiskey in a fruit-jar-shaped bottle like a Mason jar called "Georgia Moon."

The Mattingly & Moore Dist. Co., RD No. 277

J. G. Mattingly built this distillery with Thomas S. Moore in 1877 a short distance southwest of Bardstown on the old Jackson Highway, or U.S. 31E. The location was just above the present location of Barton's entry gate. The plant had a mashing capacity of 250 bushels per day, warehouses of 7,500 barrels, and produced the Belle of Nelson brand.

In 1881, Mattingly sold to a company composed of John

Simms, president; Tom Moore, secretary; and R. H. Edelen, treasurer. However, the brand was sold to Bartley-Johnson Co. of Louisville. The new owners adopted the brands Mattingly & Moore Bourbon and Morton's Spring Rye. Tom Moore withdrew his interest in 1889 and built his own adjacent distillery, which is the site of the present Barton Brands.

In September 1916, the firm of Simms, Moore, and Edelen, operating the Mattingly & Moore Distillery along with the F. G. Walker Distillery on the Boston Road, became insolvent, and the property was sold. R. H. Edelen bid $18,000 for the Walker plant but was rejected as a bidder because of a warehouse receipt scandal he was involved in, and the next month Hermann Bros. of Louisville purchased the plant for the original bid by Edelen. They had been distributors of the Tom Moore brand for years. They were given the option to buy all the 1911-12 crops of Walker whiskey, Jim Beam having already purchased the 1913-14 crops. The warehousing had been increased to 25,000 barrels, but daily mashing remained the same.

A few years after the onset of Prohibition, the warehouses burned, and the federal agents, suspecting arson to cover up theft of the barrel goods, surrounded the premises with National Guard troops until the hoops had been counted. However, no one was ever charged, and the outcome was not disclosed.

Mr. John Mudd later converted the office building to a residence. Even in the late 1920s some of the copper tanks and distillation equipment were still in the deteriorating distillery building. All remnants of the distillery were removed to make room for the renovation and reconstruction of the Tom Moore Distillery after repeal of prohibition.

The Early Times Distillery, RD No. 276

John Henry "Jack" Beam was born in Washington County on November 11, 1839. He was the son of David Beam and the grandson of Jacob Beam, who migrated from Maryland to Manton in 1795. His brother D. M. Beam operated the original Washington County distillery, and about 1856 he moved the operation and established the Beam plant near Bardstown, which later became the James B. Beam Distillery RD No. 230.

Jack Beam operated the Washington County plant for a short time and then moved to Early Times station on the Bardstown-Springfield branch of the L&N Railroad, which was completed March 19, 1860. The new plant was 50-bushel capacity and the brands were Early Times, Jack Beam, and A.G. Nall. Pierce, Hurt & Co. contracted to distribute the products, and during the panic of the 1880s they gained control, with B. H. Hurt becoming president and Jack Beam vice president and distiller. The plant had been increased to 100 bushels by this time, but by 1891, owing to increased demand, their capacity was increased to 400 bushels per day.

Jack Beam died on May 11, 1915, and his nephew John W. Shaunty became president. Edward D. Beam, Jack's son, was also connected with the company, but he died a couple of months before his father at age forty-two.

Operations ceased about 1918, and in 1920 S. L. Guthrie

bought out the distillery and farm. Guthrie had started there as a young apprentice office worker in 1907. Guthrie sold the Early Times brand to Brown-Forman, and the whiskey was bottled for medicinal purposes.

John Shaunty died in 1922, and sometime later Mrs. Shaunty took up with a young man by the name of Desmond. She was conned into believing he was going to marry her. They left together on a trip to Atlantic City, where he proceeded to bilk her of a considerable amount of money and some jewelry, and promptly deserted her. She was left stranded, and Lewis Guthrie made a trip to New Jersey to bring her home. Jodie Tharp, a nephew of Mrs. Shaunty, inherited the Shaunty estate when she died. This included the residence on North Third Street, or "Whiskey Row," in Bardstown.

When Jack Beam was in his later years he married Anna Figg Brown, a much younger woman, and when he died, he left her a considerable portion of his farm. She later married a Dr. Ball, an optometrist in Louisville. Years later, sometime in the early 1960s, she sold her portion of the farm to Geoghegan & Mathis for an extension of their rock quarry. Part of the farm was retained by the Beam family and inherited by Barbara Beam Boblitt, a granddaughter of Jack Beam. Her husband Viella operated the farm for a number of years. After his death, the Twyman Keene family bought the farm, which included one of the old warehouses. With the ricks removed, it served as a barn for both cattle and hay storage. A portion of this was recently sold to Creel Brown's heirs for a golf course and subdivision.

Churchill Distillery, RD No. 13

This distillery was one of the newcomers after Prohibition. It was built in 1934 by Bernard Milton and William and Sidney Frentz, all of Louisville. It is situated on KY 61 between Boston and Lebanon Junction just off the L&N Railroad. The plant was originally called Churchill Downs, but the racetrack objected, so they dropped the Downs portion of the name. Stanley Muir was employed as distiller.

Barton bought the distillery in 1951 and operated it for a short time as County Line Distillery and then sold it to James B. Beam in 1953. Beam expanded the plant to what is now their largest distilling operation. They have no bottling facilities, but their mashing capacity is about 10,000 bushels per day, right at 1,000 barrels, and storage includes 4 houses of 42,000 barrels each and 22 houses of 20,000 barrels each, making a total of more than 600,000 barrels.

A tornado ripped through the area on April 3, 1974, destroying one warehouse completely and dumping the contents of 20,000 barrels in a heap with a resultant loss of 5,200 barrels. Partial damage was sustained by four other houses, including roofs and side metal. Wilson Creek nearby ran a stream of low proof whiskey for some time. The plant lay in the floodplain of the Rolling Fork river and frequently flooded until improvements were made to the highway and flood walls were installed to keep out the water.

Booker Noe, grandson of Jim Beam, had been distiller and manager of this plant since the acquisition by Beam, until his recent retirement. N. D. Johnson was an assistant to Booker and also

Bob Briney, a grandson of Henry Craven, who had been distiller at Double Springs until it closed.

Fairfield Distillery, RD No. 42

Lewis Guthrie operated a bottling house on Market Street in Louisville in 1935-36. In 1936, he built the Fairfield Distillery on the Charlie Mac Greenwell farm east of Bardstown on U.S. Highway 62. Investors in the venture were Harlan Mathis, John Newman, Bethel Kelly, and Dick Hermann. Cliff Buzick built the first warehouses.

McKesson Robbins bought the distillery in 1942 and operated it under the War Production Board, making high proof spirits for defense, but they sold out to Schenley in 1945. Schenley continued the operation of the bottling house until 1956, using Guthrie's Pride of Nelson brand as well as "Chapin & Gore" and "Old Jim Gore" owned by McKesson. Mashing operations were discontinued in 1955, and their distiller, James "Pinch" Simms, was transferred to Chapeze to open up that plant for a six-month period while the George Dickel Distillery was being built in Coffee County, Tennessee. Simms was transferred to the Bernheim plant later. J. B. Guthrie, a brother of Lewis Guthrie, ran the bottling operation until it shut down, and then he retired. Bob Werner of New Haven was warehousing superintendent. Schenley continued to maintain the property and the warehouses until they sold to Heaven Hill, who were only interested in the nine houses which had space for 128,148 barrels.

The distillery, bottling house, and other buildings have all been dismantled.

Greenbrier Distillery Co., RD No. 239, Double Springs, RD No. 51

R. B. Hayden operated this plant prior to its purchase by Brown Bros. It was built on the headwaters of Mill Creek near Woodlawn. John and Charles Brown were operating there in the late 1870s using the "R.B. Hayden" brand.

In 1883, Wm. Collins & Co. was formed by Wm. Collins and J. L. Hackett to operate the distillery as the Greenbrier Distilling Co., still using the R.B. Hayden brand and adding "Greenbrier." Collins left the company, and Hackett became president and G. McGowan secretary. In 1891, the distillery was rebuilt, and the same year they built the Cane Run Distillery in Louisville.

Operations continued until Prohibition, and in 1922 the last remaining whiskey in storage was removed to the George T. Stagg concentration warehouses in Frankfort for bottling as medicinal whiskey. Schenley acquired the Greenbrier label, but it was never used after prohibition.

About 1935, since all the buildings had deteriorated, the entire plant was rebuilt as Greenbrier RD No. 51. Jim Conway, a local automobile dealer, and associates contracted with Grigsby Dones to construct the distillery building and Ray Parrish the warehouses. The local investors held it for only a very short period and then sold to Wathen Bros. It changed hands a number of times, and I remember that sometime in the late 1930s it was acquired by a company called Bird Distilling Co. I often wondered if this was a play on Irvin Cobb's book *Red Likker*, the story of a fellow named Bird, who had a distillery in McCracken County before prohibition.

Sid Flashman bought the plant later and made whiskey spasmodically. I think he depended more on purchasing distressed whiskey on warehouse receipts produced at various distilleries, but he maintained a fairly consistent bottling operation. John Huber, a former National Distillers employee, was manager; Ed Coomes, maintenance engineer; Bob Briney, distiller; and Henry Whelan, warehouse supervisor.

Flashman continued a bottling operation until the early 1960s and then moved to the old General Distillery in Louisville. When Standard Brands gave up the 21 Brands Distillery in Frankfort, he moved everything to that location. However, this undertaking was short-lived, and he sold out to Abe Schaecter, who moved the operations to the Medley plant that he had previously bought in Owensboro.

When Flashman gave notice that the plant in Nelson County would be closed out, a very disastrous thing happened. Ed Coomes and Henry Whelan were riding to work together with two other employees, Bernard Coomes and a fellow named Weathers. Weathers, apparently distraught at losing his job, went berserk, pulled a gun, and killed Ed and Henry. He would have killed Bernard except for the fact Bernard jumped out and ran. Weathers was declared insane and was committed.

The plant fell into disrepair and was eventually dismantled, after which American Greetings bought the property and established one of their greeting card plants there.

D. T. Brooks Sugar Valley Distillery, RD No. 162, B. McClaskey & Son, RD No. 442

The distillery was originally built in 1806 on Jacks Creek a short distance from Bloomfield off Kentucky State Road 1066. No record is available of its early operations until 1889, when David T. Brooks made the brand Sugar Valley, distributed through Templet and Washburn in Louisville. Late that year he sold to Bodine Mc-Claskey & Son. Although they had a warehouse capacity of 2,500 barrels, it seems they only produced a few hundred and then discontinued.

W. B. Samuels & Co., RD No. 241

W. B. Samuels purchased a 50-bushel house at Samuels Depot on the Bardstown-Springfield branch of the L&N Railroad in 1869. His business was successful, and by 1895 he had increased to 228 bushels, with brands W.B. Samuels Bourbon and Eureka Rye. George R. Burks of Loretto was a junior partner in 1896.

The company was reorganized in 1916, and J. B. Armstrong became president. They contracted with C. P. Moorman & Co. of Louisville to produce "Old R.H. Cutter." The plant closed with Prohibition and never reopened. The buildings gradually disappeared.

Until recently some of the old stone foundations remained, but the old pond for cooling water has dried up completely.

W. B. Samuels was the father of Harry Samuels, a resident of Samuels, and the grandfather of W. H. "Sammy" Samuels, a well-known automobile dealer in Bardstown. Several of his descendants still live in Bardstown.

Gwynn Springs, RD No. 371, Silas Jones Dist. Co., Crigler & Crigler, International Distillery

When the Bardstown-Springfield branch of the L&N Railroad was completed on March 19, 1860, it ran very close to this distillery at what was named Hunters Depot. It lay about one mile west of the Jim Beam plant No. 230. Jeff McGee and John B. Stoner operated it from the late 1840s until 1880, when it burned. It was rebuilt as a 65-bushel house in 1885, and Jeff D. McGee became the sole owner. The distillery had previously operated under the name Gwynn Springs, but the name was changed to Silas Jones. "Gwynn Springs" brand was discontinued and "Silas Jones" became the main brand.

In 1902, Crigler & Crigler operated the distillery and they produced the brands Crigler and Woodland. N. M. Uri, who was a brother-in-law of Isaac W. Bernheim and a partner in Bernheim and Uri, RD No. 9 in Jefferson County until 1892, began operating this plant in 1903 as International Distillery, producing "Old International," "Brookwood," "Old Roman," and "Proctor Knott." Uri died in 1909, but the plant continued to operate until Prohibition, when it was closed and never revived.

H. McKenna, RD No. 111

Henry McKenna emigrated from Ireland and settled in Fairfield in 1855. He built a flour mill and distillery on his farm, which was the main part of Fairfield. In short order, he found the whiskey business more lucrative and discontinued the mill to devote full time to whiskey making. His two sons, Jim and Stafford, followed him in the business and continued after their father died in 1893. Whiskey was made continuously until prohibition, when all the barrels remaining in the warehouses were moved to Louisville Public Warehouse for bottling as medicinal whiskey.

The premises remained more or less intact during prohibition, and after repeal the distillery and warehouses were renovated. Jim and Stafford remained at the helm after resumption of operations, but Stafford died in 1935 and Jim in 1941. Jim's son, Dr. Henry McKenna, was made president, and Marcella, daughter of Stafford, was secretary and treasurer. Tom Gilkey, who married Stafford's daughter Frances, was the plant manager until he died in 1939. At this time, Tom Mooney, who had married another of Stafford's daughters, Helen, moved from Cincinnati and took over the management. Ben Constantine, an in-law of Stafford McKenna, was the bottling superintendent and Coleman Bixler, the distiller. Bixler left in the late 1930s to become distiller at H.

E. Pogue RD No. 22 at Maysville. Bixler was also the last distiller at J. W. Dant RD No. 169 in Marion County when they ceased operations in 1948. Sam Simpson, a son-in-law of Coleman Bixler, became distiller; when Seagrams bought the plant in 1942, Sam moved to Tom Moore RD No. 12, where Herman Bixler, brother of Coleman, had been.

After prohibition was repealed, H. McKenna started back using the old original sour mash method of making their mash one day and then souring it overnight, breaking it up and completing it the next day. As far as I know, the only other distillery using this method was George Dickel, when they operated for a short time in Frankfort, Kentucky. When Schenley rebuilt the Dickel plant in 1956 near Normandy, Coffee County, Tennessee, they employed the same method for several years.

Seagrams produced high proof spirits for defense purposes after they bought the distillery in 1941, and after the war they went back to producing bourbon. After a number of years they operated this distillery as an experimental plant but shut it down in 1974 and sold the property to Tom Elder. Cleophas Greenwell, who had been one of the early employees after McKenna started operating after prohibition, was the last one to leave. He retired in the mid-1970s. Dr. Henry McKenna went to South Bend, Indiana, as company physician for Studebaker.

The city of Fairfield utilizes one of the buildings, and a car lot is set up in front of the old distillery building and boiler room, but most of the operating buildings have fallen into disrepair, and the warehouses have been dismantled. One of the houses had been constructed of dressed longleaf yellow pine, and I am sure somebody salvaged some valuable timber.

Sales of H. McKenna whiskey were handled by Charles F. Miller Co. of Cincinnati after prohibition. Miller had financial troubles, and T. W. Samuels, his main product line, bought him out about 1939. McKenna switched to Somerset Importers. Joe Kennedy was a member of that firm, and he made frequent visits to the distillery back in the late 1930s. Kindred Irish, I suppose.

Marcella McKenna related an interesting story to me. It seems her father Stafford and Uncle Jim, needing cash to operate the distillery, would peddle warehouse receipts to anyone who had the cash to buy them. If they saw some farmer plowing the fields and he looked like a good prospect, they would stop the car and trudge across the field to sell him a barrel or two. Several years later, after aging the whiskey, they would either sell the whiskey back to the distillery at a nice profit or interest some wholesaler to take it off their hands. One day a farmer pulled up in front of the office with a team of mules hitched to the wagon, dismounted and came into the office, and presented his warehouse receipt for one barrel. "Miss Marcy," he said, "I came after my barrel of whiskey." Apparently he didn't know or had forgotten the rules had been changed, and Marcella made an effort to explain to him that it was necessary to have the barrel dumped and regauged, bottled in an authorized bottling house after all the taxes were paid, and sent through a wholesaler before he could get the whiskey. She apparently wasn't getting through. He had a warehouse receipt and expected to pick up his whiskey in bulk. Finally she shunted him off to Fred Creech, who was the storekeeper-gauger on the premises. Fred must have satisfied him because he came out of the government office, climbed on his wagon, and left. It was not until a couple of years later that she saw an order from a Louisville wholesaler for the barrel of whiskey.

Boone & Brother's Distillery, RD No. 422
Thixton-Millet & Company

R. B. Hayden operated a distillery on his farm just off the old Gilkey Run Road, which has been rerouted and is now KY 49.

Around 1885, Charles H. Boone and his brother Nicholas purchased the plant and Frank N. Boone became distiller. These Boones were descendants of Wattie Boone, who was purported to be one of the first distillers in Nelson County and was a cousin of Daniel. They enlarged the plant by 1895 to 71 bushels per day and had a warehouse of 2,000-barrel capacity.

Charles Boone was a partner sometime later in the Wiggington & Boone Hardware Store located on what is now Third and Flaget streets, the present location of the Farmer's Bank. The old building served as a junk dealer's shop by a Mr. Patterson in the early 1930s and also as a dry-goods store before it was razed to make room for a DX Service Station. Charles Boone's home was torn down in the mid-1930s to provide a space for Conway's Ford Motor Company, but it is now a parking lot.

Charles Boone has many descendants left around Bardstown

including Drs. Charles and Harry Spalding and Jack Tharp, who are grandsons.

It appears that Wattie Boone, who settled on Pottinger's Creek where it empties into the Rolling Fork River in 1776, began making whiskey shortly thereafter. Stephen Ritchie settled around the same time on the Beech Fork some ten miles away and also began making whiskey but discontinued not long after.

Most of the Boones in southern Nelson County can trace their ancestry back to Wattie, particularly the ones in New Haven, Howardstown, and New Hope. Bill Samuels, Jr., is married to the former Nancy Johnson whose mother was Margie Boone, daughter of Will Boone, a direct descendant.

Orene Parker, a distributor of Covington, who had been a part owner of F. M. Head & Company RD No. 405 near New Hope in 1872-83, purchased an interest in the company and sold the output through his wholesale house. Their brands were Old Boone and Parker's private label "Old Maid."

In 1903, the distillery was purchased by Thixton-Millet & Company. About 1912, they moved it to Chicago, Kentucky, now St. Francis, incorporated it with Boone, Ballard & Osborne RD No. 11, and changed the name to Thixton-Millet.

The Old Boone name was purchased by Marvin Padgett from Seagrams, and when he took control of the John P. Dant Distillery RD No. 39 at Meadowlawn, he changed that name to Old Boone. When Pat Buse bought the plant he continued to use the name until it was closed out.

Willett Distilling Company, RD No. 43

Thompson Willett, who had been associated with the Bernheim Distillery in Louisville with his father, Lambert, left after repeal of prohibition in 1936 to build the Willett Distilling Company along with his brother Johnny. This distillery was built near the site of the Boone Brothers and later Thixton-Millet RD No. 422 before Prohibition. Lambert had bought the farm and operated a cattle and hog business.

Thompson became president, and Johnny, an engineer who had designed the plant, was in charge of construction. The plant was completed and fully equipped, and the mashing of 300 bushels was first made on March 17, 1937.

In building and equipping the plant, they installed a charged beer still and operated it until 1947, when it was replaced with a columnar or coffee still. They developed the Old Bardstown brand and confined their sales mostly to Kentucky.

Lambert stayed with Bernheim until 1942 and then left to manage the farm and assist in overseeing the distillery operation. Paul and Bill Willett both served in the Army Air Force during World War II. They returned after the war, and Paul took over the bottling and Bill the distillery. However, Bill left a few years later to pursue other interests, and they hired Charlie Thomason as distiller. Mr. Thomason, an Anderson County native and a relative of the Bonds, had been a distiller there at a number of distilleries, both before and after prohibition. Charlie Willett, a Navy veteran of World War II, established a wholesale house after he was released from service and distributed Willett products along with some other distillery brands.

Robert Willett, also a veteran of World War II and an Army Air Corps pilot, had been practicing law in the Washington, D.C., area, returned home in the 1970s, and joined the company.

In view of the oil crisis of the 1970s, the Willetts decided to convert the distillery to a fuel alcohol plant. The conversion was completed, but interest in small operations abated, and the project was dropped.

No distilling operations are carried on at the plant, and most of the equipment has been salvaged. At present, Evan Kulsveen, son-in-law of Thompson, is operating a specialty bottling business in the bottling house. The four warehouses are still standing, but most of the other buildings have been razed.

Heaven Hill Distillery, RD No. 31

Another newcomer after Prohibition was the Old Heaven Hill Springs Distillery built in 1935 on the W. J. Smith farm on KY 49 two miles south of Bardstown. Principals in the original organization were Dick Nolan, Harlan Mathis, Marion Muir, Joe Beam, and the Shapira brothers, Gary, George, Ed, Dave, and Mose. The Shapiras operated a wholesale and retail line of dry goods in several towns in central Kentucky.

The distillery started out with a mashing capacity of 500 bushels and by the start of World War II had four warehouses with a capacity of about 48,500 barrels. During World War II, they installed a rectifying column and were engaged in producing high proof spirits for defense. During this time the Shapiras bought out the other interests and obtained full control.

Harry Beam, the youngest son of Joe Beam, stayed on as distiller and was followed by Earl Beam in September 1946. Earl Beam was the son of Park Beam and brother to Carl (Shucks) Beam, the master distiller at James B. Beam at Clermont. Park Beam was a brother of Jim Beam and had been a distiller at several distilleries in the county.

As soon as the War Production Board released the distilleries from grain allocations and Office of Price Administration ceiling prices were lifted in December 1946, the plant was expanded to 2,600 bushels. Since there was no whiskey production during World War II except for a couple of holidays that were allowed, the inventory in the warehouses was practically depleted.

With the increase in mashing capacity it was necessary to build additional warehouses, and the first one was completed in 1947. After that they built a 20,000-barrel house about every year until they ended up with 24 houses, including the original four, with a total capacity of 488,700 barrels. The distillery and warehouses were built on the farm, which was leased from the Smiths for 99 years. Whenever a new warehouse was built, it was necessary to renegotiate a new lease, and of course, the price went up each time.

After one such negotiation took place, Ed Shapira mentioned to me that when the distillery was first built, the Smiths had offered most of the farm for $3,500. The offer was declined because of an insignificant clause in the contract giving the Smiths rights to ten barrels of slop every day that they operated.

At the same time that the distillery was expanding, a new dryer house with evaporators for recovery as dark grains was installed and finished in early 1947 with the help of Reconstruction Finance Corporation. A new 427 H.P. Henry Vogt water tube boiler was also installed to provide additional steam required, because the three 250 H.P., HRT boilers couldn't carry the additional load.

The Marshall Plan was established by George C. Marshall, former Chairman of the Joint Chiefs of Staff during World War II and then Secretary of State. The plan got under way in 1947 and along with it a Citizen's Food Committee was formed to feed the starving people of Europe, who were trying to get back on their feet after the devastation of the war. The committee was headed by a man named Luckman, who was in charge of Lever Brothers, a subsidiary of Unilever of Great Britain.

In order to conserve grain to send to Europe, he called for a voluntary suspension of operations in the distilleries for sixty days, from October 25 through December 25, 1947. All of the distilleries complied at once, but Heaven Hill Corporation of Los Angeles, the sales agency of the distillery, headed by Oliver Jacobson and Harry Homel, sued the distillery for breach of contract that they held with a number of their customers. The court ruled that a voluntary suspension was not grounds for breach of contract. As a result, Heaven Hill called all employees back after about a week and resumed operations.

The news media immediately got involved and proceeded to castigate the distillery for refusing to abide by the original plan, even though they were abiding by the court order. It was only a very short time before public opinion forced them to shut down.

They remained closed through December 25 and then resumed mashing. In the meantime, a grain allocation was ordered for all the distilleries, and, apparently to punish Heaven Hill, they deducted from Heaven Hill's quota the number of bushels that they had mashed from October 26 until they shut down. The quota was very small, and as a result, they were only able to mash a few days in January 1948. At the end of January all quotas were abolished.

A devastating fire started in "I" warehouse about 2:00 p.m. on November 7, 1996, and quickly spread to six other houses, completely destroying all of them and their contents of about 105,000 barrels. The capacity of the seven houses was 108,500 barrels, which indicates that they were 97 percent full.

Burning whiskey ran off the hillside through drainage ditches and entered the creek below, causing the fire to spread to the fermenting room, distillery, warehouse office, and shop. The dryer house and boiler room were spared. Luckily the warehouse location records were in a fireproof safe, and they too were spared.

The fire destroyed approximately 14 percent of the total whiskey in storage, which was partly owned by customers holding warehouse receipts. A dollar value has not been placed on the loss at this time, but it will run into the millions.

As I understand it, the distillery is to be rebuilt, but at this time, no completion date has been set, and whiskey is being produced for them under their supervision at James B. Beam and Early Times of Brown-Forman.

The Bureau of Alcohol, Tobacco, and Firearms has spent considerable time sifting through the residue in an attempt to determine the cause of the fire. They do know that it was not lightning even though a thunderstorm and heavy rain broke out shortly after. The last report issued a few months ago was that it was absolutely impossible to determine the cause due to the intense heat that was generated, destroying any clue that might have led to the conflagration.

Max Shapira, Ed's son, has been in charge of operations since the death of his father, and George, the last remaining brother of the original five, who was president, died a short time after the fire. Parker Beam, Earl's son, is the distiller and he is assisted by his son, Craig. Earl (Jack) Doyle was warehouse superintendent for many years and on his retirement in 1976, Kenny Ice replaced him. Henry Shain, who was employed by John Shaunty at Early Times Distillery near Woodlawn before Prohibition, was bottling superintendent from 1946 until his retirement in the early 1960s. Maurice Edelen replaced him and, at present, Bill Osborne is in charge.

Heaven Hill has enlarged their bottling operations over the years with a new facility and has acquired the brands Elijah Craig,

Evan Williams, and seventy others bought from United Distillers, the U.S. operations of Guinness. They now own such famous brands as J. W. Dant, Cabin Still, Ezra Brooks, Yellowstone, Henry McKenna, and J. T. S. Brown, as well as a line of gins, brandies, and liqueurs.

In addition to their new bottling operations, the plant has a new boiler room constructed in the mid-1960s, the distillery had been increased to 4,600-bushel capacity, and additional warehouse space purchased. They now own nine warehouses at the old T. W. Samuels RD No. 145 containing 165,874 spaces, the old Fairfield Distillery RD No. 42 with nine warehouses and 128,648 spaces, and very recently the Glencoe RD No. 4 warehouses of which there are four with 52,524 spaces. The grand total of their warehousing is 687,246 barrels.

Charlie DeSpain was plant manager from July 1945 until July 1972 when Bob Murray replaced him. After Charlie finished school at Speed, University of Louisville, as a chemical engineer, he had a short stint with Brown-Forman, and in July 1935 he joined Bill Samuels Distillery at Deatsville. When T. W. Samuels sold to Country Distillers in August 1943, Charlie moved to James B. Beam at Clermont. After less than two years at Beam, he left to become manager of Heaven Hill.

Before World War II, Ray Parrish built warehouses "A," "B," and "C," and Cliff Buzick built warehouse "D." All of these houses were burned. After the war Mickey McGuire built three houses and Howard Farnsworth built the remainder. As of April 28, 1999, Heaven Hill has bought the Bernheim Distillery, RD No. 1. See Jefferson County distilleries, under Bernheim Bros. & Uri, for more information.

J. T. S. Brown Distillery, RD No. 29

The J. T. S. Brown name originated in Jefferson County in 1870 with the wholesale firm organized by George Garvin Brown and his half-brother John Thompson Street Brown, Jr., and was transferred to the Old Prentice plant RD No. 8 in Anderson County in 1904, where it remained until Prohibition.

I spent some time with William Cross, who was distiller at J. T. S. Brown in Nelson County from 1942 to 1950, when the plant closed.

William was born in Breckinridge County in 1913 and moved to Louisville when he was three years old. When he was eight, his family moved to Nelson County where his father worked on the farms of Jack Beam and John Shaunty at Early Times. He says that he can remember the Early Times Distillery's bottling some whiskey for medicinal purposes during the prohibition period.

According to William, Creel Brown acquired part of the John Shaunty farm and Warehouse "A" from John Shaunty's widow and the Jack Beam heirs. In 1935, Brown built a distillery with a capacity of 217 bushels. Location of the distillery was approximately four miles northeast of Bardstown on the Bardstown-Springfield branch of the L&N Railroad.

He installed a 36-inch beer still and four fermenters and produced their first whiskey on Christmas Day 1935. During World War II, they thickened their mash and ran 225 bushels. Since they did not have a rectifying column, they only distilled at about 140 proof, and the product was transferred elsewhere for redistillation to 190 proof for defense purposes.

Sometime after 1950, Brown sold his interest in the distillery to someone named Farvet but retained the farm, which is currently being subdivided by his heirs. An eighteen-hole golf course is included in the project. Farvet sold to William Morrison, who later sold to Alvin and Bob Gould, who then moved the brand back to Anderson County, but to the Ripy plant RD No. 27 at Tyrone. The Goulds used the brand until they sold the plant to Austin Nichols and Tom McCarthy on July 1, 1972, for the Wild Turkey operation. The brand lay dormant from 1972 until 1991, when Heaven Hill bought it along with a number of other brands from United Distillers.

None of the purchasers of the distillery operated the plant after Brown sold it, and the last whiskey was produced in 1950. At present, no remnants of the distillery are standing. The original warehouse of 11,000 barrels, along with an additional one that Brown built, are also gone.

In addition to William Cross as distiller, the only other employees on record were James Moxley and Billy Keene. Sue Keene kept the books. J. C. Sparrow, who had been a Navy pilot during World War II, came in after the war as a bottling superintendent.

J. H. Mahoney, Walnut Hollow, RD No. 432

Samuel Elliott writes in the supplement of the *Nelson County Record* of 1896 about this distillery located at Howard's Mill on the Rolling Fork River a few miles from New Haven. The distillery was first established by Fred Bray in 1831 and run by James Mahoney until 1888. At this time, James H. Mahoney, son of James, formed a partnership with Miles A. Howard and operated until 1895, when Mahoney bought Howard's interest.

Capacity of the distillery was 20 bushels and the distiller was Richard Bowling, a very astute black man who had been making whiskey since 1845. Their brand was Walnut Hollow and while it was distributed locally, plans were to enlarge the operation in order to extend their distribution to the south and west. In 1896, he sold his entire production for the next three years to an Indiana firm.

The company did not survive Prohibition.

Ford Brothers, RD No. 461

Another distillery described by Samuel Elliott in the *Nelson County Record* of 1896 was run by R. Monroe Ford. The distillery was located on the waters of Davis Run, one mile north of New Haven on what was then the Bardstown–Green River turnpike. The road later became Jackson Highway and is now U.S. 31E.

The distillery had a capacity of fifty bushels per day. The brand was Pride of Nelson, which was distributed throughout the South and West. This brand was used after prohibition by Lewis Guthrie, who established the Fairfield Distillery RD No. 42.

Richard Bowling became an apprentice in the distillery of E. L. Miles at New Hope in 1880 and later joined Mr. Ford as his distiller. Green Price served as his assistant. He should not be confused with the Richard Bowling who was distiller for J. H. Mahoney.

Monroe Ford was married to a granddaughter of Wattie Boone, who was a sister of Charles H. Boone of Boone Brothers Distillery RD No. 422 located right outside Bardstown off the Gilkey Run Road.

D. S. Wood Distillery, RD No. 19

On the 24th of November, 1896, D. S. Wood bought seven acres of land from George A. Edmonson on Stephens Run in Nelson County near Chaplin. On this land John H. McBrayer had apparently built a distillery, which was also conveyed in the same contract. The contract appears a bit garbled saying the distillery was owned by Edmonson, but if terms of the contract were not met, the distillery would revert to McBrayer.

On the same day, David S. Wood entered into an agreement with Morgan Edelen as co-partner, with Wood furnishing the capital for operation and Edelen as manager and distiller. Edelen was to be paid $30 per month, and the two were to share equally in profits or losses. The distillery was to produce whiskey under the name Pride of Nelson.

Records show that this brand was being produced at Ford Brothers near New Haven at this time, but I cannot find any information regarding an arrangement between the two. It is unlikely that there was any infringement, and it is possible that Ford could not produce a sufficient quantiity in his 50-bushel house to meet the demands in distribution through the South and West and they were merely making whiskey for him. However, I have copies of warehouse receipts numbers 10 and 11 showing that D. S. Wood Distillery sold 10 barrels of whiskey to John H. McBrayer on October 1, 1897, showing serial numbers 209 to 218 produced in June 1897.

Mr. Edelen related to me that the distillery was burned not too long after they started operating, because residents of Chaplin were opposed to the production of whiskey. If he told me how long they operated I have forgotten because this story comes to me from nearly sixty years ago. He did say that he held no grudge about the loss and made no effort to pursue it further. He said the distillery shouldn't have located there in the first place.

D. S. (Davey) Wood was a well-known businessman in Bardstown and at one time owned a farm west of town on the Boston Road or U.S. 62. The property was subdivided beginning about 1913 and called Maple Hill after the sugar maples he planted off the right of way. When the road was improved later and the right of way widened, all of the trees were removed, much to the dismay of the property owners.

Davey Wood was the father of D. J. Wood, who was an officer with the Wilson & Muir Bank of Bardstown for many years, and also Ada Wood Rodman.

The atlas of Nelson and Spencer counties, Kentucky, published in 1882, of the Balltown precinct number 8 shows the H. A. Miles Distillery near the mouth of Landing Run Creek where it empties into the Beech Fork. The farm where this distillery was located was later occupied by the Dick Hite family.

The Chaplin precinct number 2 shows the following:

- Cokendolpher Distillery located southeast of Chaplin on the Mclean branch of Ashes Creek.
- Blanton Distillery on Chaplin River south of Chaplin near the covered bridge.
- L. Bodine-S. O. & A. McMakin east of Chaplin on the Chaplin fork of Ashes Creek.

These distilleries are not otherwise identified on descriptions of Nelson County plants, but may have been operated under a different name at the time, and no registration number has been found.

Reason Price, RD ?

This distillery appears on the 1882 Nelson-Spencer County Census, but no information is available except that it was located on the Toll Gate Road, now KY 457 near New Hope. There is also a reference to a brand of whiskey in 1883 called Price & Willett, which could have been a product of this distillery. However, another distillery called Price and Thompson RD No. 30 has surfaced at Blincoe in Washington County in 1898. Research has failed to connect these operations.

Scott County
6th District

Buffalo Springs Distillery, RD No. 105

Prior to 1853 a woolen mill was established at Stamping Ground, a small community northwest of Georgetown, and in that year it was converted to a distillery by one Robert Samuels. Apparently he was not a full-time whiskey maker and only made a barrel "every once in a while." This was typical of some of the earlier producers, who were not interested in being in the commercial trade.

About 1868 the Crigler family of Cincinnati purchased the plant and began producing about fifteen barrels a day under the name of Buffalo Springs. The company name became Mullins, Crigler & Company. Soon after, however, the name was changed to A. B. Mullins Company.

In 1890, Moorin-Powers, a Kansas City firm, purchased the plant and continued producing whiskey using the formula of the Crigler family. It soon gained a wide reputation, particularly in the West. The Buffalo Springs brand was a sour mash bourbon, and they also made a rye whiskey under the name "Old Stamping Ground." Shortly after Prohibition was repealed, a group of entrepreneurs headed by James B. O'Rear purchased the property and completely rebuilt the distillery. O'Rear, who had been schooled in mechanical engineering, undertook to design a new distillery, and it was completely modern in every way. The new plant included a refrigeration system that would allow them to operate year-round if it became necessary.

O'Rear had been employed by the Frankfort and Cincinnati Railroad and was not a whiskey distiller himself. He married Miss Agnes Saffel, a granddaughter of Colonel E. H. Taylor, Jr., and his sister was married to W. E. Bradley, who was associated with the Old Crow operation, both being well-respected whiskey families. The other members of the firm consisted of Chester B. Morris of Lexington, secretary and advertising manager; Pat Sullivan, Frankfort, treasurer; P. L. Wright, Stamping Ground auditor; and Otis Beam, son of Joseph L. Beam of Bardstown, distiller. The distillery building was made from local limestone rock and had a mashing capacity of 1,200 bushels and warehouse storage space of 25,000 barrels.

Schenley bought the plant in the early 1940s and continued to run it for a period. O'Rear stayed with Schenley and established an office in the McClure building in Frankfort. The warehouses were used for storage until about 1960, and in 1970 a tornado hit the area, destroying some of the buildings. The solidly built distillery building was spared.

Local investors bought the property, and at last report Obey Wallen of Georgetown was offering it for sale at $100,000.

Recently, some of the residents of Stamping Ground headed by Colleen Schrandt were attempting to buy it and preserve it as a historical site.

The Penfield Distillery Company, Juniper Springs

In 1936, the Tom Bixler Company was organized and a distillery was built west of Georgetown on the North Fork of the Elkhorn, but it was soon sold to a Cleveland, Ohio, firm. They only made a small quantity of whiskey in the ten years that they owned it and then shut it down. The entire plant was dismantled sometime in the 1960s.

R. H. Risk, RD No. 149

R. H. Risk built a very small distillery of 16-bushel capacity on Lytle's Fork near Josephine in the north-by-northwestern area of Scott County. All I can learn is that it was established in 1874.

J. M. Stone

I cannot resurrect any information on this distillery, except that it was located on the South Fork of the Elkhorn Creek about two miles southwest of Georgetown.

Springhurst, RD No. 40, Old Colonel

This distillery was built after repeal of Prohibition as a 1,000-bushel operation, and their storage consisted of three warehouses with a capacity of 27,000 barrels.

Seagrams leased the plant in 1942 from a Mr. Wiley with provisions that the property would revert to the owner at a time to be determined when they ceased to operate or had no further use for it. They continued operations for grain neutral spirits during World War II and closed out all activities in 1947. For a period of about four years they subleased the warehouses to Bob Gould, who had taken over the Ripy RD No. 27. Seagrams held on to the property until 1958 when they terminated the lease and returned the property to Wiley, much to his dismay. He had expected to finally sell it to them. The office was later converted into a residence, the warehouses were used for a period for other purposes, and the distillery burned.

Lemmons Mill

Lemmons Mill on the north fork of the Elkhorn about three miles east of Georgetown was the site of a flour mill, but later it was converted to a distillery. The venture apparently was not successful, and it reverted to a mill about 1882. The building was vacant for a number of years, and eventually it was torn down.

Trimble County
6th District

The Snyder Distillery Company, RD No. 63
The Susquemac Distillery Company

James Snyder built a distillery in 1840 about 1.5 miles north of Milton on the Ohio River. He ran the distillery until his death in 1872, with brands Snyder and Richwood. His son, W. T. Snyder, took the helm and ran it until July 1879, when the distillery burned to the ground, with a reported loss of $60,000.

The distillery was rebuilt the following year, and a contract was let with James Levy & Brothers of Cincinnati, Wholesale Liquor Dealers, to handle distribution. They already controlled the Cedarbrook RD No. 44 production in Anderson County, as well as some other Kentucky distilleries. The name was changed to Susquemac Distillery Company, making the brands Richwood, Tea Kettle, Crab Orchard, and Susquemac Rye. The "W. T. Snyder" brand became the property of the Boone County Distillery RD No. 8 at Petersburg, which was owned by Frieburg and Workum of Cincinnati and was later part of the trust.

In 1913, Ferdinand Westheimer & Associates purchased the distillery from Levy Brothers with all the brands and operated it until Prohibition. In 1914, the directors of the company were Morris F. Westheimer, D. I. Johnson, Harry M. Levy, Sidney S. Hillman, and Lewis S. Rosenstiel. After prohibition was enacted, the whiskey in inventory was bottled by American Medicinal Spirits.

There seems to be a conflict on the brand "Crab Orchard," and it is possible that Levy had some interest in the Crab Orchard plant in Lincoln County, hence the use of the name by Susquemac. After repeal of prohibition, National Distillers used the Crab Orchard brand for a period.

The distillery at Milton was not revived until an effort was made to put it back in operation in 1948. Paul Cummins Dant, who was the only son of Paul Francis and Lucille Cummins Dant, inherited a considerable amount of money when his father died in 1936. He bought the premises of the Richwood distillery and proceeded to rebuild and re-equip the dormant plant. Jean Yeager, a daughter of Arthur Dunn, was living adjacent to the distillery at that time, and since Dunn had been employed by the Old Darling distillery in nearby Carrollton, she related that he was teamed up with Paul Dant in the endeavor. Further, according to Walter "Toddy" Beam and Jack, his brother, their father, Guy Beam, along with another son, Burch, were employed as well, due to their expertise in the field. Apparently, Paul C. Dant, whether due to his age or inexperience, was not able to complete the project and soon abandoned the idea. The only remnants remaining are a distillery foundation and one other building.

Richard Johnson and John Cade operated a basket factory there for a period of time, but it has since gone out of business.

Union County
2nd District

J. M. Lancaster,
Mutual Distillery Company,
Union County Distillery, RD No. 6
John G. Roach & Company

J. M. Lancaster, a brother of Sam Lancaster of Nelson County, operated this distillery prior to 1878 on the Ohio River at Uniontown. He sold the plant in 1878 to John G. Roach after Roach had sold the Old Time Distillery RD No. 1 in Louisville to Anderson Biggs. The brands at this time were Old Log Cabin and Rich Grain.

In 1890 the distillery burned, but the warehouses were saved. Loss was reported at $50,000. Roach then sold to KD & W and returned to Louisville to establish the John G. Roach Distillery RD No. 8 in 1892, using the same brands. KD & W rebuilt the distillery and operated as the Mutual Distillery Company and later, in 1905, as Union County Distillery Company.

Washington County

According to family records, Jacob Beam migrated from Maryland to Kentucky around 1795. He settled in Washington County near what is now Marion County just west of the village of Manton. He set up a distillery on Hagans Schoolhouse Road south of Hardin Creek, which he and his son operated for a number of years.

William Medley was born in Washington County, Kentucky, in 1816 after his father migrated from Maryland. He died in 1853. Sometime prior to his death, he set up a distillery on Cartwright Creek near St. Rose. His son George E. was born in 1850 and started his career with Mattingly & Moore near Bardstown before he moved to Daviess County and purchased the Daviess County Distillery.

The only other record available on Washington County Distilleries is a census map of 1877, which shows two other distilleries. One was called the Ross Distillery, located in precinct No. 7 on the

Springfield Pike out of Glenville. The other was located on twenty acres of land in the same precinct on the Little Beech River and was called J. P. Bush. No registration numbers can be found on any of these, and it is clear that the Beam and Medley operations were no longer in existence in 1877, since they are not shown on the census map.

Woodford County
7th District

E. H. Taylor Jr. & Sons Company, RD No. 53
Old Taylor Distillery

J. Swigert Taylor built this distillery on Glenn's Creek about five miles across the line from Frankfort. Beginning about 1850 and continuing until 1884, his nephew, E. H. Taylor, Jr., managed the plant, making the "J. S. Taylor" brand. He was active in managing a number of other distilleries and also the Oscar Pepper estate. He built the O. F. C. RD No. 2 and Carlisle RD No. 113 distilleries in Franklin County and operated under the name of E. H. Taylor, Jr. & Company. The panic of 1882 was a drain on finances, and he obtained backing from West Coast investors to purchase the J. S. Taylor Company. He changed the name to E. H. Taylor, Jr. & Company and began producing the Old Taylor brand.

Production ceased with Prohibition, but the inventory on hand was bottled for medicinal purposes by American Medicinal Spirits. After repeal, the plant was purchased by the newly formed National Distillers. American Brands bought the plant when National Distillers left the whiskey business in 1985. It now displays the sign "James B. Bean Distilling Company" and is only used for storage.

W. A. Gaines & Company, RD No. 106
Old Crow Distillery

Oscar Pepper built a distillery on Glenn's Creek near Millville in 1860. He produced the Old Crow brand and Old Oscar Pepper at his original plant a few miles up Glenn's Creek at what is now Labrot and Graham.

Pepper died in 1864, and E. H. Taylor, Jr., became executor of the estate and guardian of his minor son, James E. Pepper, who was then fourteen years old. In the early 1870s, James E. Pepper managed the plant under the tutelage of E. H. Taylor. Taylor, along with W. A. Gaines and others, organized the W. A. Gaines Company to succeed Gaines, Barry and Company, which was operating the Hermitage Distillery RD No. 4 in Frankfort. They purchased the Old Crow Distillery shortly after.

On February 17, 1887, W. A. Gaines & Company was incorporated in Kentucky. The charter specified a life of twenty-five years, and Marshall J. Allen was elected president; 600,000 shares of stock were authorized, half of which went to the incorporators, and par was set at $1. In August 1919, with Prohibition on the horizon, the capital stock was reduced to $50,000. The company was liquidated in 1922, but it was not until 1926 that the assets were completely sold, and bottling continued until then.

A.M.S. bought the plant in 1935 and, after renovating it, turned it over to National Distillers, which operated it for a number of years. National Distillers went out of the whiskey business in 1985 and sold the plant to American Brands. James B. Beam continues bottling and storage at the plant.

Old Oscar Pepper Distillery, RD No. 52
Labrot and Graham

Elijah Pepper and his brother-in-law, Mr. O'Bannon, operated a distillery in Versailles around 1800. Pepper dissolved the partnership in 1817 and built a distillery on Glenn's Creek a few miles above Millville. His son Oscar Pepper inherited the property a few years later, and in 1838 he established the Old Oscar Pepper brand. Elijah Pepper had a well-known distiller by the name of James Crow since 1820, and in 1860 Oscar Pepper built another distillery a few miles down Glenn's Creek at Millville called Old Crow RD No. 106. Here he produced the Old Crow brand in deference to their old distiller. Oscar Pepper died in 1864, and E. H. Taylor became executor of the estate and guardian to Pepper's minor son, James E. Pepper.

Taylor rebuilt the Old Oscar Pepper plant in 1874, and in 1878 it was sold to Leopold Labrot and James H. Graham of Frankfort, who renamed it Labrot and Graham, with the brand Old Oscar Pepper. Mr. Graham managed the plant and Labrot the sales until Graham died in 1908. Labrot continued until 1915 when the company was succeeded by a corporation consisting of T. W. Hinde of Chicago; D.

K. Weiskopf of Republic Distilling Company, Cincinnati; Robert A. Baker, son-in-law of Labrot; and Carl Weitzel of Chicago.

The plant was closed with Prohibition, and the whiskey was moved to a concentration warehouse by 1922. Frankfort Distillery bottled the brand for medicinal spirits. The distillery was rebuilt in 1935 by R. A. Baker and others, operating as Labrot and Graham and bottling the brands "L & G" and "R. A. Baker." Sometime around late 1939 or early 1940, they sold a considerable amount of four-year-old bulk whiskey to T. W. Samuels Distillery RD No. 145 at Deatsville—a transaction which they needed badly to support the increasing demand for their 90 proof tax-paid bottling. In July 1940, the distillery was sold to Brown-Forman for $75,000 and an option to buy 25,673 barrels of whiskey, which Brown-Forman needed. Brown-Forman used the plant for a while, producing "Kentucky Dew," which they later bottled in Louisville.

The plant lay idle for many years and the premises were listed as an experimental farm by the Browns until they decided to revive the plant. The renovation was completed in October 1996, and it is quite a showplace. Production has resumed on a very limited scale, and the brand being produced is Woodford Reserve. Judging by the amount of whiskey being made, they are not likely to flood the market. The stills are a copper, pot-type that has not been used for bourbon in this country for many years, but is still being used for Scotch and Irish whiskeys. Dave Scheurich, a former Seagrams man, is in charge of production and plant manager.

W. J. "Jeff" Frazier, RD No. 50

Jeff Frazier built a distillery on Grier's Creek, a tributary of the Kentucky River, southwest of Versailles in 1855. His son, George H. Frazier, was associated with him for a while but left to join J. M. Waterfill in the early 1860s to purchase the RD No. 41 plant across the river in Anderson County.

W. J. Frazier produced the "W. J. Frazier-Old Line Hand-Made Sour Mash" on a very limited scale, depending on weather and other conditions. In 1907, he sold the plant to O. J. Carpenter of Lexington, but on April 11, 1908, the distillery burned. Warehouses were not affected, and the distillery was rebuilt, adding a new 14,000-barrel warehouse in 1911. Whiskey remaining in the warehouses when Prohibition was enacted was moved to Louisville Public Warehouse and bottled for medicinal use. Later the distillery was salvaged, but some buildings were left for farm use.

Johnson Miller, RD No. 32,
J & F Laval,
John T. Barbee

Johnson Miller operated a small distillery on Grier's Creek southwest of Versailles in 1834, but the gold rush in California in 1849 lured him away, and he sold the farm and distillery to Jacob and Ferdinand Laval. They operated the plant successfully, making about 500 barrels a year, but in 1892 they sold to John T. Barbee, who had been associated with John G. Roach at the Union County Distillery in Uniontown.

Barbee used his own brand name "Old Barbee" under the John T. Barbee Company. Barbee died in 1900, the same year that H. A. Thiermann died. Thiermann was a major stockholder in Barbee's company and was also president of Rugby Distillery RD No. 360 in Louisville. After Barbee died the plant continued to run until 1912, when a Mr. Voldering, then president of the company, died, and the distillery reorganized with John C. Weller Company of Louisville. John C. Weller Company was also associated with the Burks Spring plant RD No. 440 of Loretto in Marion County. John C. became president, and Ed M. Babbitt vice-president. The plant was dismantled after all the whiskey had been removed to concentration warehouses at George T. Stagg in Frankfort when Prohibition began. The whiskey was bottled for medicinal purposes. Schenley acquired the brand but only used it for a short time after repeal.

Glen Arme Distilling Company,
S. J. Greenbaum,
Midway Distilling Company,
Woodford Distilling Company,
Park & Tilford, RD No. 50

S. J. Greenbaum sold the distillery buildings in Midway to James Cogar for a grain storage facility in 1877. Greenbaum is recorded as operating a distillery in Jessamine County in 1880. In

1893 he was producing "Belle of Anderson" as well as "Belle of Lexington" at the Woodford County Distillery in Midway, apparently having bought it back and resumed distilling. Greenbaum died in November 1897, and the operation was continued by his heirs. Fire destroyed five warehouses containing some 47,000 barrels of whiskey on August 5, 1908, and the following year the company bought the William Tarr plant RD No. 1 in Lexington to replace inventory and warehouse space lost in the fire.

The company reorganized in 1912 as Belle of Anderson Distillery, with Morris Greenbaum as president and J. Lincoln as secretary and treasurer. Their brands included Belle of Anderson, Glenarme, Jessamine, Arlington, and Woodford. They became bankrupt in 1915, and the following year Cincinnati parties reorganized under the name Midway Distilling Company with Louis Fleckheimer as president and Daniel Weiskoff as distiller and manager. Production was discontinued with Prohibition.

Fire destroyed the entire plant, including the cattle pens, in 1925, and the premises were left vacant until shortly after repeal, when the distillery was rebuilt as Woodford County Distilling Company, with a capacity of 600 bushels per day. Seagrams attempted to buy the operation early in World War II, but was rebuffed by the federal government as being too large already. However, Schenley, retaining Tom Dewey as their attorney, succeeded in buying it.

Schenley changed the name to Park & Tilford, which name originated in Tell City, Indiana, and the name was also given to the Bonnie Brothers plant RD No. 6 in Louisville. Henry Bell was manager and Jack Reilly was his assistant, but they were replaced by Desmond Beam and his nephew Charles.

In the late 1960s, when Schenley had no further use of the warehouses for storage, they donated the property to Midway College as a tax write-off. At that time, part of the buildings were dismantled, and the equipment was salvaged. Midway College disposed of the property, and the only part left standing is a grain bin and a portion of the distillery, which is being utilized as a hardware store and an antique shop.

The James Cogar who operated the grain storage facility in 1877 was the father of James Cogar who was in charge of the restoration of Colonial Williamsburg. Earl Wallace prevailed on him to move to Shaker Village at Pleasant Hill in Mercer County for the restoration there. When he died he left his home, a valuable collection of antiques, and library to the village.

Index

Index

CPSIA information can be obtained at www.ICGtesting.com
Printed in the USA
LVOW12s0014260913

354190LV00005B/161/P